Our Reformed Church
Service Book

*To my 'tutor' and friend
Dr. C. Trimp
professor emiritus
at the
Theological University
of the
Reformed Churches
in
The Netherlands*

Our Reformed Church Service Book

by

G. Van Rongen

**INHERITANCE PUBLICATIONS
NEERLANDIA, ALBERTA, CANADA
PELLA, IOWA, U.S.A.**

Canadian Cataloguing in Publication Data
Van Rongen, G., 1918-
  Our Reformed Church service book

  ISBN 0-921100-52-3

  1. Canadian Reformed Churches. Book of praise : Anglo-Genevan psalter. 2. Canadian Reformed Churches—Liturgy. 3. Canadian Reformed Churches—Catechisms. I. Title.
  BX9598.Z5V36 1995   264'.0857'71   C95-910779-7

Library of Congress Cataloging-in-Publication Data
Rongen, G. van.
  Our Reformed Church service book / by G. Van Rongen.
     p. cm.
  ISBN 0-921100-52-3 (pbk.)
  1. Canadian Reformed Churches. Book of Praise.
  2. Reformed Church—Canada—Liturgy—History. I. Title.
  BX9427.R67 1995
  264'.04271—dc20   95-31942
                                                                    CIP

Cover Picture by Dick M. Barendregt

All rights reserved © 1995
by Inheritance Publications
Box 154, Neerlandia, Alberta
Canada T0G 1R0 Tel. & Fax (403) 674 3949

Published simultaneously in U.S.A. by
Inheritance Publications
Box 366, Pella, Iowa 50219
Tel. & Fax (515) 628 3804

Printed in Canada by
Premier Printing Ltd. Winnipeg, MB

CONTENTS

PREFACE
- *Book of Praise* 11
- A complete church service book 11
- The intention 12
- The covenant 12
- Taught how to respond 13
- The task 13

1. THE BIBLE
- Limited task 15
- Early stages 15
- Anglo-Saxon 15
- Anglo-Norman 16
- Wyclif 17
- Tyndale 17
- Coverdale 18
- Other versions 19
- Geneva Bible 19
- Roman Catholic Bibles 20
- AV or KJV 21
- Later editions 23
- RV 24
- ASV 24
- RSV 25
- Other versions 26
- NEB 27
- NASB 28
- KJIIV 28
- NIV 29
- NKJV 30
- Canada 31
- Australia 36
- In conclusion 41

CHURCH SINGING
- 2.1 singing
  - Before the Reformation 42
  - The Reformation 43
  - Geneva 44
  - The Old Version 45

Scotland	45
New versions in England	46
New versions in Scotland	46
North America	48

2.2 Hymn singing
What is a hymn?	51
Songs of praise	52
Pre-Reformation hymn singing	53
The Reformation	54
England	56
Scotland	57
Further developments	58
North America	60
The Christian Reformed Church	61

2.3 *Book of Praise*
Our own churches	62
On our way	63
Reports	64
Book of Praise, Provisional Edition	65
Supplement 1967	67
Toward a complete song book	69
1972: First Complete Edition	70
Improvements	71
1984: Revised Edition	73
Toward the final edition	74

3. CREEDS AND CONFESSIONS
3.1 In Biblical times
"Hear, O Israel . . .!"	76
The New Testament	77
Fixed formulas	77
Sacred deposit	78
Faith defended	78
Liturgy	79
Bible and creeds	79

3.2 The Apostles' Creed
Baptismal interrogations	80
Declaratory forms	82
Rule of faith	82

Received Text	84
Our churches	84
Christian	88
I.C.R.C.	90

3.3 The Nicene Creed
Nicea, 325	92
Constantinople, 381	93
Acceptance	94
Our churches	95
I.C.R.C.	96

3.4 The Athanasian Creed
Name	97
Contents	98
History	98
Use	98
Our churches	99
I.C.R.C.	100

3.5 The Belgic Confession of Faith
Name and character	100
Author	101
Adopted	103
Our churches	104

3.6 The Heidelberg Catechism
Catechisms	105
The Palatinate	105
Editions	107
Translations	107
Dutch	108
English	109
America	110
Our churches	110

3.7 The Canons of Dort
Complex situation	111
The Reformation at stake	112
Precursors	113
Arminius	114
Remonstrants and Contra-Remonstrants	116

Conflict 118
Dordrecht 1618-1619 120
After "Dort" 123
Our churches 124

4. ORDERS OF WORSHIP
Suggested only 126
Two orders 126
History 127
"Middelburg 1933" 129
"Kampen 1975" 131

5. LITURGICAL WRITINGS
5.1 Introduction
  Liturgy 133
  History 133
  Wittenberg, Basel, and Zurich 134
  Strasbourg 135
  John Calvin 135
  London 136
  The Palatinate and Petrus Dathenus 137
  The Netherlands 138
  Dordrecht 1618-19 and after 139
  During the last one hundred years 139
  Our churches 140

5.2 Liturgical Prayers
  Prayer forms 142
  Three types of prayers 145
  Confessional prayers 145
  Illumination prayers 147
  Intercessory prayers 149
  The first prayer 152
  The "long prayer" 153
  The "Prayer of Bucer and Calvin" 156
  A Prayer after the Sermon 158
  Prayers concerning the Catechism preaching 159
  Prayers before and after meals 160
  Prayers for the sick and spiritually distressed 164
  Morning and evening prayers 166
  Prayers for ecclesiastical assemblies 168

5.3 Liturgical Forms
5.3.1 Introduction 171

5.3.2 Forms for Baptism
   Baptismal history in a nutshell 172
   The history of the Form for Infant Baptism 175
   The original Form 177
   The structure of the current Form 180
   Its text 180
   Title 180
   "In" or "into" 180
   Two parts 182
   Grounds for infant baptism 183
   Baptismal Prayer 184
   Flood Prayer 184
   Him 186
   Address 186
   Questions 187
   Sanctified in Christ 187
   Here in this Christian Church 188
   Parents 190
   Thanksgiving Prayer 190
   The history of the Form for Adult Baptism 190
   Its text 191
   Doctrinal part 191
   Baptismal Prayer 192
   Questions 192

5.3.3 Form for the Public Profession of Faith
   A young Form 193
   Reformation 194
   Confirmation 194
   Shorter catechisms 195
   John Calvin 196
   London and the Palatinate 197
   The Netherlands 198
   Its text 200
   To forsake the world 201

5.3.4 Forms for the celebration of the Lord's Supper
   The history of the Lord's Supper in a nutshell 204
   The history of the Form for the celebration of the Lord's Supper 207

Its text 208
The "catalogue of sins" 213
The Lord's Prayer in our Form 214
Reformation 216
The abbreviated Form for the celebration of the Lord's Supper   217

5.3.5 Forms for excommunication and readmission
Order 218
Institution 218
Church discipline in history 219
The story of the Forms 220
Structure 222

5.3.6 Forms for ordination or installation
The offices in Scripture 222
The offices in Church history 224
The story of the Forms 225
Our churches 227

5.3.7 Form for the solemnization of marriages
Marriage in history 227
The history of the Form 230
Our churches 235
Solemnization or confirmation? 236

6. CHURCH ORDER
Character and purpose 237
Historical roots 238
A Reformed Church Order developed 241
Church and State 243
Our churches 245
Contents 247

7. IN CONCLUSION
A unity 248
Church Order and liturgy 248
Church Order and worship orders 248
Church Order and Confession 249
Church Order and Bible 250

PREFACE

Book of Praise

The book you have just started to read is about another book, one that could be called *Our Reformed Church Service Book*. The sentence you have just finished reading may sound a bit strange, for it contains the word "book" no fewer than *three* times. It may be even more strange to hear that most of us do not even possess a copy of the book which I have in mind — at least, not in a single volume.

When I speak of *Our Reformed Church Service Book*, I am not simply referring to our beloved *Book of Praise*. There are two reasons why these are not to be regarded as separate titles for one and the same book.

In the first place, the *Book of Praise* has a sub-title, which reads: *Anglo-Genevan Psalter*. Strictly speaking this sub-title refers only to the metrical version of the 150 Psalms. In other words, it does not even cover half of the contents of this booklet — no more than 309 of its 670 pages.

The second reason is a more important one. For even the main title of the whole book, the *Book of Praise* — let alone its sub-title — would not be suitable for a "Reformed church service book," because an essential part of such a book would still be missing.

Perhaps it has occurred to you by now that the essential section I am referring to here is the Bible itself. Indeed, the most important part of a church service book is the Bible. All the other sections are based on it. If the other parts were not based on it, we could not even call it a church service book, let alone a *Reformed* church service book. After all, what is a Church without the Bible?

A complete church service book

All these considerations may lead us to the conclusion that, indeed, the majority of church members do not possess a complete Reformed church service book. Only some of us purchased a certain volume containing the Revised Standard Version of the Bible along with the *Book of Praise*, published by Premier Printing Ltd. of Winnipeg.

The intention

It is my intention to deal with the various sections that together make up such a book. The main question we should like to answer is: Why do we use all these sections — not just the Bible, the metrical Psalms and the hymns, but also the liturgical forms and prayers? This is an important question indeed. For are the weekly worship services not a culminating point in our lives?

Where do all these documents come from? What is the origin of the English translation of the Bible which we use in church?

There is value in knowing the history of the various sections and documents which our church service book contains. In tracing such history we are instructed in all sorts of interesting aspects of church history. We learn about the history of the English Bible, and of Psalm- and Hymn singing in the English language. We get an answer to the question how our creeds and confessions came into being. And we learn about the background of our liturgical forms and prayers, even our Church Order.

The covenant

My aim is not just to supply some historical data; rather, with the help of the information which this book provides, I hope we can make ourselves more aware of the great riches which our service book comprises. For only then we shall indeed participate in the worship services with spiritual joy because — as we have already stated — these services are culminating points in the communion with our covenant God.

Yes, here is the word *covenant!* For it is in this great framework that the contents of our church service book must be considered. They are meant to function in the covenant communion which a gracious God has established between Himself and those who believe in Him.

In the Holy Scriptures He speaks to us, addressing us with promises, exhortations, and admonitions, whatever our needs are. In our Psalm- and hymn singing, our creeds and confessions, our liturgical prayers and other ceremonies, even in maintaining Scriptural Church Order, we are responding to His word. The divine message and the congregational response reflect what occurs when covenantal communion with our God is experienced in a church service.

Taught how to respond

All of this is a matter of grace. Here again the Holy Scriptures prove to be the essential part of our service book, for it is in these Scriptures that God has taught us how to respond to His message.

The Bible also includes the book of Psalms and other songs. It contains prayers, and what we can call credal fragments, even credal or confessional songs, which are the roots of our own creeds and confessions. Our response rests on the Bible itself. This general principle applies not just to our liturgical forms but also to our Church Order.

Certainly, the Bible alone is infallible: the rest of our church service book manifests weaknesses and shortcomings of all sorts. But our church service book is nevertheless a treasure, for our churches — and this was the case already in the early part of their history — have learned to listen with respect and in awe to what the LORD says to us, and to respond to His Word with thankfulness in the whole of their church life, especially in their liturgical answers to the Scriptures.

The task

The task which we have set for ourselves in the following pages is to study the various sections of our Reformed Church Service Book in the light of our covenant communion with our God. If His blessing rests upon this study, we will be able to participate in the worship services with an increased spiritual joy and gratitude.

1. THE BIBLE

Limited task

It bears repeating that the Bible is the most important part of our Reformed Church Service Book. All the other sections are based on it.

There are many interesting questions that could be explored here, questions regarding the Bible as a book, its two Testaments, the different ways in which God has revealed His Word in prophecy, in dreams, in visions, in the preaching of Christ and His apostles, and so forth. And then there are further questions about the various literary styles of the Bible books, as e.g. historical books, gospels, epistles, etc. Interesting as these questions may be, I do not propose to take them up here. Neither will I discuss questions pertaining to the process whereby the canon came to be acknowledged. Thus I will not comment on the difference between canonical books and apocryphal books, or on other such matters. All these questions have been dealt with in a great number of other publications.

Freely acknowledging the special and unique character of the book that provides us with our materials, I will restrict myself to the history of the English versions of the Bible. This history is indeed an interesting one.

Early stages

In the early stages of their existence, our churches in Australia, Canada, and the United States of America used a translation of the Bible which is known in North America as the King James Version (abbreviated as KJV) and in other countries as the Authorized Version (abbreviated as AV).

This rendition of the Scriptures dating from the year 1611 is not, however, the first and oldest translation of the Bible into the English language. It was preceded by a few other versions and also by some translated Bible fragments. It was even consciously based on older English versions.

Anglo-Saxon

We read somewhere the following lines: "The history of Bible-translation into English is the history of the movement from a clergy Bible to a laity Bible; it is at the same time the history of the formation of the English language from a mixture of French, Anglo-Saxon, and Anglo-Norman."[1]

In the first part of this sentence I would like to replace the phrase "laity Bible" with "the people's Bible." Yet it is perfectly true that for ages the Bible was almost exclusively in the hands of the clergy. The reason for this was the fact that a Latin version was in use.

Since the latter part of the seventh century, there has been gradual change in this situation. From that time onward, we find occasional reference passages being translated into Anglo-Saxon or Old English. There were also some paraphrases and metrical versions of favourite passages in this language.

According to the Venerable Bede, a famous historian of the eighth century, a young herdsman called Caedmon, who lived in the previous century, must have heard such translated passages. Even though he himself was illiterate, he put them into poetic forms. Some of the songs he sang have been preserved.[2]

Bede himself is said to have translated the gospel according to John — at least in part. Alcuin, who became Charlemagne's religious adviser, also did some translation work. King Alfred the Great (849-901) was the first of a series of royal persons who were involved in this sort of activity. In his introduction to the Code of Saxon he included an abbreviated English rendering of the Ten Commandments and also a translation of some other parts of the Bible. When it came to the complete Bible, however, only a Latin version was available.

Anglo-Norman

After 1066, the year that inaugurated an era of Norman dominion in the country we now call England, similar efforts were undertaken. However, the translations into Anglo-Norman that were made did not reach the majority of the people.

And so the situation remained virtually the same. Only the language underwent a certain development.

---

[1] *New Encyclopedia*, Funk & Wagnalls, 1990, Volume 4, 55.

[2] Bede, *Ecclesiastical History of the English People*, IV, Chapter 24.
Also: J.H. Skilton, *The New Bible Dictionary*, Grand Rapids, 1974, 369; S.M. Houghton, *Sketches From Church History*, Edinburgh, 1980, 46.

Wyclif

The real story of the English Bible had a double start. The first start came in the fourteenth century, and the second in the sixteenth century.

As for the first start, the first complete English Bible was published approximately in the year 1385. It was called *The Wycliffe Bible*, named after the well known "precursor of the Reformation," John Wyclif. He himself may have done some of the translation work; at the very least, he sponsored this publication.

This Bible was distributed in handwritten copies only, even after the invention of printing in Germany — or in The Netherlands, if the claims of some Dutch patriots can be believed. Therefore we must not claim that with the publication of this work, the Bible had become "the people's Bible." Moreover, it was a translation from the Vulgate, the Latin "clergy's Bible."

Yet, this work was considered to be a danger to the power of the clergy. That it was indeed considered in such terms is evident from what happened in the year 1408, when the Synod of Oxford, at the instigation of archbishop Thomas Arundel, forbade further translation of the Bible into English without the approval of the proper ecclesiastical authorities.

Tyndale

We now move ahead to the era of the printing press and something of even greater importance — the Reformation. Here we encounter the name of William Tyndale, a fervent opponent of the doctrine and practices of the Church of Rome.

It was no wonder that this man had to flee to Hamburg, on the continent, never to return to England. His English version of the New Testament was printed — yes, indeed, as the first part of the Bible to be printed in English! — at Cologne, and it was smuggled into England. It was a direct translation from the Greek original text — and in this respect, too, it represented something new. In 1530 Tyndale's version of the Five Books of Moses was published. This work was followed by translations of other parts of the Old Testament. However, Tyndale could not finish the translation of the entire Bible. After his arrest at Vilvoorde he died a martyr's death. His last prayer proved that he still had his native country and its spiritual interests at heart, for he asked that the Lord might open the eyes of the English king.

It has been claimed by some that before he had to flee to the continent, Tyndale studied at Cambridge under Desiderius Erasmus of Rotterdam. Whether this is true or not, he was certainly influenced by Erasmus, who, as a scholar, stimulated many people's interest in the classical languages and texts, including the Bible.

Apart from the two aspects of the history of English Bible translation mentioned above — that of the Bible becoming "the people's Bible," and that of the development of the English language — there is also a third aspect worth noting, namely, that the interest in, and study of, ancient texts and manuscripts led to an increased interest in the Holy Scriptures, which meant that efforts were made to serve the ordinary people. Together with the invention of printing — a fourth aspect — this movement strongly promoted the Reformation's cause.

This name, "Reformation," brings us back to Tyndale. His Bible version was also characteristic because of its marginal notes. They were very provocative because of their anti-Roman content. King Henry VIII once described them as "the pestylent glosses in the margentes."

Another aspect worth noting is his use of colloquial language. The word "Church" was replaced by "congregation." Tyndale strongly disliked the frequent use by the Roman Catholic clergy of the Latin word *ecclesia*, just as Martin Luther, whom he is said to have met at Wittenberg, hated the word *catholicam* or "catholic," and, following a tradition of the Middle Ages, replaced it in the Apostles' Creed with "Christian." Other illustrations are Tyndale's rendering of *caritas* as "love" rather than as "charity"; the use of the term "Good Frydaye" in Matthew 27:62 rather than "Next day, that is, after the day of Preparation"; of "ester holydayes" (Easter holidays) for "the days of Unleavened Bread" in Acts 20:6; and of the name "Whitsuntyde" for "Pentecost" in I Corinthians 16:8.

Coverdale

The next name we come to in the history of the English Bible is that of Miles Coverdale.

With his work a step forward was made, but also a step backward. His version of 1535 was the first complete translation of the Bible printed on English soil. However, it was not based purely on the original texts, but on the Vulgate, on Tyndale, on Martin Luther's German version, and on the work of Leo Judae, Zwingli's friend and fellow-worker.

That this Bible — though prepared on the continent — could be printed in England was only possible because there had been a change in attitude on the part of the king and the Church. In the year 1534 the Canterbury Convocation of the Church of England petitioned King Henry VIII to have the Bible translated. The resulting translation was dedicated to this king as a reward for granting his royal consent. Those who possess a copy of the Book of Common Prayer can find Coverdale's translation of the Psalms in beautiful prose. It is still used in the Church of England!

Other versions

Both "Tyndale" and "Coverdale" were used by other translators, e.g. John Rogers, alias Thomas Matthews, who in the year 1537 published what is known as the Matthews Bible. A revision of this version by Richard Taverner was issued in 1538; it is known as the Taverner's Bible. However, these were what we call private versions.

In the same period the Church became more and more aware of the fact that providing the people with a good Bible translation was the task of the Church itself. This process led to the publication of the Great Bible, prepared by an official commission in the year 1539. It owed its name to its large format. It is said to have exercised an enormous influence not only on the people but also on the subsequent history of the English Bible. Church as well as State sought to make it the only permissible Bible version, but these efforts were not very successful because other translations were still popular.

Its second edition is also known as Cranmer's Bible, because Thomas Cranmer, the well-known archbishop of Canterbury, wrote its Preface. It was "authorized for the use of every Church, and for distribution among the people." Necessary revisions were undertaken by a number of scholars along with the bishops of the Church of England. This sixth edition is therefore known as the Bishop's Bible. However, it was not a real success and used mainly as a pulpit Bible.

Geneva Bible

During the reign of Mary Tudor, the Bibles were taken out of the churches. Many adherents of the Reformation had to flee to the continent where a number of them settled in Geneva. There the Geneva Bible was produced, influenced by Theodore Beza, John Calvin's successor.

This English version also occupies an important place in the history of the English Bible. The New Testament portion, which was a translation by William Whittingham, published in the year 1587, was the first Bible version with a division into verses. The verses had been introduced by Robert Stephanus in the fourth edition of his Greek New Testament (1551).

Another feature is that the words which were introduced to clarify the meaning of a sentence but were not found in the original were printed in italics — a method which was adopted later by other versions, such as the Authorized or King James Version of 1611 and the Dutch *Statenvertaling* of 1637. In the marginal notes there was a return to polemics, indicating the heretical character of the Roman Catholic doctrine and practices. A point of minor importance gave this version the popular name "Breeches Bible." It got this name from its translation of the word used for the first clothes worn by Adam and Eve (Genesis 3:7). In the year 1559 the translation of the book of Psalms was published, and in 1560 the whole Bible became available. When Mary Tudor was succeeded on the throne by Elizabeth I, the Reformation in the Church of England was restored, and the complete edition of the Geneva Bible was dedicated to the new queen. However, this did not mean that it was officially endorsed.

Roman Catholic Bibles

The Church of Rome tried to regain some lost ground and break the influence of the above-mentioned versions of the Bible. This effort resulted in the publication of the Douay or Rheims-Douay Bible (1582-1609). This translation project followed the example set by the French Roman Catholics in translating the Vulgate, the officially and exclusively authorized Bible of the Church of Rome.

Not until the twentieth century were a number of versions that were actually based on the Hebrew and Greek original texts published within the Church of Rome. Worthy of mention here are the Jerusalem Bible (1966) and the New American Bible (1970). During the years 1945 to 1949 Ronald A. Knox published a Vulgate-based English version, the Knox Bible.

AV or KJV

We have now arrived at a very important moment in the history of English Bible translation, the moment which led to the birth of the Authorized or King James Version. This version owes the latter name to James I, who, having been King James VI of Scotland since 1567, became the King of England and Ireland when Queen Elizabeth I died childless in the year 1603.

King James claimed it was the divine right of kings to take control not only of the State but also of Church life. In accordance with this policy, he played a role in ecclesiastical affairs, but his efforts brought him into conflict with the English Parliament.

King James is also known for delegating a number of English theologians and others to the well known Synod of Dordrecht of 1618-1619. In the Preface to the Canons of Dort, he is given some credit for its outcome.

However, in regards to Church matters, he is more frequently mentioned with respect to the Bible translation. The story starts at the Hampton Court Conference, which he convened in the year 1604, thereby alienating the Nonconformists. At that conference Dr. John Reynolds, a Puritan within the Church of England and the president of Oxford's *Corpus Christi*, made the suggestion that a new translation of the Bible should be made to replace the various versions that were then in use. After some initial opposition this suggestion was adopted by the conference, with the king giving his enthusiastic approval.

Fifty-four men, who were the greatest scholars in Greek and Hebrew and other fields in those days, were appointed. They were divided into six groups, called "companies," two groups coming together at Westminster, two in Cambridge, and two in Oxford. One of the Westminster groups had to translate the books of Genesis to Kings; the other the New Testament epistles; the first Cambridge group had to produce a translation of I Chronicles to the Song of Solomon; the second "company" the new version of the Apocryphal books; Oxford I had to deal with Isaiah to Malachi; and Oxford II with the four gospels, Acts, and Revelation.

The new translation was supposed to be a revision of the Bishops' Bible, with its language to be modified slightly as the "truth of the original" or emphasis required. It was also to be based on the Hebrew and Greek texts. At the same time, other versions such as those by Tyndale and

Coverdale, the Matthews Bible, the Geneva Bible, and versions in other languages were also used. As the Dedication to King James says, "out of the Original Sacred Tongues, together with comparing of the labours, both in our own and other foreign Languages, of many worthy men who went before us, there should be one more exact translation of the Holy Scriptures into the English Tongue."

The task as set was reflected in the membership of the six companies. Among the prominent members was Dr. Lancelot Andrews, former chaplain of Queen Elizabeth I, a great scholar in Latin, Greek, Hebrew, Chaldee, Syriac, Arabic, and fifteen "modern" languages, somewhere called "one of the rarest linguists in Christendom." Further, there was Dr. Adrian Saravia, a Spaniard, professor at the Leyden University in the Netherlands, "that learned foreigner," with his knowledge of Spanish and Dutch scholars. Dr. John Reynolds was a member of the Oxford Old Testament company. He was a Hebrew and Greek scholar. It is said that "his memory and reading were near to a miracle." Until his death in 1607 he worked on a translation of the Old Testament prophets. Dr. George Abbot of the Oxford New Testament group was considered to be the head of the Puritan party within the Church of England. He was a strong opponent of Archbishop William Laud's efforts to introduce a new, Romanizing liturgy. Dr. Abbot encouraged the Dutch States General to dismiss professor Vorstius of Leyden because of his Arminian teachings. The second Cambridge committee included John Bays among its members. At the age of five years he had begun to read Hebrew, and when he was fourteen years old he was admitted to St. John's College at Cambridge, where, after having studied Greek for ten years, he became chief lecturer in this language, his lectures starting at 4 A.M.(!)

The method followed was that each company member independently translated the Bible books allotted to his group. Once this had been completed the committee had to come to agreement on the text to be presented to a revisionary committee consisting of twelve men selected from the six companies.

Some of the adopted rules were: Old ecclesiastical words such as "Church" and "charity" must be kept — instead of Tyndale's "congregation" and "love." Apart from this restriction, Tyndale's style was to be followed. Words not found in the Hebrew and Greek original, but which were added to clarify the meaning of the sentence concerned, had to be printed in different type. The 1611 edition was printed in "black letter" (gothic); the insertions were set in a smaller and different type (roman). Marginal notes were not to be theological and controversial but textual only.

The result of undertaking this gigantic task was the publication of the new version in the year 1611. In a Dedication — which can still be found in many editions of the AV or KJV — King James was highly praised for his sponsorship and invited to grant his royal authorization. However, no record of such a royal authorization, not even an ecclesiastical one, is known, although the title-page of the first edition included the words "appointed to be read in Churches."

Called somewhere "the noblest monument of English prose,"[3] this Bible became known as the Authorized Version. On the American continent the name King James Version is used. This use of this name seems to originate from the revision committee which in the year 1946 objected to the word "authorized."

In an introductory statement entitled, "The Translators to the Reader," we read: "Truly (Good Christian Reader), we never thought from the beginning, that we should need to make a new Translation, not yet to make a bad one a good one, (. . .) but to make a good one better, or out of many good ones one principal good one."

Later editions

Already in the year 1613 another edition of the AV or KJV was published. It included more than three hundred changes. Minor changes in wording were included in the editions of 1626 and 1638. In the second half of the eighteenth century, however, a more thorough and extensive editing was undertaken at the Universities of Cambridge and Oxford. This work resulted in a revision of the text, including modernization of spelling, expression, and punctuation. In 1873 a sixteen-page list containing all the variations from the 1611 text was published .

Taking all this into consideration we must draw the conclusion that the AV or KJV which was used by our churches in the first decades after their establishment is not exactly the same as it was when first published.

---

[3] Preface to the Revised Standard Version.

RV

The AV or KJV had to compete for some time with the Geneva Bible, which was popular among the Puritans. But at last the KJV prevailed, and for more than two and a half centuries it was *the* English Bible.

At the end of the nineteenth century the Canterbury Convocation of the Church of England took the initiative for a revision. It was thought that in the meantime better manuscripts had been discovered, e.g. the Codex Sinaiticus and the Codex Vaticanus.

Eight general principles were adopted. Two of them were: (1) to introduce as few alterations as possible in the text of the Authorized Version, consistent with faithfulness; (2) to limit, as far as possible, the expression of such alterations to the language of the Authorized and earlier English versions.

Two companies were established — one for the Old Testament, one for the New Testament. Each company had to go over the text twice.

The work started on June 22, 1870. The New Testament was completed on November 11, 1880. The text is based on the theories of Westcott and Hort, who deviated from the "received text" of Erasmus, which had been used until that point. It was claimed that the manuscripts they used, namely, the Codex Vaticanus and the Codex Sinaiticus, were older and therefore better. The Old Testament was completed on June 20, 1884, and published on May 19, 1885; the translation of the Apocryphal books was published in the year 1895. The influence of the textual theories of Westcott and Hort can clearly be seen in this version.

ASV

The English translators of the RV sought the assistance of scholars in North America. Consequently some American companies were established as well. It soon appeared that they wished to publish an American revision, but they agreed not to do so within fourteen years after the RV was published.

The fruit of their labours diverged from the RV in hundreds of details. Reports of these divergences were sent to England, although their proposals were not always accepted. The American revisers, too, were strongly influenced by Westcott and Hort.

The ASV was published in the year 1901. Although it was given the name "American Standard Version," it was never "standardized" or "authorized." One of its peculiarities is that the artificial name "Jehovah," which originated in the Middle Ages, was introduced for "the LORD" or "God."

RSV

Another version of the Bible in the English language is the Revised Standard Version. Its title-page makes clear what this version claims to be. It says: "The Bible, containing the Old and New Testament, Revised Standard Version, translated from the original tongues, being the version set forth A.D. 1611, revised A.D. 1881-1885 and A.D. 1901, compared with the most ancient authorities and revised A.D. 1952." Since 1971 a "second edition of the New Testament A.D. 1971" has been added.

This means that the RSV claims to be a revision of the AV or KJV via the RV and ASV. Thus it is a revision of an alternative revision. The Preface therefore praises the KJV, referring to the revisers of 1881 who had expressed their admiration for "its simplicity, its dignity, its power, its happy turns of expression, (. . .) the music of its cadences, and the felicities of its rhythm."

However, it was also realized that the KJV had some grave defects. They stemmed partly from the progress that had been made in the field of Biblical studies and the discovery of what were claimed as being more ancient manuscripts. These new discoveries were made after the RV and ASV were published, in and following 1931. The defects in the KJV also had to do with the further development of the English language.

The initiative was taken by a Committee of the International Council of Religious Education — now the Division of Christian Education of the National Council of the Churches of Christ in the United States of America. It represented forty churches in the U.S.A. and Canada. Thirty-two scholars were invited to establish the revision committee. Two groups were formed, for the translation of the Old Testament and the New Testament respectively. Their work was to be reviewed by an advisory board of fifty representatives of the participating churches; but before this was done the two groups had to review each other's work. All changes were supposed to be agreed upon by a two-thirds majority of the whole committee.

Among the committee members were such men as Moffatt of New York's Union Seminary, and Goodspeed of the University of Chicago, whose names we will meet again shortly.

The task included the requirement that it should "embody the best results of modern scholarship as to the meaning of the Scriptures, and express this meaning in English diction designed for use in public and private worship. It should preserve those qualities which have given the King James Version a supreme place in English literature."

The New Testament was published in 1946, the entire Bible in 1952, and a second edition of the New Testament — including some minor changes — in the year 1971.

The name "Jehovah" — used in the ASV — had been changed back to "the LORD" and "God."

General acceptance of the RSV was hindered by a number of objections. To some its English — in accordance with the rules preserving much of the dignity of the AV or KJV's language — was too old-fashioned. Others had difficulties with the textual theories on which the New Testament translation, in particular, was based. There were also those who — to say the least — hesitated to accept this version as reliable because almost all the committee members were exponents of "higher criticism."

A new edition, published in 1990, and known as the NRSV, makes use of "inclusive language" to reduce the number of masculine references — which means that it has been influenced by today's feminism.

Other versions

In the course of the twentieth century some other translations were published, and also some paraphrases. I will discuss some of them because of the role they have played in the life of our Churches. As for others, I restrict myself to mentioning their names and editions.

The latter include: R. F. Weymouth, 1903, 1943; James Moffatt, 1901, 1913, 1922, 1934; Goodspeed, 1923, 1945; W. G. Ballantine, 1923; C. B. Williams, 1937; the Berkeley Version of Gerrit Verkuyl, 1945, 1959; H. J. Schonfield, 1955; Kenneth S. Wuest, 1956-1959; J. B. Phillips' New Testament in Modern English, 1958; The Amplified New Testament, 1958; and Good News for Modern Man, or Today's English Version, 1966.

NEB

At the 1946 General Assembly of the Church of Scotland, a proposal by one of the presbyteries to approach other churches about undertaking a translation of the Bible in contemporary English was discussed. This resulted in a conference held at Westminster in October of the same year, which was attended by delegates of the Church of England, the Church of Scotland, and the Methodist, Baptist, and Congregational Churches. At a second conference, held in January of 1947, the University Presses of Oxford and Cambridge were also represented. A joint committee was appointed, to which even more churches and the University Presses were invited. The Roman Catholic Church sent observers. Three panels were established, for the Old Testament, the New Testament, and the Apocrypha respectively. A special panel consisted of a number of literary advisers.

The New Testament in this translation was published in 1961, and the entire Bible in 1970.

It was indeed intended to be a new translation, not a revision. This may explain its name. It was called "New" because in the history of the Bible in the English language, versions such as Tyndale, Coverdale, and in particular the Authorized Version or King James Version were known as "the English Bible."

The "New English Bible" therefore belongs to the group of "modern speech" versions. It was meant to replace the AV or KJV because of the latter's archaic language. Another justification offered was that it would incorporate "the gain of recent biblical scholarship."

As for the underlying manuscripts, the panel of scholars adopted those which "to the best of their judgment seemed most likely to represent what the author wrote."

Regarding the translation they stated: "It should be said that our intention has been to offer a translation in the strict sense, and not a paraphrase, and we have not wished to encroach on the field of the commentator." However, it was added: "But if the best commentary is a good translation, it is also true that every intelligent translation is in a sense a paraphrase."

According to the translators, the rendering is "into the natural vocabulary, constructions, and rhythm of contemporary speech." Another feature worth noting is that this version does not use italics for insertions.

It has not gained the wide recognition of the RSV and NIV, let alone of the AV or KJV.

NASB

In the year 1971 the California-based Lockman Foundation produced the New American Standard Bible, the New Testament section of which had been published in 1963. It claimed to be a continuation of the ASV tradition, but in a more contemporary form, incorporating the most recent findings in textual and language studies.

It was prepared by a panel of fifty-eight anonymous scholars from a great variety of churches, all acknowledging the infallibility of the Bible as the Word of God.

The aim of these scholars was "to adhere as closely as possible to the original languages of the Holy Scriptures, and to make the translation in a fluent and readable style according to the current English language." Their method of translation was basically formal equivalence.

A few particulars of this translation are: Insertions were usually printed in italics; and God is addressed as "Thee," "Thy," and "Thou," and Christ usually as "You."

KJIIV

The year 1971 also saw the publication of the King James II Version. It was meant as a kind of rehabilitation of the AV or KJV, although in a somewhat modernized form — this over against the RV, ASV, and RSV as "truly updated revisions of the King James Version." The "major purpose" of "both the English and the American Committees" was, according to the author of KJIIV, Jay P. Green, "to supplant the King James Version."

His own aim and method is clear from the following excerpts from what Green calls "the gains of the King James II Version":

1. A strong effort has been made to keep all the majesty, beauty and glory that is inherent in God's Word, and which even its enemies admit were brilliantly incorporated in the original King James Version;

3. A pre-study of textual criticism encompassing more than 1000 hours convinced us the best text was that used by Tyndale and the KJV scholars.

4. This Bible is translated word-for-word in an attempt to give a literal rendition of each and every one of God's words. Lately, the "translators"

and paraphrasers have claimed this was impossible without destroying readability. In this Bible, you will see it is not only possible, but it is desirable;

6. This Bible has easy-to-understand language. It can be read by elementary school children with relative ease. It is not, however, in basic English.

7. This Bible has far fewer words added for sense, and they are in italics.

NIV

The New International Version is another new translation.

Its New Testament was published in 1973, the whole Bible in 1978, and a revision in the year 1984. Its brief history runs as follows. The 1954 General Synod of the Christian Reformed Church in North America rejected the RSV as a replacement of the KJV. The General Synod of 1956 appointed a committee that had to study the possibility of sponsoring a new translation in cooperation with other conservative churches. This resulted in discussions held with the Education Division of the National Association of Evangelicals. In the year 1965 a conference was held at Palos Height, Illinois; it was followed a year later by a Chicago conference. A committee on Bible Translation, consisting of fifteen persons, was established. As soon as the New York Bible Society — now the International Bible Society — appeared to be willing to act as a sponsor, more than a hundred scholars from colleges, seminaries, and universities were willing to be enlisted. In church background they were Anglican, Christian Reformed, Methodist, Presbyterian, Baptist, Lutheran, and so forth. Included were Americans, Canadians, Englishmen, Australians, and New Zealanders.

These men divided themselves into twenty teams, consisting of translators and consultants. To each team an English stylist was added. The General Editorial Committee and the Committee on Bible Translation edited the drafts — which means that altogether there were three revisions. The final approval was to be given by the Committee of Fifteen.

The goals were: an accurate Bible translation, having clarity and literary quality. There must be continuity with the long tradition of Bible translation into English. The result should not be a word-for-word translation, for "faithful communication of the meaning of the writers of the Bible demands frequent modifications in sentence structure and constant regard for the contextual meaning of words." Obvious Americanisms and Anglicisms were to be avoided. Yet there is a British edition with some slight differences of idiom and spelling.

The translation of the Old Testament was based on the *Masoretic Text*, but the Dead Sea scrolls and older translations such as the *Septuagint* and the *Vulgate* were consulted. For the New Testament the underlying text was an eclectic one, the choice having been made "according to accepted principles of New Testament textual criticism."

The Tetragrammaton YHVH was rendered as "LORD" (all capitals), and the Hebrew name Adonai as "Lord." Where both are found together it says: "Sovereign LORD."

In cases of uncertainty, insertions are in brackets, but there are no insertions in italics, except in the book of Psalms, where there are italicized headings, but these are not part of the official NIV text.

There are footnotes for alternative translations or for cases of textual uncertainty. These footnotes refer to "Some manuscripts" etc.

The NIV intends to continue to improve itself. Five year assessments are made.

Since all the participants are subscribers to the authority and infallibility of the Bible as God's Word in written form, it is nice to know that this version is widely available. In English-speaking countries it is used in many churches.

NKJV

The name "King James Version" is included in the name of another translation of the Holy Scriptures. In 1975, one hundred thirty American scholars were commissioned to produce a revision of the AV or KJV. The initiative was taken by Thomas Nelson Publishers in Nashville.

The management of this publishing house was very suspicious of some of the manuscripts which were used in revisions of the AV or KJV and modern translations. Therefore the appointed revisers held that they should not base any changes in the AV or KJV text on these manuscripts, which were not available to the translators of the 1611 version.

The NKJV was published in 1982. It was promoted as "the greatest publishing event since 1611." Reviewers, however, regret the fact that manuscripts which had become available since the publication of the AV or KJV were not used but were even deliberately ignored. They are of the opinion that the language is too strongly reminiscent to the AV or KJV's Jacobean English. It must be appreciated that there are no liberal tendencies, but there is an inclination to support certain outspoken theories on the Millennium. On the other hand, "Thou" and affiliated nouns have been replaced by "You." Insertions are in italics.

Canada

Several of the above-mentioned Bible versions have played a role in the brief history of the Canadian Reformed Churches and the Free Reformed Churches of Australia.

At the National Synod of 1954, held in Homewood, the Canadian Churches decided to recommend "to the Churches in the present situation the use of 'the Authorized King James Version,' because the Scriptural nature of this version has not been disputed."

The double formulation of the name of this version is taken over from a proposal that was made by the Classis East of these churches. It is an indication of how infrequently Church services were held in the English language at that time. I will not take up the question whether it was Canadian influence or similar proof of being unfamiliar with this version when we read the same double name in one of the Australian documents . . . .

The inclusion of the words "in the present situation" was taken from Classis East's proposal, in which some reservations regarding the RV, the ASV, and in particular the RSV were stated: "that the Scriptural nature is beyond doubt, cannot be said of the Revised Standard Version." The Classis therefore stated concerning the KJV: "In the present situation it is therefore to be preferred."[4]

The Synod of Homewood-Carman, held in 1958, had to deal with a request of the professors of Calvin Seminary at Grand Rapids for "cooperation in investigating the feasibility and desirability of sponsoring or facilitating the early production of a faithful translation of the Scripture in the common language of the American people." Synod stated that it was

---

[4] *Acts*, Articles 50, 64, 71.

not competent to undertake this, but advised senders to contact individual members of the churches who would be able and willing to share in the work of preparing a new translation.[5]

The same Synod decided to appoint a committee with the mandate to study the question whether the RSV could be recommended for use by the churches,[6] but apparently it forgot to execute this decision.

However, at the General Synod of Orangeville, held in 1968, the point was raised again by way of a proposal presented by the church at Burlington. From this proposal it may be obvious that within the churches there was the inclination to look for a Bible version which could replace the KJV because of the latter's archaic language. At the same time, people were also aware of some criticism of the RSV. All of this was echoed in Burlington's proposal "to appoint a Committee with the mandate to study the desirability of corrections of the Revised Standard Version, and to contact the "Standard Bible Committee," publisher of this translation, in order to bring our wishes to attention."

Synod first of all declared that "from the several later versions of the Bible the Revised Standard Version be chosen." The grounds for this statement were the following:

a. The Revised Standard Version has the merit of not being a complete new, a 'revolutionary' translation, but is meant as a 'revision' of the King James Version. It 'is not a new translation in the language of today. It is a revision which seeks to preserve all that is best in the English Bible as it has been known and used through the years' (Preface R.S.V.);

b. It does not have the weakness of a strongly personal translation like others, e.g. Phillips;

c. Its English will for many years to come remain sufficiently modern to meet the needs expressed in the overture and requests mentioned above;

d. The editors of the Revised Standard Version are in the process of preparing an improved edition of the Revised Standard Version, which will be published in the near future.

Synod did not feel free to comply with a request to "declare that with a view to the testing of the Revised Standard Version it is desirable that, besides the recommended King James Version also the Revised Standard

---

[5] *Acts*, Articles 30, 34, 48.

[6] *Acts*, Article 35.

Version be used in our Churches." One of the grounds for this negative response was: "An improved edition of the Revised Standard Version is planned; the Churches should await its publication."

Synod further decided to appoint a Committee with the mandate to study the Revised Standard Version as to faithfulness to the original text and Scriptural nature; to evaluate the criticisms of the Revised Standard Version; to contact the Standard Bible Committee which is preparing an improved edition of the RSV, a committee which welcomes all worthwhile contributions; and to solicit any help that it needs from persons who are considered competent in this field. It also recommended that members of the Churches, especially the ministers, be requested to take part in testing the RSV and be asked to submit their remarks to the Committee appointed.[7]

This Committee reported at the General Synod of New Westminster, held in 1971. The discussion also included a number of reactions to this report in the form of overtures and comments. The final result was that Synod declared "that no valid reasons have been adduced why the Revised Standard Version should be declared unacceptable for use by the Churches." The Committee on the Revision of the RSV was continued. Part of its mandate was "to receive, scan, and judge the criticism received and to pass it on to the Standard Bible Committee."[8]

The whole matter came to a provisional end at the General Synod of Toronto, held in 1974. Having declared that no valid reasons had been adduced to state that the RSV would be unacceptable, it decided "to leave the use of the RSV in the freedom of the Churches." The Committee on the RSV was continued and mandated "to continue the work of checking the R.S.V. and to pass on their criticism to the R.S.V. Bible Committee."[9] Proposals to undertake studies of other modern translations, e.g. the NASB and the NIV, were rejected.

At the next Synod, however, the General Synod of Coaldale, which met in 1977, there were overtures from several churches, requesting that the mandate for the Committee on the RSV be broadened and that the NASB and NIV be investigated as well. Synod decided to comply with these

---

[7] *Acts*, Article 45.

[8] *Acts*, Article 33.

[9] *Acts*, Article 182.

requests. Changing the name of the Committee to "Committee on Bible Translations," it added to its mandate: "to make a comparative study of the NASB and the NIV with the RSV and the KJV, in order to determine which one translation can be positively recommended for use by the Churches, whereby the criteria are: faithfulness to the original text, and linguistic character of the translation." Synod further declared that "pending this study only the use of the KJV and the RSV is in the freedom of the Churches."[10]

To the formulation of the previous Synod's decision it added that the use of the RSV was left in the freedom of the Churches, "though with discretion and care."[11] This declaration was apparently based on some findings of the Committee on the RSV to the effect that there are proofs of unscriptural and evolutionary influences. All the same, this Committee was of the opinion that "it is proven that all orthodox doctrines can be accurately formulated on the basis of the RSV."

The recommended use of the RSV had some consequences for the contents of the Book of Praise. This became apparent at the General Synod of Smithville, held in 1980, which decided that the RSV would be used "for the Scripture quotations in the linguistic modernization of the Creeds and the Liturgical Forms as much as possible." It further recommended "to the Churches the use of this translation in the worship services and for catechism instruction in order to come to uniformity of practice." However, it was left "in the freedom of the Churches to use the K.J.V. and the N.A.S.B., if the acceptance of the Revised Standard Version meets with insurmountable objections." The Committee on Bible Translations was reappointed, with the mandate "to continue to make recommendations to the Standard Bible Committee for changes necessary" in the RSV.[12]

As for the work of this committee, its contact with Prof. B. M. Metzger, the secretary of the RSV Bible Committee, resulted in the impression that the second version of the Old Testament and the third version of the New Testament would be based on more "conservative" texts.

Since that time, the work has come to a standstill. The Synods of Cloverdale (1983) and Burlington (1986) could only reappoint deputies

---

[10] *Acts*, Article 105.

[11] *Acts*, Article 104.

[12] *Acts*, Article 111.

with the same mandate.[13] Only at the General Synod of Winnipeg, held in 1989, was there again some activity in this respect. Deputies reported that the time schedule was too tight to make submissions to the RSV Bible Committee since this Committee was to give its work to the publisher by the middle of 1988. In the meantime, a couple of churches had expressed their concern about the direction the RSV Committee was taking: it proposed the elimination of "masculine-oriented language so far as this can be done without altering passages that reflect the historical situation of ancient patriarchal culture, and of masculine society." One church also proposed the scrutinizing of the new edition of the RSV as well as the latest edition of the New King James Version as a possible alternative translation for future use in the Churches. New deputies were appointed with the mandate to scrutinize the NRSV Bible as soon as it becomes available: they were to consider faithfulness in translation, particularly with regard to the use of so-called inclusive language. No further response was given to the proposal regarding the NKJV that came from the Church of Carman, apparently because Synod considered that "based on information received from the RSV Bible Committee, there will not be substantial changes in the forthcoming edition of the RSV."

At the General Synod of Lincoln, held in 1992, the Committee reported that the RSV will go out of print within a few years, although Premier Printing informed Synod that it might be able to reprint this version. Synod agreed with the Committee for Bible Translations that the NRSV "is unacceptable for use in the churches." It decided to continue the committee with the mandate "to do a comparative study of the NASB, NIV and NKJV, making use of past studies, in order to determine which one translation can be positively recommended for use by the churches, whereby the criteria are: faithfulness to the original text and linguistic character of the translation"; furthermore "to investigate the direction of the Bible Societies/Publishers behind different translations and whether there is the possibility to suggest improvements in the translation of the Bible Societies/Publishers which can be incorporated into future editions; as well, to investigate the future availability of the translations." The Committee was instructed "to give due consideration to the decision of Synod Bedfordale 1992, regarding Bible translation."

---

[13] *Acts*, Articles 115 and 60 respectively.

After having discussed a lengthy Report tabled by the committee appointed by the previous synod, the General Synod Abbotsford 1995 decided to "recommend the NIV for use within the Churches," to "leave it in the freedom of the Churches if they feel compelled to use another translation," "to continue the Committee on Bible Translation which would receive comments from churches and/or members about passages in the NIV in need of improvement, scrutinize those comments, and pass on valid concerns to the NIV Translation Centre. The committee should also glean from previous synod reports as well as from the Report and its appendices any recommendations for change which need to be presented to the NIV Translation Centre. The letters which were sent to Synod expressing concerns about certain Bible passages should also be sent on to the Committee." Furthermore it was decided to "send a copy of the Report of the Committee on Bible Translation and Synod's decision to our sister churches in Australia."[14]

Australia

The story of the synodical decisions regarding the Bible translation to be used in the Free Reformed Churches of Australia is not as lengthy as the story of the decisions made by their Canadian sister Churches.

Their first Synod, the Synod of Armadale (1954), decided to appoint deputies who were charged to investigate which English version of the Bible was most to be preferred for use in the worship services. The deputies were instructed to inform themselves about the results reached by the Churches in Canada, in order that in this respect there would be as much uniformity as possible in the English-speaking countries.[15]

The next Synod (Armadale, 1956) decided to recommend to the Churches — and here is that double name again! — "the Authorized King James Version," since the Scriptural character of this version is undisputed.[16]

The Acts of the Synod of Albany, held in 1962, make mention of the existence of deputies for the study of the New English Bible (Article 24).

---

[14] *Acts*, Article 72.

[15] *Acts*, Article 16.

[16] *Acts*, Article 36.

Apparently they had been appointed by consultation among the Churches in between 1959, the date of the previous Synod, and 1962. The NEB New Testament was published in the year 1961. The deputies informed Synod that they had commenced their work.

The next Synod, that of Launceston (1964), decided to appoint deputies once again for the investigation of the NEB, but it broadened their mandate: They had "to investigate which versions of the Bible may be considered for use in our Church services."[17]

The Synod of Armadale (1966) was of the opinion that it was indeed urgent to find a usable Bible translation for Church services. It appeared to be difficult to carry out "the instruction to independently test the NEB." Therefore Synod resolved to appoint new deputies with the instruction to investigate further which Bible translation could be considered for use in Church services.[18]

The next two Synods reappointed deputies because they had been unable to finalize their task. The Synod of Albany, held in 1968, added to their mandate the instruction that they should contact their Canadian colleagues.[19]

In the year 1972, at the Armadale Synod, there was a report at last. Objections had been raised against the RSV. Therefore Synod decided to further broaden the deputies' mandate by instructing them to include in their examination such translations as the NASB and the King James II Version by Jay P. Green.[20]

At the Albany Synod of 1975 it appeared that deputies were of the opinion that the NIV and the KJIIV must be rejected — the former because "the dynamic equivalent method of translation does not do full justice to the inscripturated, inspired Word of God," and the latter because of several weaknesses. Synod agreed with their judgment and decided to instruct new deputies "to study fully the New American Standard Bible (N.A.S.B.) and the Revised Standard Version (R.S.V.), taking into account the many objections against the R.S.V. (raised) over the last years"; further "to compare them with each other and with the Authorized Version (A.V. or

---

[17] *Acts*, Article 18.
[18] *Acts*, Article 50.
[19] *Acts*, Article 40.
[20] *Acts*, Article 47.

K.J.V.) in order to find which translation is to be preferred." A point of special interest is that Synod decided "to counsel the Churches to be alert as regards the possible use of new translations by members of the congregations."[21]

The Launceston Synod of the year 1978 adopted a proposal "to appoint new deputies with the instruction to contact the translators of the updated King James Version, to be published by Thomas Nelson Inc., Nashville, Tenn., to obtain further information on this version," and to evaluate it when published, comparing it with the RSV. They were to abandon the evaluation of the NASB.[22]

These deputies were unable to table the required evaluation at the next Synod, that of Armadale (1980). New deputies were given a somewhat lighter mandate. Synod repeated the warning of 1975 that the Churches should "remain alert so that unreliable translations do not gain a foothold in our families."[23]

At the Kelmscott Synod of 1983 it was stated that the KJV was not suitable because of its archaic language. The RSV was deemed to be a reliable, accurate, and acceptable translation, in clear contemporary English, and therefore suitable for use in public worship and for instructional and family use. Consequently, it was recommended for these purposes. Meanwhile, the use of the AV was still in the freedom of the Churches if the use of the RSV met with insurmountable objections. Deputies were appointed to monitor developments regarding the use of the RSV in Churches, and to do the same as far as the work of the RSV Translation Committee was concerned.[24]

At the Launceston Synod of 1985, the last part of this mandate was reaffirmed for new deputies. In addition, the deputies were to study materials produced by Synods of the Canadian sister Churches, and also the material placed before this Launceston Synod. The latter consisted of some objections to the RSV, which, as the deputies reported, was being used by all of the Free Reformed Churches of Australia. These objections were raised against: (a) the influence of modern/liberal translators who were not

---

[21] *Acts*, Article 52.

[22] *Acts*, Article 42.

[23] *Acts*, Article 36.

[24] *Acts*, Article 35.

committed to the divine authority of Scripture or to the divinity of Christ; and (b) omissions and substitutions compared with the KJV.[25]

The Synod of Albany (1987) had to deal not only with the deputies' report but also with additional objections to the recommendation to use the RSV. The text underlying this translation was questioned, and also its faithfulness. Synod charged newly appointed deputies "to investigate once more the NIV & NASB and to investigate the New KJV to see if any one of these translations would be better than the RSV. The reports of previous deputies and the reports of the deputies of our Canadian sister-churches can be consulted and used for this investigation." The following criteria had to be used:

1. Faithfulness to the original Hebrew, Aramaic and Greek texts;

2. Readability and suitability for worship services, for instruction and for memorization;

3. Consistency in maintaining the unity of the Scriptures.

Meanwhile, the decision of the 1983 Synod to recommend the RSV for use in the Churches was upheld and maintained.[26]

The Synod of Armadale (1990) had to discuss a lengthy report which dealt with the underlying text, the method of translating, the criteria for suitability, the forthcoming 1990 edition of the RSV, the NASB, the NKJV, and the NIV. Among the Synod's decisions was the following:

3. as regards the underlying text, to accept the premise that there is room for a careful eclectic method;

4. to declare at this time already that the NASB, NKJV and NIV are deemed better translations than the RSV;

5. to express caution over the DE (dynamic equivalent) approach to translation;

6. to appoint new deputies with the following instructions:

    1. to explore, in consultation with (in the first instance) the sister-churches, the feasibility of the churches themselves undertaking the task of translating the Bible;

    2. as regards the NASB, NKJV and NIV translations: to supplement the 1989 report and:

        2.1 to further study (. . .) the suitability of NASB and NKJV to replace the RSV;

---

[25] *Acts*, Article 73.

[26] *Acts*, Article 109.

2.2 to further evaluate the NIV (...), in respect of its methods of translation;

2.3 to make use of previous deputies' reports including those of our Canadian sister-churches;

2.4 to monitor developments in these translations;

2.5 to send relevant suggestions and improvements to the Committees on Bible translation concerned, and await and evaluate any replies on these;

2.6 to invite comments from the churches on these translations;

2.7 to consult with the Canadian Reformed Churches to see whether a common approach can be reached.

All in all, this added up to a great deal of work for the deputies. It is therefore no wonder that the very last line of the deputies' instruction included some reservation regarding the time required to complete their task. It reads: "to report, and if possible make recommendations, to next Synod."[27]

Surprisingly, the deputies tabled a lengthy report at the Bedfordale Synod, held in 1992. On the basis of this report, Synod decided to recommend to the churches that the NKJV be used for study, instruction, and family purposes. This recommendation was not supposed to be taken to mean final endorsement of this version for use in the worship services, although room for such use was left if consistories so desired. Synod also mandated new deputies to continue studies of the NKJV in comparison with the NIV, to determine whether the NKJV could be endorsed as a final recommendation to the churches. As for the latter part of this mandate, the following areas of study were included: whether Old Testament sources are properly used, and the extent and seriousness of the loss of reliability resulting from the method of translation that was chosen. The Canadian Committee was to be contacted in order to urge "the brotherhood in Canada to reach a similar decision."

As for the RSV, apart from other objections against it, there was also the obstacle of the 1971 version being replaced by the 1990 edition, the NRSV. Another stumbling-block was the fact that the 1971 version was no longer available in bookstores.

This decision caused a shift of attention toward the NKJV, although room for study and use of the NIV was maintained.

---

[27] *Acts*, Article 138.

In conclusion

It is to be appreciated that both federations of Churches are diligent with regard to the question of Bible translation and are on the alert regarding problems related to the source manuscripts and translation. For the Holy Scriptures, acknowledged and confessed by both Church federations as the infallible, inscripturated Word of God, play a very prominent role in communion and communication between the LORD God and the people of His covenant.

2. CHURCH SINGING

In the year 1542 John Calvin published his Genevan Psalter. He introduced it in a "Letter to the Reader." In this letter we find the following words:

> As for the public prayers, there are two kinds. The one is prayed by speaking only, the other by singing. This is no recent invention, for, as the history books may prove, this is how it was done right from the beginning of the Church.

Praying by singing is a response to God's Word. But we must realize that it is the same Word of God that teaches us how to formulate this response. Our covenant God has given us a complete book of Psalms along with other biblical songs.

We will briefly review the history of Church singing and see that these biblical examples have indeed been followed, although they have been neglected as well. We will do so in two different sections — the first one on Psalm singing, the other on hymn singing.

2.1 Psalm singing

Before the Reformation

Although I just mentioned the name of John Calvin, I will not begin with him. I want to concentrate on Psalm singing in the English-speaking countries, which means that we have to start in the days before his time.

In the year 596 a certain Augustine — not the well known Aurelius Augustine — landed at Thanet in England. He was accompanied by forty monks, among whom were a number of musicians, most likely trained at the *Schola Cantorum* in Rome. They had all been sent out by Pope Gregory the Great, the alleged "father" of Gregorian chant. England had to be conquered and made to submit to "Rome."

At his conversion King Ethelbert presented them with a Church building at Cambridge. Since that time Augustine has been regarded as the first archbishop of Canterbury, the leader of the Church of England. One of his first activities was the establishment of a *Schola Cantorum*, which in turn led to the introduction of the Gregorian chant throughout England during the eighth century, followed by Scotland in the ninth century. However, for congregational singing the Gregorian chant was unsuitable.

The same must be said about the ancient Sarum tunes, which originate from the liturgy of the Salisbury diocese. This liturgy, which was in use before Augustine's arrival, did not differ fundamentally from the Gregorian chant. The former tunes were even "adopted" by the latter.

However, there is a kind of pre-reformation heritage in the ballad tunes, and in the songs used by the followers of John Wyclif, called Lollardic songs. Both groups of songs became more widely used in the days of King Henry VIII. And this observation already brings us to the reformation of the English Church.

The Reformation

Augustine's success in submitting the Church of England to the Pope's jurisdiction was undone by King Henry VIII's act of divorcing not only Catharine of Aragon but also the Church of Rome. In the process he himself became the head of the Church of England (1533).

In spite of the fact that the monastery system was disbanded and the Gregorian chant seriously affected, we cannot say that his actions led to a real reformation of the Church. Genuine reforms in the liturgy were made under his successor, Edward VI (1547-1553). From then on the liturgy would be in the vernacular. The Mass was simplified, and the daily services were reduced to Morning Prayer and Evening Prayer.

However, the need for a new Church book was strongly felt. The result was the publication of *The Book of Common Prayer* in the year 1549. This book replaced the missals, couchers, grailes, hymnals, antiphoners, portuasses, primers, journals, ordinals, epistollers, gospellers, and others. Its second edition of 1552 was of a more reformative character, having been influenced by Martin Bucer and John Calvin. The Book of Common Prayer includes Coverdale's version of the Psalms, a version which, after so many centuries, is still used in this context, although not for congregational singing.

Congregational singing was stimulated by John Merbecke, whose work, *The Book of Common Prayer Noted*, was published in the year 1550 in cooperation with Thomas Cranmer, the Reformed archbishop of Canterbury. It was an effort to provide congregations with some simple music.

A few years earlier Thomas Sternhold, groom of the robes to King Henry VIII, had tried to write sacred ballads. He wrote metrical versions of the Psalms, almost exclusively in common metre, with the help of his disciples Hopkins and Norton. This version may be referred to when, in the first edition of *The Book of Common Prayer*, we read the following sentence: "that it be lawful (. . .) in churches (. . .), chapels or oratories and other places to use every day Psalme or prayer taken out of the Bible (. . .) not letting or omitting thereby the service or any part thereof mentioned in the said book."

Geneva

We now go first of all to Geneva, where William Farel and John Calvin tried to win the City Council for the introduction of congregational singing. However, their proposal, together with other proposals, backfired: in the year 1538 they were exiled.

Nevertheless, on his return in 1541 Calvin introduced his selection *Aulcuns Pseaulmes et cantiques mys en chant*, which he had compiled, together with Clement Marot, during his stay at Strasbourg. Soon afterwards it was replaced by a selection of fifty Psalms and Scriptural songs, written by Marot. In 1562 these efforts were brought to completion with the help of Theodore Beza, drawing on tunes by Louis Bourgeois, the still unknown "Maitre Pierre," and Matthias Greiter.

I have mentioned these publications because they served as examples for the Anglo-Genevan Psalter. This Psalter may be named as one of the positive fruits of the flight of Scotsman John Knox and others to the continent. Under the guidance of Knox, refugees from the British Isles, in the year 1556, produced for their congregational life at Geneva, *The Order of Geneva*, or, *The Book of Common Order*, a part of which bore the title, *One and Fiftie Psalmes of David, in English Metre, 37 of which were made by Thomas Sternholde and the rest by others,"* (seven by John Hopkins, and seven by Whittingham, John Calvin's brother-in-law). In the year 1561 some more Psalms were added by William Kethe and others, the total then being eighty-seven Psalms. This selection is known as the "Anglo-Genevan Psalter."

Whittingham's version of Psalm 124 is still well known. It was sung during a service attended by the members of the House of Commons at the end of World War II. It is said that Winston Churchill, then Britain's Prime Minister, was deeply impressed by it. This version was included in the first edition of the *Book of Praise*. Our present tune of Psalm 134 was used for Psalm 100, and is still known as "The Old Hundredth."

The Old Version

After the interim under Queen Mary, reprints of Sternhold and others were published. A newcomer in this field, John Daye, issued the Daye's Psalter in 1562. This included forty-four old Psalm versions by Sternhold and Hopkins, twenty taken from the Anglo-Genevan Psalter, and eighty-six new versions, mainly by Hopkins. It was semi-officially sanctioned by the Church of England.

However, there was a major disadvantage: almost all the Genevan tunes were replaced by "Common Metre" tunes. This edition is called the "Standard Edition," and is even better known as the "Old Version."

Scotland

There was a similar development in Scotland. Sternhold's version, which was introduced in 1550, was replaced the next year by a more extensive Psalter, in versions by Sternhold and Hopkins. In the meantime John Knox had returned to Scotland. The First General Assembly adopted the *Book of Common Order*, which resulted in the *Anglo-Genevan Psalter* being expanded to the *First Scottish Psalter* of 1564. This Psalter included thirty-nine Psalms by Sternhold, thirty-seven by Hopkins, sixteen by Whittingham, twenty-seven by Kethe, and thirty-seven by others.

While the English Old Version had only sixty-two tunes, the Scottish version had one hundred and five, forty-two of which were taken from the *Anglo-Genevan Psalter*, thirty-one being "French" or (altered) "Genevan."

That this version became very popular is evident from the fact that sixty-four editions were published between 1564 and 1644 — some of them printed in Middelburg and Dordrecht, The Netherlands. Bassandine's edition of 1575 for the first time bore the title *The CL Psalmes of David*. Consequently the whole Church service book was called *The Psalms Book*.

Musical deterioration did, however, creep into the Scottish Psalter, as we will soon see.

New versions in England

After the Old Version, several other Psalters were published. One of them was John Daye's version in four musical parts, "suitable to be performed with the help of various musical instruments." This note indicated a development in a non-reformative direction. Another was Thomas Este's version, the first Psalter containing names for the tunes. A third one was George Whither's work — authorized by the King, although this authorization was annulled by the Privy Council on request of the publishers of the Old Version.

In that year *His Majesties Poeticall Exercises at Vacant Hours* were published. They were from the hand of King James, the man who lent his name to the King James Version. The King appeared to have "some time off" every now and then. Having been corrected during King Charles's reign by Alexander of Menstrie and appearing in 1631, this publication carried the official name *The Psalmes of King David translated by King James*. Through this title, the latter was put on the same level as the former. This publication was popularly known as "The Menstries Psalms."

The work of Francis Rous, speaker of the House of Commons, was anonymously printed and published at Rotterdam in 1638, with a second edition under his name appearing in 1641. Four years later this edition was revised so drastically that Rous could no longer grant his permission to have it carry his name. Therefore it was also known as the "Westminster Version." It met with competition from William Barton's version of 1645. Politics entered the field of Church singing when the House of Commons placed Rous's version under its protection, and the House of Lords did the same with Barton's work.

The deadlock was broken by the publication of the Psalter of Tate and Brady in the year 1696. It was dedicated to King William III of Orange and has since then been called *The New Version*. Musically it deviates from real reformative congregational singing because its tunes are mainly in Common Metre.

New versions in Scotland

The development in Scotland does not produce a more favourable picture. The various editions of the *First Scottish Psalter* contained fewer and fewer tunes. In the 1612 edition there were only twelve of them left, thus called "Common Tunes." However, some efforts to reform Church singing were undertaken. In this context I should mention a selection of harmonizations and various old French tunes included in *The Great Scottish Psalter* by Edward Miller (1635). It is to be regretted that many of these tunes, derived from the Psalters of Calvin and of Knox, were mutilated because they were transformed into Common Metre and Long Metre tunes. Of greater importance is the fact that in Scotland Rous's work was revised several times. In 1650 it was introduced as *The (Second) Scottish Psalter*. However, it was published without any tunes! One month later Oliver Cromwell's troops entered Scotland, which event had some serious consequences for Church life. Due to extreme Puritan ideas, Psalm singing was replaced by Scripture-readings. The old tunes, passed on orally, were soon forgotten. The 1661 edition included no more than a dozen tunes in Long, Common and Short Metre. Other factors that promoted further decay were the general poverty and analphabethism of the people. The precentor, or "uptaker-of-the-psalm," was given another name: "he that takes up the line," for first the precentor sang a line to the people, and only then did the congregation do the same. No organs were used.

Not everyone was happy with this situation. Therefore efforts for improvement were undertaken. However, they were promptly opposed by a "Resistance to Change Movement." A wrong direction was taken when some "great precentors" introduced choirs. There was some improvement when a lecture on Psalmody, delivered in the year 1854 by William Carnie, resulted in the establishing of a "General Association for the Improvement of Psalmody."

The year 1929 saw the appearance of a revised edition of the Psalter-Hymnary. It included Psalms, paraphrases, and metrical versions of Scripture sections, many hymns, all fully harmonized, suitable for choir or congregation to sing in four parts. However, there were no fixed tunes, so that for every song a choice had to be made from a large number of options.

Looking at the whole picture we reach the conclusion that, as far the musical aspect is concerned, Psalm singing in Great Britain cannot be regarded as truly reformative in character.

North America

In earlier days the northeastern part of what we now call the United States was called "New England." This may explain the use of the name "New England Psalmody."

It was very unfortunate that Ainsworth was neglected by the Puritans who settled in the Massachusetts Bay colony. He was one of the leaders of the Pilgrim Fathers. He had strong objections against the English Old Version. In 1612, during his stay in The Netherlands, he wrote a Psalm Version partly on the Genevan tunes of the Dutch Psalter. The Puritans were not happy with the Sternhold-Hopkins Psalter and therefore published their own version, the *Bay Psalm Book* or *Bay Psalter* (1640). The 1651 edition, introducing itself by the name *New England Psalm Book,* also included the songs of Moses from Exodus 15 and Deuteronomy 32, the songs of Deborah and Hanna, the Song of Songs in metrical version, and the songs from Isaiah and Habakkuk's prophecies.

The *Bay Psalter* came into being after much internal trouble: Some of the Puritans were of the opinion that singing was worldly, others that only "recognized Christians" were authorized to sing, while the rest of the congregation was only allowed to respond to it by their "Amen." A third opinion was that only men were permitted to sing, and a fourth that the singing of Psalms, in particular, was forbidden. In spite of this variation in opinion, the *Bay Psalter* was accepted in the long run. Only its ninth edition included some tunes, written by Playford.

The *Bay Psalter* was written by a number of ministers, the most prominent of them being John Cotton. It was printed within ten years after the arrival of the first Puritans. It was also the very first book printed in America, because the ship which brought some more migrants in the year 1638 had a complete printing press on board.

When, "Ainsworth" became too difficult for the people to sing, because of the lowering of the standard of congregational singing, the Pilgrim Church adopted the *Bay Psalter*.

The level of Church singing was indeed very low. The use of musical instruments was not allowed. Efforts for improvement were undertaken, e.g. by the establishing of song schools, by stimulating schoolteachers, and by means of sermons and pamphlets. But there was also some resistance to these efforts, for example, from the side of the precentors who did not want to lose their job.

As soon as instruction books were published, the tradition of "reading the line" slowly disappeared, though not without resistance. Growing nationalism and opposition to the policy of the English government also manifested themselves in musical form: during the War of Independence William Billings — whom some have called the first real American composer — interpreted and paraphrased the Psalms in a really nationalistic and political way.

Psalm singing was replaced more and more by hymn singing, in spite of the opposition to the latter from the side of those who had Puritan origins. The remnants of Psalm singing and Psalm versions were minimal, e.g. in rather free versions, with some Arminian influences, by Isaac Watts.

Turning now to the Dutch and Scottish migrants, I should mention first of all that the former brought with them Petrus Dathenus's Psalm version, which was, however, soon replaced by the version of 1773. When the worship services were held more and more in the English language, the consistory of the New York congregation, in the year 1767, published an amended New Version (English). It is said that these Psalms were adapted to the Genevan tunes, but these tunes were mutilated, and many of them were replaced by Common Metre tunes. Moreover, the tune of the Genevan Psalm 134 had to serve for some twenty other Psalms!

The Presbyterians used the *Second Scottish Psalter* of 1650. But in 1872 it was replaced by, *The Psalter, Scottish Version of the Psalms revised, and the New Version adopted by the United Presbyterian Church*. This song book had some "grand old tunes," but also "many of modern date." A new edition appeared in 1887, with more modern versions, some Psalms having more than one rhyming.

Where as the 1927 version is still in use in some American churches, the Christian Reformed Church (established in 1857) adopted the older version until it was replaced by the *Psalter Hymnal*. But even this Church borrowed a great deal of its Psalm section from the United Presbyterians, whose Board of Publication and Bible School held the copyright.

The background of this development is as follows: in the year 1900, at the instigation of the United Presbyterian Church, a "Joint Committee" consisting of representatives of seven Presbyterian Churches, the Dutch Reformed Church, and the Christian Reformed Church, was established. The aim was to rehabilitate Psalm singing — a very commendable aim indeed! The committee's findings were published in the years 1905 and 1909. However, the Churches did not immediately or integrally adopt them — which may be clear from their respective song books, which consisted mainly of hymns.

The Christian Reformed Church, for example, continued the use of *The Psalter*. When in the year 1911 a certain Rev. van der Werp published his work, *The psalms, new metrical versions with tunes, old and new*, which was a kind of mixture of "1905" and "1909," with the addition of some special versions by E. A. Collins — one of the contributors to "1909" — this publication did not gain general support. It was only in the year 1928 that the Synod of this Church appointed a committee to study the possibilities of the renewal of the song book.

It was not even the matter of *The Psalter* that dominated the scene, but the growing desire for the use of hymns in public worship. Therefore it is no wonder that the final outcome was the appearance of the *Psalter Hymnal* in the year 1934, which included no less than 327 versions of Psalms or of "selected stanzas," and 141 hymns. The 1946 edition had 310 "Psalms" and 179 hymns. The great majority of these Psalm versions were adopted from "1909." Only thirty-four Psalms were set to Genevan tunes. Their text was written by Mr. Dewey Westra — whom we will meet again at a later stage — and the Revs. S. G. Brondsema, E. A. Collier, B. Essenburg, and William Kuipers. In the 1946 edition the tunes lost their original rhythm, because after the appearance of the first edition "many of our people were disappointed because of the rhythmic setting which was given to these chorales." The "desire of many to sing these tunes just the way they used to be sung from the Dutch Psalter (namely, as plain chorales, with all the notes of equal length) found official expression in a decision of the Synod of 1946 that in the next edition of the *Psalter Hymnal* these melodies should be printed as plain chorales" — which was definitely not an improvement, rather, to the contrary!

When considered from a Reformed point of view, the history of Psalm singing on the North American continent is, in terms of the text as well as in terms of the musical content, not a joyful one. We must therefore be very grateful that in the publication and use of the *Book of Praise*, Scriptural Psalm singing was restored.

2.2 HYMN SINGING

What is a hymn?

We are all familiar with the distinction between Psalms and hymns. Hymns, to us, are all those songs suitable for congregational singing which are not found in the book of Psalms.

It is not my intention to create confusion in the minds of the readers, but it is a matter of fact that in biblical times this distinction was not so strongly made.

In the ancient Greek translation of the Old Testament, called the Septuagint, the word "hymn" is used in the titles of Psalms 6, 54, and 55. The whole second selection, consisting of the Psalms 42 to 72, is called "David's hymns" in the final verse of Psalm 72. The same name, or the verb "hymn singing," is used in reference to Psalms 22:23 and 25; 40:3; 65:1 and 13; 100:4; and 148 passim.

In the meantime it may be significant that the terms "hymns" and "hymn singing" are used for what in our English versions has been translated as "praise." These terms, then, were used for what can be called songs of praise to God. It is not strange, therefore, that we find the same term, "hymn singing," describing what we are told the Saviour and His disciples did when they concluded their Passover celebration with the singing of a "hymn," according to the custom of those days. This was most likely the so-called Egyptian Hallel, the Psalms 113 to 118 (Matthew 26:30; Mark 14:26). The same is said of Paul and Silas, who prayed and were "hymn singing" in the Philippian prison.[28] Consequently the apostle cannot be making a sharp distinction into three different groups of songs when, in Ephesians 5:19 and Colossians 3:16, he speaks of "Psalms and hymns and spiritual songs." It is remarkable that Psalm 76 is typified by each of these three names.

Nevertheless, I will maintain the distinction between Psalms and hymns, considering the latter to be those sacred songs which are not found in the book of Psalms.

Actually, I should mention two more groups and distinguish them from the hymns. I am thinking of the so-called canticles or odes, which refer to a series of songs found in the Bible but outside the book of Psalms, e.g.

---

[28] Acts 16:25.

the two songs of Moses (Exodus 15 and Deuteronomy 32) and the songs of Deborah and Hanna. The second group includes the paraphrases — biblical texts put into metrical version for congregational singing. However, I will restrict myself now to what we usually call hymns.

Many people do not make the above-mentioned distinction between hymns, canticles or odes, and paraphrases. I do make this distinction and go ever further. Without making an effort to formulate a precise definition of a hymn, we can already, on the basis of the above-mentioned biblical data, draw the conclusion that a hymn, in the Scriptural sense of the word, is a song of praise to God.

For those who want to follow these biblical indications, what I have established here would make it impossible to include in their Hymnary many of the Methodist hymns, for example. The difficulty with these hymns is that they concentrate on man's religious feelings and experiences, putting man — rather than God — into the centre. In other words, if the hymn section of a Church service book includes songs of praise to God, it can rightly carry the name of *Book of Praise*.

Songs of praise

Augustine — and this time I am referring to the well-known Aurelius Augustine — asked the question in a commentary on Psalm 148: "Know ye what a hymn is?" He answered the question himself by stating: "It is a song with praise of God." Further explaining this definition, he added: "If thou praisest God and singest not, thou utterest no hymn. If thou singest and praisest not God, thou utterest no hymn. A hymn, then, containeth these three things: song (*canticum*), and praise (*laudem*), and that of God. Praise, then, of God in song is called a hymn."[29] (We had better forget that Augustine, appealing to Psalm 148:14, added: "Also songs of praise to the saints are called hymns!")

It is therefore no wonder that a Hymnary from the tenth or eleventh century says in its preface: "Whatever poems, then, are sung in praise of God are called hymns. A hymn, moreover, is linked with those who sing and praise, which from Greek into Latin is interpreted *laus*, because it is a song of joy and praise; but properly hymns are those containing the praise of God."

---

[29] John Julian, *A Dictionary of Hymnology*, London, 1907, 640.

Alas, this principle has been neglected in the course of the history of hymn writing and hymn singing.

Pre-reformation hymn singing

Before the Reformation, hymn singing was not just a matter of congregational singing. The text was either in Greek or in Latin, the languages of the clergy.

The use of hymns originates from the Eastern Church. When the Western Church took them over, many Greek hymns were translated into Latin, although a number of them were maintained because in certain regions Greek was still in use, e.g. in parts of Italy, Germany, North Africa, and the South of Gaul.

The earliest Western Latin hymns date back to the days of Hilary, bishop of Poitiers in Gaul, and of Pope Damasus, and on to the beginning of the fourth century. Then the well-known bishop of Milan, Ambrose, arrived on the scene. The "Ambrosian hymns" were written for congregational singing. This may be proved from the story which tells us about the church building being besieged by enemies who were deeply impressed and scared off by the singing of the congregation!

The Ambrosian hymns had been set to simple tunes which were suitable for congregational singing. They were addressed to God who was considered to be present in the congregation. Their texts were often derived from daily happenings in nature, because the visible world was thought to run parallel to the invisible world. From Milan these hymns were spread all over Western Europe. They also reached England.

Hymns that used the same style — at least at first — were written and promoted by Pope Gregory the Great, and also, as far as England is concerned, by Beda Venerabilis, the great historian.

Since the eleventh century, however, the character of the hymns changed. Augustine would no longer have called them all by that name, for many of them no longer praised God — not even Mary or other saints. Rather, they became meditations on Christ's passion and wounds, penitential exercises, and sacramental songs. As for the first-mentioned group, we may remember that even until our own days such a song as *O Haupt voll Blut und Wunden* (O Sacred Head Now Wounded) has maintained itself.

Another turn for the worse was the fact that the hymns were used more and more in the context of the Mass. This development resulted in the composing of a large number of Latin hymns at the beginning of the fourteenth century — really a culminating point in this respect. Some of them were translated into the vernacular and sung by the people, although not in church. But in the sixteenth century, Pope Pius V and the Council of Trent reduced the number of hymns to be used in the celebration of the Mass to four. Among them were the well-known titles of *Veni Sancte Spiritus* and *Dies Irae*, to which the *Stabat Mater* was added in 1772. Experts are of the opinion that the quality of most of these Latin hymns was poor.

Apart from these hymns there were also metrical versions of the Ten Commandments, the *Pater Noster* (Lord's Prayer), the *Gloria in Excelsis* (song of the angels from Luke 2), and the Creed.

It all seemed so pleasant. But we must not forget that in the meantime the priest had imposed himself between God and the congregation — the priest sung the Scripture lessons and the prayers in Latin, later assisted by a choir and even by soloists. All that remained for the congregation was simply "Amen" as a response, and a few Ambrosian hymns.

A last point to be mentioned is that, as far as England was concerned, before the Breviary came into use at the end of the eleventh and the beginning of the twelfth century, Hymnaries were used. These Hymnaries (collections of Latin hymns) sometimes included interlinear Anglo-Saxon translations so that the congregational members would be able to follow the singing in their own language. Some of these hymnals were combined with the Psalter and the Scriptural canticles.

Looking at the whole picture, we reach the conclusion that a reformation was urgently needed because the congregation was unable to participate properly in the worship of God. In His grace God granted His Church this reformation.

The Reformation

Reformed congregational singing has its cradle in Martin Bucer's Strasbourg. Since our church service book, the *Book of Praise*, claims to be representative of this type of singing in modern times, I will concentrate on that city and on John Calvin's Geneva.

Hence I will not pay great attention to Martin Luther and the hymn singing of the Lutherans. This reformer introduced congregational singing, and we owe to him and his followers a large number of hymns and beautiful tunes, some of which are to be found in our *Book of Praise* — Hymns 24, 33, 41, 47, and 62.

As for Ulrich Zwingli, he was a good musician, yet he did not tolerate any music in church, being of the opinion that producing it was a "good work" in the Roman Catholic sense of the word. It was no wonder, then, that organs were removed from the church buildings. However, it seems that later he adopted a more lenient attitude and expressed himself more than once in favour of congregational singing.

In Strasbourg Martin Bucer made a plea in his publication of 1524, *Grund und Ursach*, for congregational singing. He used to defend the purifying of the liturgy. In the same year, and in 1525 the two volumes of his *Teutsch Kircheampt mit lobgesangen und gottlichen psalmen wie es die gemein zu Straasburg singt und halt ganz Christlich* were published. This work contained a number of Psalms, and metrical versions of the Lord's Prayer, the Creed, the Ten Commandments, and the Miserere (a penitential song). It was enlarged in the next two decades, resulting in the official songbook of the Strasbourg Church dating from the year 1541. It included many "free songs" for the festive days, a large proportion having been adopted from Martin Luther's Wittenberg.

We still use a few tunes which originate from Strasbourg. A quick look in the *Book of Praise* above Psalms 36 and 68 and the Songs of Mary and Zachariah, will reveal this.

It was at Strasbourg that for the first time in his life, John Calvin heard congregational singing. He had tried to introduce it in Geneva, where William Farel's songbook of 1533 was available — including a version of the Ten Commandments — but the City Council strongly opposed him in this and in other matters. As the minister of the congregation of French refugees at Strasbourg he adopted this liturgical element from the German-speaking congregation. In 1539 he published his book *Aulcuns Pseaumes at Cantiques / mys en chant*, its title revealing that some hymns were included, the Ten Commandments, the Creed, and the Song of Simeon — the latter being used at the conclusion of the celebration of the Lord's Supper.

After his return to Geneva, Calvin published a number of Psalm versions by Clement Marot (1543), to which the same hymns were added, as well as the Lord's Prayer, a Prayer before meals, and a Prayer after meals.

Theodore Beza, who in 1551 had completed the metrical version of the book of Psalms, published a booklet in the year 1595 containing the so-called Canticles or Scriptural Odes, its title reading *Les Saincts Cantiques Recvellis tant du Vieil que de Nuveau Testament, mis en rime francoise*. It included metrical versions of Deuteronomy 26:3; the songs of Moses (Exodus 15 and Deuteronomy 32); the songs of Deborah, Hannah, and David in II Samuel 1:19 (his lamentation on the death of Saul and Jonathan); the song of II Samuel 7:18 (expressing his gratitude for what he could do in view of the establishing of the temple); his last song (II Samuel 23); the songs of Isaiah 5, 12, 26, and 38; the Song of Jonah; Habakkuk 3; and the Songs of Mary, Zechariah, and Simeon.

From Strasbourg, and in particular from Geneva, the congregational singing — including a modest form of hymn singing — spread all over the continent and the British Isles. Refugees played a significant role in this development.

England

Due to its beginning, the Reformation in England had a special character. King Henry VIII wanted to divorce his wife, and subsequently he broke with the Pope. Yet, many ceremonies and other pre-Reformation practices were maintained. This may explain the continuous influence of the Latin hymn used in the daily offices.

Some of them were translated. Coverdale's *Goostly Psalms and Spiritual Songs*, most likely published in the year 1539, had three hymns based on the well known "Veni Creator," and another based on "*Christe, qui lux*." This may also be the fruit of the Lutheran influence on the English situation in the initial stages of the Reformation: Martin Luther maintained much that dated from the pre-Reformation days. Still, even today we can find a Common Metre version and a Long Metre version of *Veni Creator* in the *Book of Common Prayer*. As for our own *Book of Praise*, it includes a Latin hymn dated from the thirteenth century in an altered translation by James R. Woodford made in 1852 (Hymn 32), and another hymn (44), which is partly based on the seventh century Latin hymn, in a translation adapted by J. M. Neale in 1851.

However, as soon as Bucer and Calvin began to influence Church life in England, the development in the field of Church singing started to run parallel to that in the Reformed Churches on the continent. Other influences were reduced to a bare minimum, which may serve to explain the fact that the remnants of the translated Latin hymns are rudimentary. Congregational singing consisted almost exclusively of Psalms, with the addition of English versions of the continental hymns, canticles, or paraphrases. This is why, in the Old Version of 1560/2 we can find: the songs of Mary and Simeon, the Creed, the Lord's Prayer, and the Ten Commandments, together with a metrical version of the response, "Lord, have mercy upon us;" further: the Lamentation of a Sinner, the Hymble Sute of a Sinner, a Prayer unto the Holy Ghost (before the Sermon), and a Thanksgiving after the receiving of the Lord's Supper. Daye's *Complete Psalter* of 1560/1 included, before the Psalms: a Song of the Three Children, and the Humble Sute of a Sinner, and after the Psalms: The Complaints of a Sinner, and a Lamentation. George Whiter's *Hymns and Songs of the Church* (1623) included some paraphrases, e.g. the Song of Songs, and hymns for all the festivals, the Lord's Supper, seasoned weather, the King, etc. *The New Version* (1696) had the Canticles, the Creed, the Ten Commandments, the Lord's Prayer, an Easter Anthem, and the Song of the Angels (*Gloria in Excelsis*). An interesting feature of Whither's collection of hymns is that it carried the King's patent. It was to be bound with every copy of the metrical Psalms, just as the latter was to be bound together with every copy of the Bible. The owners of the Old Version offered strong resistance against its publication because they had many copies still in stock. They were successful, for in 1633 the Privy Council ended the royal patent. Further, it earned the Pope's contempt: "this wretched Whiters!"

Scotland

The development in Scotland was fundamentally the same. This is why in *The Great Scottish Psalter* of 1635 we find the following hymns: the Ten Commandments, A Prayer, The Lord's Prayer, Veni Creator, The Song of Simeon, The XII Articles of the Christian Beliefe, The Humble Sute of A Sinner, The Lamentation of A Sinner, The Complaint of A Sinner, The Song of the Blessed Virgin Mary, The Lamentation, The Song of Moses

(Deuteronomy 32), A Thanksgiving after Receiving the Lord's Supper, and A Spiritual Song.

Further developments

As we can see, among the above-mentioned songs there are already a few which are not directly based on biblical texts. In the long run this development led to requests made for more "free hymns."

Via a number of "precursors," we have now come to the man who is called "the first modern hymn writer," Isaac Watts (1674-1748). In the year 1707 he published his *Hymns and Spiritual Songs in Three Books*. The first volume contained a number of paraphrases, the second contained 170 songs "Compos'd on Divine Subjects," and the third volume was written in view of the Lord's Supper. Later on he published another 40 hymns in his *Divine Songs attempted in Easy language for the Use of Children*. In our *Book of Praise* there are a number of hymns from his hands: Hymn 23, in a revised and supplemented version of 1978, Hymn 42, Hymn 54 (partly), Hymn 55 (adapted in 1978), and Hymn 61 (altered).

At the close of the seventeenth century, hymns were cautiously admitted into the worship of Nonconformist Churches, the Baptists being the first. Before this time they had considered singing as something carnal! Hymns were introduced — as we have just noted — especially in view of the celebration of the Lord's Supper.

Great hymn-writers were the Wesley brothers. John Wesley was the first to publish a series of hymns in his *A Collection of Psalms and Hymns* (1737). They were written for use in the Church of England, for at that time he was an Anglican missionary in Georgia, together with his brother Charles. A new edition appeared in the next year after his return to England. In May of 1738, the Methodist movement was born, frequent singing being an essential part of its worship.

His brother Charles wrote approximately 7000 hymns. One of his best-known songs is "Hark! the herald angels sing." Our *Book of Praise* includes two hymns written by Charles Wesley: Hymn 37 (altered), and Hymn 64.

In many of his hymns, the emotional aspect plays a dominant role. In the selection *A Collection of Hymns for the use of the people called Methodists* (1779), John Wesley wrote: "The hymns are not carelessly jumbled together, but carefully ranged under proper heads, according to the experience of real Christians. So that this book is, in effect, a little body of experimental and practical divinity." Proof of this subjectivistic trend is given by the section-titles in the book's respective parts. We quote those of Part III: Praying for Repentance, For Mourners convinced of Sin, For Persons convinced of Backsliding, for Backsliders recovered; and those of Part IV: For Believers Rejoicing, Fighting, Praying, Watching, Working, Suffering, Seeking for full Redemption, Saved, Interceding for the World. Similar headings are in its Supplement, published in 1780 and 1784. Honesty requires us to add that in these collections several hymns by others have been included, among them some by the "more objective" Isaac Watts. It should also be noted that the Supplement opens with a selection of Psalm versions.

The Methodist Hymn Book of 1904 includes many of the great hymns of the past, with the emphasis falling on personal experience and evangelistic enthusiasm. There are also songs for children, along with hymns on the Church, on Christian philanthropy, temperance, etc.

Augustus Montague Toplady (1740-78) enjoys a reputation for having been the Calvinistic opponent of Methodism. To him we owe, among others, the selection *Psalms and Hymns for Public and Private Worship* of 1776. One of his best known hymns is "Rock of Ages."

During the eighteenth century the hymns were mainly sung during meetings. Most of them were written for people who were not familiar with the specific "Church language." Tunes did not differ widely from the popular songs of those days. The result was that the people paid more attention to the tunes than to the text. An extreme consequence of this phenomenon is the singing of Henry Frances Lyte's, "Abide with me" before the start of the annual soccer Cup Final in London's Wembley stadium!

With this hymn we have arrived in the nineteenth century, for it was written in the year 1847. During the nineteenth century the hymns entered more strongly into the Church services. This resulted in an increased production of hymns. The most important hymn book of this period was Joshua Pratt's, *Collection of 1829*, which supplied material for American Hymnaries. There were even several "schools": The Florid-School of Hymne-Tunes, The Modern Hymn Tune, The Later Hymn School, and others. Scotland was a bit slower in this respect, but at last hymn singing was introduced in its Church services — with the exception of the Free Church of Scotland and the Covenanters maintaining "exclusive Psalmody."

The Oxford Movement in the Church of England, led by John Henry Newman — who after his conversion to Roman Catholicism was appointed as a cardinal — represented a new impetus. It restored some hymns of the ancient Church but also produced new ones. To Newman we owe the hymn "Lead, kindly light."

A great number of Hymnaries were published. This awakened a desire to have the best hymns collected into a single book. The result was the publication in 1861 of *Hymns Ancient and Modern*, which was a great success. This selection was officially adopted by the Church of England. Supplements appeared in 1889 and 1916. More frequent choir singing required the setting of the music in four parts.

The Methodist Church continued its use of the Wesleyan *Collection of Hymns*. The edition in my personal library was published in 1894.

As for Scotland, Methodist and other influences caused an increase in the number of hymns that were included in the Hymnaries of the Church of Scotland. This is obvious in the *Church Hymnary* of 1898.

In the year 1929 a revised edition was published. A certain form of traditionalism can be seen when we learn that the voluminous songbook opens with the *Scottish Psalter, 1929*.

This revised edition included (apart from *The Psalms of David in Metre*, the Second Scottish Psalter) a number of paraphrases. Then, however, follows *The Church Hymnary, Revised Edition*, containing no less than 707 hymns and a few doxologies. The above mentioned traditionalism is visible again when, at the end, we find a number of *Ancient hymns and canticles*.

North America

For a long time the situation on the North American continent was fundamentally the same as that on the British Isles. This is no wonder, because the immigrants brought with them their respective songbooks.

During the eighteenth century there was almost exclusive Psalmody. As we have already seen, the first book ever printed in New England was the Puritans' *Bay Psalter*, which was also called the *New England Version* after its second edition was issued. It included a number of canticles and a metrical version of the Song of Songs.

Hymn singing became more frequent as a result of the numerous editions of Isaac Watt's *Psalms and Hymns*, published toward the end of this century. For a long time this collection was used by the Presbyterians, who, however, adopted a Hymnal in 1871. This hymnal was revised and enlarged in 1982 to 679 hymns.

The Methodists had their own collections, the Southern Methodists adhering more closely to the Wesleyan hymns than their Northern counterparts.

The Dutch Reformed Church used its own Psalm version of 1767. It was succeeded by collections of Psalms and hymns in 1789, 1814, 1831, and 1850. In 1869 all these publications were superseded by *Hymns of the Church*.

New hymns were written by men like Lowell Mason and William Bradbury. But since their tunes were copyrighted, the door was open for the introduction of *Hymns Ancient and Modern*.

In Mid-America and in the southern States a new brand of music came into being because several Churches required very simple tunes for their evangelizing activities. These tunes influenced the Sunday School Song and Gospel Song.

With the introduction of organs and pianos, unison singing changed into part singing.

Ira D. Sankey adopted these songs for his evangelistic campaigns. This meant that they were introduced in England as well.

For later campaigns new music was required, which resulted in new Gospel Song selections. As soon as those types of songs were introduced in Church Hymnaries, Church singing underwent a process of deterioration.

The Christian Reformed Church

Turning now to the Christian Reformed Church, we see from the "Foreword" to its *Psalter Hymnal* of 1934 that this Church had until that year only sung "the Old Testament Psalms (. . .), barring a few exceptions mentioned specifically in Article 69 of the Church Order." Before it was revised in 1932, this Article mentioned: "the 150 Psalms of David, the Ten Commandments, the Lord's Prayer, the Twelve Articles of Faith, the Songs of Mary, Zacharias, and Simeon, the Morning and Evening Hymns, and the Hymn of Prayer before the Sermon." However, in the Psalter only the Songs of Mary, Zacharias, and Simeon were found.

The "Foreword" further states that the Christian Reformed Church was not opposed to hymn singing as such, yet practical considerations kept it from engaging in this practice. One was "aware of the unsound or unsatisfactory character of many current hymns," and "feared that in an environment where the Psalms are seldom sung, the introduction of hymns in public worship would lead to the neglect of those deeply spiritual songs of the Old Testament which the Church should never fail to use in its service of praise."

I do not know how to reconcile this statement with the fact that in 1890, at the time of the unification with the "True Protestant Dutch Reformed Church," which seceded from the Dutch Reformed Church in the year 1822, no fewer than 52 hymns were added. It may be that in practical Church life they were hardly ever used.

Nevertheless, the desire to use hymns in public worship gradually became stronger, so that at the Synod of 1928 action was taken and a committee was appointed to study the matter from every angle. In 1930 this committee offered the text of 197 hymns, from which a selection was then made.

The same committee was also charged to thoroughly revise the English Psalter which had been used until then. The Psalter consisted of 413 songs. Some of them had to be "eliminated as unsatisfactory, especially as regards the tunes." In their place came "metrical versions of not fewer than twenty-five and not more than fifty Psalms which can be sung to the best tunes of our Dutch Psalter." For Synod desired "that our rich musical heritage should be preserved."

The Synod of 1932 approved the changes made in the Psalter, and adopted nearly all the 138 hymns submitted by the committee. The text of Article 69 of the Church Order was revised accordingly. In 1934 the first *Psalter Hymnal* was published.

2.3 BOOK OF PRAISE

Our own Churches

During the first years after their institution the Canadian Reformed Churches and the Free Reformed Churches of Australia were compelled to use material supplied by others.

This material consisted mainly of the above mentioned *Psalter Hymnal*. I say "mainly," because in at least one Australian congregation Psalm versions from English or Scottish origin were used every now and then. However, "borrowing" from the *Psalter Hymnal* was limited to the "34" which were set to the Genevan tunes. No hymns from that selection were used, except the songs of Zechariah and Simeon, the Lord's Prayer, and A Mighty Fortress.

On our way

The very first body to become active in this field was the Classis West of the Canadian Reformed Churches. In November of 1953 it formulated a proposal for the following year's National Synod regarding preparations to be made for the acceptance of an English version of the Bible, the *Psalter Hymnal*, and the text of the doctrinal standards and liturgical forms.

Classis East of February 1954 followed with a similar proposal. However, it did not refer to the *Psalter Hymnal* in particular, but spoke more generally of the "Psalter."

The first synod that dealt with the material was that of the Free Reformed Churches of Australia, held at Armadale in the month of April, 1954. It appointed deputies with the mandate "to investigate if and to what extent the existing metrical versions in English and the existing translation of the Three Forms of Unity can be used in our Church services." The deputies were instructed "to inform themselves about the results gained by the Churches in Canada, in order that in this respect there may be as much uniformity as possible in the English-speaking countries."[30]

Returning to the Canadian scene we read in the Acts of the National Synod of Homewood (November 1954) that the above-mentioned Classis East had also decided to leave the use of the *Psalter Hymnal* in the freedom of the Churches. Regarding this decision a letter was tabled by Br. M. M. de Groot together with another brother. I mention this name because, as one of the deputies for an English Calvinistic Psalter, he has played a significant role regarding the musical section of our Church service book. These two brothers apparently saw that the classical decision could open the door to un-Reformed influences on the life of the Churches. Although Synod was of the opinion that the letter was not an appeal, it informed the brothers that the matter would be dealt with while the overtures of Classes East and West were discussed.

---

[30] *Acts of Synod 1954*, Article 17.

This discussion resulted in the decision to leave the use of the 34 rhymed versions of the *Psalter Hymnal* in the freedom of the Churches, "as long as we are not able to reach a definite solution of this important matter."

The Synod further decided "to appoint a committee with the instruction to study the whole matter of the rhymed versions of the Psalms in the English language."[31]

Reports

The Synod of 1956 of the Australian Churches reappointed deputies, who wrote an extensive report, mainly on the history of Church singing. The report also included a lengthy evaluation of the *Psalter Hymnal*. It came to the conclusion that this collection could not be used by the Churches because as a whole it was not an acceptable kind of hymnbook. Among the grounds for this conclusion were the following considerations. The biblical Psalms had been mutilated by the omission of many historical parts. The text of the metrical versions had been subjected to Pietist and Methodist influences, while the great majority were set to hymn tunes. As for the "34" Psalms, objection had to be made to the tunes, which were robbed of their original rhythm, although the congregations were supposed to be familiar with the original rhythm, so that this objection was not insurmountable. Many of these "34" had been reduced to "Selected Stanzas." More generally, it could be said that they were not acknowledged as "songs of the covenant and the Kingdom." The final conclusion was that they could only be used in the "emergency situation" then in existence, for no other material was available.

This report was published in serial form as a kind of Appendix to the successive issues of *Una Sancta*, the magazine published within the Free Reformed Churches of Australia. Therefore in the later stages the deputies were able to refer to the work undertaken by the Canadian committee, with which intensive contact was maintained at that time.

From their side, the Canadian colleagues used a substantial part of the historical section of the Australian report when, in turn, they published relevant findings for their Churches and the Synod of Homewood-Carman of 1958.

---

[31] *Acts*, Article 56.

This report was written in the Dutch language (still in wide use at that time) under the title *Op weg naar een Engels Reformatorische Psalmberijming* (On our way toward an English Reformative Psalm version).

Except for a section written by Br. M. M. de Groot on a number of the Rev. G. van Dooren's metrical versions, the report was from the hand of the Rev. van Dooren. The fact that the initiative was taken by this committee member who, at later stages, had done so much for successive editions of the *Book of Praise*, may serve to underscore the committee's conclusion, which was the same as that of their Australian counterparts.

In harmony with these conclusions, Synod appointed new deputies, with the following instructions: "to compose a Psalter in the English language including, if possible, other hymns of the Scripture in accordance with the directives contained in the report of 1956; and to make use of material available in the Psalter of the Christian Reformed Church and other Psalters in as much as the versification is faithful and tunes answer the Church-musical norms." The committee was further charged to compile a sample collection, to forward it to the Churches at least one year prior to the next General Synod, and request them to take it as such into immediate use.

This decision was made in spite of the fact that two Churches had proposed leaving the use of the Christian Reformed Psalter and some of its hymns in the freedom of the Churches. Synod was of the opinion that the committee in its report had brought forward some very important objections to the *Psalter Hymnal*.

From this report we may learn that for some time a small booklet — popularly called "the green booklet" — had been used, containing the "34" Psalms.

As for the co-operation with the Australian deputies, Synod "considered it desirable that deputies, for uniformity's sake, shall closely co-operate with sister Churches in other English-speaking countries."[32]

Book of Praise, Provisional Edition

In the history of our Church service book, 1961 was a very important year. That was when the first edition of the *Book of Praise* was published.

The wishes of the Churches in their first synods were realized. For the booklet carried not only the name now so familiar, and so suitable for

---

[32] *Acts*, Articles 172, 209.

Church services, which according to our Saviour's saying of John 4:24 are characterized by the word "worship" — but also the subtitle: "Metrical Psalms and Paraphrases compiled by order of Synod 1958 of the Canadian Reformed Churches including Liturgical Forms and the Heidelberg Catechism."

"Metrical Psalms" it said, but not yet — as in the 1982 edition — "Psalter." For the booklet included only eighty-two Psalms — most of them set to the Genevan tunes. And "Paraphrases," because as far as the hymn section was concerned the deputies wanted to keep as close as possible to the text of the Bible. There were fifteen of them: the Ten Commandments; Isaiah 9:2-8; Isaiah 53; the Lord's Prayer; the Song of Zacharias; Nahum Tate's version of Luke 2:8-14; the Song of Simeon; Romans 8:34-9; I Peter 1:3-5; Revelation 5:9-13; 7:13-17; and 5:9-10; A Mighty Fortress; Te Deum; and Praise ye the Lord. Many of them were also set to Genevan tunes.

A number of versions were, with permission, adopted from the *Psalter Hymnal*, others were taken from *The Book of Psalms* and *Psalter 1767*. Some of the Rev. G. van Dooren's metrical versions were included.

The author who contributed almost half of the Psalms was Mr. Dewey Westra, who had also written metrical versions for the *Psalter Hymnal*, namely some of the "34." Originally the committee had high expectations of what he could do for the completion of the Psalter, but at a later stage some difficulties pertaining to copyright, amendments, and remuneration arose, so that the co-operation had to be terminated.

It was no wonder that the Acts of the General Synod of Hamilton 1962 made mention of enthusiasm and gratitude regarding the appearance of this first product of the committee's labour. However, at the same time everyone realized that the work was not perfect. Therefore newly appointed deputies were given a mandate, to revise, wherever necessary, the Psalm versions and the Paraphrases, and to extend the booklet. They had to pay attention to the specific requirements of congregational singing; the songs must be faithful to the Scriptures, the versions be understandable, the tunes suitable for singing in public worship and of Church-musical standard. The local Churches were invited to send their remarks and proposed corrections to the committee.

When the Synod of the Australian Churches, held at Albany in January 1962, was convened, copies of the booklet had not yet arrived. But Synod was well informed about the progress made, and expressed its joy and gratitude for the fact that the publication of a provisional edition could be expected in the near future. Therefore it advised the Churches to have the "34" replaced by this edition.

However, there was a shadow. The same synod had to express its strong regret that the Canadian deputies had not, according to their mandate, compiled this Psalter in co-operation with the Australian deputies.

Deputies were again appointed and given the mandate to test the provisional edition with the help of the guidelines mentioned in the "big" report of deputies tabled at the 1959 Synod, to invite the Churches to comment on the provisional collection, to contact the Canadian deputies, and take an active part in the completion of the Psalter.

As for the hymn section it repeated Synod 1959's statement, "that it is our intention to limit the song book for the time being to a book containing a metrical version in the English language of "the Book of Psalms" and of other songs from the Bible."[33]

Supplement 1967

The fourth of the series of booklets which led ultimately to the publication of the complete *Book of Praise*, after "the green booklet," the provisional edition of 1961, and the second print of the same edition in 1965, was "Supplement 1967."

The General Synod of Edmonton 1965 had continued the committee's instruction, with the addition that other hymns must be included, namely songs faithful to the Scriptures, preferably metrical versions of suitable sections of the Scriptures, and in particular those of a poetical nature. Deputies were also charged to put certain confessional texts into rhyme.

Synod suggested that, if the committee was unable to complete the song section before the next General Synod, it could publish a Supplement.

This did indeed happen. Within two years a little booklet was compiled and published under the title: *Book of Praise. Supplement 1967. Provisional Edition. Metrical Psalms and Paraphrases*. It contained 34 Psalms and 19 hymns. As for the latter, they could not all claim to be paraphrases. Only 9 of them were based more or less on a biblical text, the others being "free songs."

---

[33] *Acts*, Article 40.

In the Psalm section there was something "new." Synod 1965 had shown some unfortunate lack of appreciation of the high quality Genevan tunes. This most likely originated from the days when, generally speaking, congregational singing was limited to a smaller or larger number of favourite Psalm-verses, which resulted in the creation of what used to be called "unknown tunes." For Synod stated that it was not necessary for the committee to set the metrical versions to Genevan tunes exclusively. In exceptional cases it was allowed that two different versions of one and the same Psalm could be made, one of them to a non-Genevan tune. The deputies, however, were of the opinion that the goal was "a complete Genevan Psalter, in which all melodies would be preserved." Therefore apparently they chose to sail, for the time being, a middle-course. In the Preface to Supplement 1967 they wrote: "In this publication are incorporated three (which should be: four) Psalms which are set to an alternative tune, because the original Psalm-tune is virtually unknown: e.g. Psalm 41a had been set to the melody of Psalm 25." Seeing the goal just mentioned they added: "Psalm 41 is also included with the original melody." The strange thing is that those who look for the latter will not find it. Due to a printing mistake it was missed. The same must be said about Psalm 129. However, the other two Psalms were indeed included twice. The Psalms 94, 112, and 129, were set to their original Genevan tunes as well as to the tunes of Psalms 105, 147, and 85 respectively. It may be clear that deputies only partly complied with the Synod's suggestion. In the first completed edition all Psalms were set to their original tunes. For this we may be very grateful. We have the impression that the deputies "policy" has been beneficial to Church singing, also in this sense that for many congregations there are very few "unknown tunes" left, or perhaps none at all. Many ministers no longer limit their choice to a kind of personal selection of Psalms or Psalm-verses. On the other hand, the ideal situation has not yet been reached, whereby all the Psalms — yes, indeed, whole Psalms as well as sections of them — are used and not just a few selected verses, sometimes taken out of their context.

As for the above mentioned alternative melodies, the Synod Armadale 1966 of the Free Reformed Churches of Australia supported the deputies, appointed by its predecessor, in their disapproval of the introduction of such melodies. They were apparently successful in keeping their Canadian counterparts from introducing these tunes. The same can be said about the inclusion of "free hymns." Therefore Synod reaffirmed the stand taken by a previous synod that the English service book should not move in a direction which may lead to a "hymn book" in the spirit of the *Psalter Hymnal*. In a general sense Synod declared that it shared the desire of Synod 1954, viz. "concerning this matter there must be as much uniformity as possible in the Churches in English-speaking countries."

Toward a complete song book

What was said in the previous paragraph about the Canadian deputies" opinion on the matter of the "alternative melodies" is confirmed by what we read in their supplementary report to the General Synod of Orangeville held in the year 1968 — for Supplement 1967 itself had the character of a report. They stated that they intended to proceed to the completion of a Genevan Psalter. This suggested that they themselves were not in favour of including "alternative melodies." They admitted that there are many non-Genevan tunes of priceless value, but these could be used in the hymn section.

This brings us to the decisions taken by the 1968 Synod. Having taken notice of the criticism expressed from among the Churches, it decided to have deleted from a new edition:

1. these rhymed versions which lack the close conformity to the Scripture-text and those which lack the simplicity and clarity of expression required for the songs of the covenant, if revision is not possible;

2. those hymns which are not thoroughly Scriptural in contents;

3. those tunes which are not considered conducive to the purpose of the singing of the covenant people, namely: "the praise of the Lord.

The deputies were given the mandate to pay immediate attention to the completion of the Psalm section; to give preference to the Genevan tunes, whereby identical tunes for different Psalms are avoided as much as possible; to replace those tunes which are hard to sing by other melodies of "priceless value" (here Synod ploughed with another man's heifer, but using this term in a sense different from that of the deputies, in this way giving another proof of "amateurism"); and "to set as target date for the presentation of a complete *Book of Praise* the year in which the next General Synod will be convened"[34]

Work was well under way when in the year 1971 the next synod was held at New Westminster. In their report deputies presented a hymn

---
[34] *Acts*, Article 87.

section. Several hymns had been deleted. The report was not meant to be scrutinized in detail by this synod, but to be considered part of the complete *Book of Praise* to be submitted to the Churches in the near future. Consequently Synod decided to receive the hymn section for information. It expressed the desire that Scriptural references be placed with the hymns. The committee was charged with the mandate to complete the *Book of Praise*.[35]

As for the Psalm section, deputies had scrutinized the Psalms that had been published in the 1961 and 1967 editions. Individual changes had been made. They assured Synod: "All Genevan tunes will be found in the complete Psalter!"

1972: First Complete Edition

Then there was a rather thick booklet, entitled *Book of Praise. Anglo-Genevan Psalter. First Complete Edition.* We cannot say: it was there all of a sudden, for many people had been involved in its preparation for almost two decades. Neither can we say: At last it was published, for the gigantic task took no more than nearly two decades.

Its Preface, dated January 1972, correctly stated in its very first sentence: "The appearance of the *Book of Praise: Anglo-Genevan Psalter* is an event of considerable significance in the life of the Canadian Reformed Churches as well as a landmark in the history of psalmody." Indeed, this book is evidence of the Churches' desire "to preserve their Calvinistic heritage."

It is no wonder then, that immediately after the Preface John Calvin's statement on public prayers is printed, made in his *La Forme des Prieres et Chantz ecclesiastiques, 1542*, in which he distinguishes between two kinds of prayers: "the one consists simply of speech, the other of song." It is the document in which he stressed that the tunes should show their own peculiar character, using the famous terms of *"poids et majeste"* (dignity and majesty), and expressed his preference for the Psalms because there are no "better or more appropriate songs (. . .) than the Psalms of David, inspired by the Holy Spirit." When we sing them, "we are assured that God puts the words in our mouth, as if He Himself were singing through us to exalt His glory."

---

[35] *Acts*, Article 28.

Besides the 150 Psalms, set to their original Genevan tunes, the book contained 62 hymns and paraphrases — though all were numbered as hymns — 10 of which had been set to Genevan tunes. Further there were: the Three Forms of Unity, the ecumenical creeds, and a number of liturgical prayers and forms, adopted from the old edition of the Dutch sister-Churches' service book.

We can imagine that in their report to the General Synod Toronto 1974 deputies wrote: "It gives your Committee much pleasure to officially present to Synod a complete Psalter with 150 Psalms, 62 Hymns and the Forms." This present writer clearly remembers how the Rev. G. van Dooren — a committee member from the very beginning — was given the floor and related the book's long and yet so brief pre-history, and how Br. M. M. de Groot — another member during all those years — on behalf of the committee officially presented to Synod a copy of all the various provisional editions and the first complete edition of the *Book of Praise*. This was a great hour!

Improvements

Again it was fully realized that the results of all the work done could not claim perfection. The committee members were the first to acknowledge this. For they recommended to the Synod Toronto 1974 that the committee be continued, also for the purpose "to be the address for remarks and criticisms." This recommendation was accepted, and the committee was charged with the mandate:

a. to invite the Churches to once again submit their possible remarks on the Psalm section to the Committee;

b. to remain diligent with respect to a possible improvement of this section of the Church Book.

A similar mandate was given regarding the hymn section. Deputies had to bring into account that "Scripture teaches us that Church singing shall have for its theme the praise of the Covenant God." They had to seriously consider John Calvin's example of reintroducing the Canticles; and attention must also be paid to the "credal fragments," and in particular to the "credal songs" in the New Testament. The committee was also instructed "to complete, and make public, a list of Scripture passages suited to be rhymed and tone-set as hymns."

Earlier, in the month of October 1972, the Synod of the Australian Churches, held at Armadale, had advised the Churches to use the Psalm section of the new *Book of Praise* as a proof-collection. The same was done regarding the hymn section as far as it was accepted. For this synod, at the recommendation of deputies, adopted only 31 of the 62 hymns.[36]

The next synod, that of Albany 1975, reaffirmed its predecessor's decisions, adding to it that it would like to see Bible songs produced suitable for use in Reformed worship, requesting the Churches to examine and try out the six Bible songs which deputies had published in the magazine Una Sancta.[37]

At the General Synod Coaldale 1977 the Canadian committee reported that work was well under way with respect to the wanted improvements, but that some more time was needed to finalise it.

"Armadale 1980" again put the finger at the desired uniformity. Therefore it instructed its deputies to continue their contact with the Canadian committee for joint consultations, in particular concerning the hymns.[38]

Two months later, in November 1980, the General Synod of Smithville was informed about the progress made by the committee. Almost all the Psalms had been revised. Deputies reported that they had deleted from the 1972 edition some hymns as being superfluous because their contents were already included in the book of Psalms. The hymn section's setup would be changed: It would follow the order of the Apostles' Creed. This resulted in inserting some songs in order to provide a broader "coverage" of each part of that creed.

Final drafts of the Psalms and the hymns were presented to Synod in respectively a Yellow Book and a Green Booklet.

Synod decided "thankfully to accept the Psalm and Hymn Section, with the understanding that room is to be left for changes, deletions and additions in future editions."

Since the committee on this section was not continued, a Standing Committee was appointed, which was urged "to use as an example for layout and music notation the Dutch *Liedboek voor de Kerken*, in order to achieve uniform notation and a suitable format."[39]

---

[36] *Acts*, Articles 22 and 46.
[37] *Acts*, Article 44.
[38] *Acts*, Articles 53–7.
[39] *Acts*, Article 22.

Briefly returning to Australia we find the Kelmscott 1983 Synod adopting the deputies' recommendation pertaining to the list of acceptable hymns: another hymn was added to it.

Back in Canada we read in the Acts of Synod Cloverdale 1983 (Article 123) that the Standing Committee was charged "linguistically to scrutinize and correct the text of the entire *Book of Praise*, wherever necessary, in order to achieve uniformity with respect to the language and punctuation."

1984: Revised Edition

The way was now clear for the publishing of the Revised Edition.

Even the Preface had undergone revision. It begins with the following sentence: *"The Book of Praise: Anglo-Genevan Psalter* has an important function within the worship services of the Canadian Reformed Churches. The word "praise" in the title reminds us of the exhortation in the letter to the Hebrews: ". . . let us continually offer up a sacrifice of praise to God, that is, the fruit of lips that acknowledge His Name" (13:15). Because of the grace and faithfulness of the LORD, the worship service is a meeting of Him with the people of His covenant. In response to His Word we offer up our sacrifices of praise in psalms and hymns. Also the creeds and confessions are the fruit of lips that acknowledge God's Name."

Many of the 150 Psalm versions were made by "own people:" W. Helder, D. van der Boom, W. van der Kamp, G. van Dooren, and W.W.J. van Oene. In a sometimes amended form a small number has been adopted from the "34," their authors being: S.G. Brondsema, W. Kuipers, and D. Westra. L.J. Lamberts is the author of another Psalm, while four Psalms are from unknown authors.

As for the hymns, the Preface no longer mentions the name "Paraphrases." It states: "Although in Reformed liturgy the Psalms have a predominant place, our Churches have not excluded the use of Scriptural hymns. They, too, constitute a thankoffering of praise when we sing of the facts of redemption by God in Jesus Christ our Lord." Indeed, Scriptural hymns sing of God's redemptive acts. This is how they are distinguished from many other hymns, and fit in our Reformed liturgy. Therefore the 65 hymns of the *Book of Praise* have been arranged in the order of the respective articles of the Apostles' Creed.

There are many authors of these hymns, among them being: W. Helder, W. van der Kamp, and W.W.J. van Oene. One hymn was written within the Free Reformed Churches of Australia, where a "workshop" at Launceston tried to contribute to the compiling of the hymn section.

Particularly in the special edition published by Premier Printing Ltd, Winnipeg, which includes the Bible in the Revised Standard Version, we have a complete Reformed Church service book. Apart from the Psalms and hymns it includes the Ecumenical Creeds, the Three Forms of Unity, two unofficial Orders of Worship, the adopted Liturgical Forms and Prayers, and the Church Order of the Canadian Reformed Churches.

Toward the final edition

In both countries, Canada as well as Australia, the song section of the Revised Edition had already been adopted by their 1983 synods. The Australian Synod of 1985, held at Launceston, took note of the fact that deputies were "satisfied with the few revisions that were made."[40] As for Canada we may be a bit surprised to read that the General Synod Burlington 1986 set 1989 "as target date for the final edition of the *Book of Praise*."[41] However, this may be explained by the fact that work at the revision of the text of creeds, confessions, and liturgical forms and prayers had not yet been finished. Besides, the inserting of the word "Christian" in the article on the Church in the Apostles' Creed required an amendment to the tune of Hymn 1A or an alternative melody.[42]

Such an amendment and alternative melodies have been submitted. The Standing Committee for the Publication of the *Book of Praise* has been mandated by the Lincoln 1992 Synod "to serve the next Synod with a detailed evaluation" of these submissions, "and carry out this part of the mandate in consultation with musical experts."

Synod Abbotsford 1995 decided to "adopt the suggestion of one of the musical advisors to give 'the alternate melody' (Zwart) a 'testperiod' in the churches as also the Strasbourg melody (Bucer) of 1539 recommended by the Standing Committee."[43]

---

[40] *Acts*, Article 59.

[41] *Acts*, Article 118.

[42] *Acts*, Article 189.

[43] *Acts*, Article 44. Furthermore it mandated the Standing Committee: "to foster an increased awareness of the existence of the *Book of Praise* among others; promote the availability of a book of harmonizations facilitating the use of the *Book of Praise* in the

The insertion of the word "Christian" may cause some confusion because, as we will learn below, the Australian churches have rejected its inclusion in the text of the Apostles' Creed.

Synod Albany 1987 of the Australian Churches — at the request of a Canadian minister serving "down under!" — decided "to introduce the probationary use of the deleted hymns by the Churches till the next synod" and to give deputies the mandate "to maintain contact with the C.R.C.[44] concerning the matter of any revision or changes to the Psalms or Hymns in the *Book of Praise*."[45] It is to be regretted that since then no further communication between Australian deputies and the Canadian committee has taken place. The old wish to have the emphasis on Scriptural songs like the Canticles is still alive!

At the Armadale 1990 Synod the whole hymn section was adopted.

"Winnipeg 1989" expressed its regret that the target date for the final edition was not obeyed by deputies,[46] and stated that the use of the *Liedboek* notation "does not compel consistories, organists, and congregations of the Canadian Reformed Churches to change the traditional practice of singing certain Psalms with the use of chromatically altered notes (*toevallige verhogingen of verlagingen*), since it is not in the province of Synod to make such a decision".[47] This may be formally correct, but in our humble opinion it does not promote the right way of using the Genevan tunes, which after so much work was done, have been presented not to the Canadian and Australian Churches only, but also to the English-speaking world!

English speaking world," and "to investigate the possibility of repeating the musical notation when a psalm or hymn continues overleaf and to make a recommendation to the next General Synod" (*Acts*, Article 44 L).

[44] = Canadian Reformed Churches

[45] Acts, Article 99.

[46] Acts, Article 60.

[47] Acts, Article 146.

3. CREEDS AND CONFESSIONS

3.1 IN BIBLICAL TIMES

"Hear, O Israel . . . !"

Somewhere we read the following statement: "the daily repetition of the *Shema*, the Christians' use of the Lord's Prayer, and the Moslems' of the First *Sura*, are all justified by psychology no less than by religion."[48]

It is not our intention to evaluate this statement, particularly not the last part of it. However, it is a matter of fact that in their compulsory prayers the "believing Jews" repeat the well known line from Deuteronomy 6: "Hear, O Israel: the LORD our God, the LORD is one." They do so in their morning and evening prayers in accordance with the command: "these words (. . .) shall be in your heart (. . .) when you lie down and when you rise up."

The true nature of these words is, however, that of a confession. With them one confesses faith in the God Who is really unique because of what He has done and is still doing for His people.

While the Jewish daily prayers quote one single line only, the confession — called *Shema*, after the Hebrew word for "Hear" — is much longer. In the morning and evening services of the synagogue it is recited in full, consisting of Deuteronomy 6:4-9, 11:13-21, and Numbers 15:37-41.

We cannot trace the origin of this tradition. It may be that in the later temple liturgy of the morning and evening sacrifices the *Shema* had its place. But it is very likely that it was used in the synagogue services during the days in which the Lord Jesus was on earth.

It is also very likely that in his first epistle to the Corinthians the apostle Paul made an allusion to the *Shema* when he wrote: "for yet there is one God, the Father, of Whom are all things, and we for Him, and one Lord Jesus Christ, through Whom are all things and through Whom we live" (I Corinthians 8:6). While the Jews confessed their faith in one God over against the polytheism of the gentiles, the apostle made his confession of faith over against Jews as well as gentiles.

---

[48] Evelyn Underhill, *Worship*, London, 1948, 14.

The New Testament

The necessity to profess one's faith was already there when the Lord Jesus was here on earth. He Himself as it were challenged His disciples in this respect when He asked them: "Who do men say that the Son of man is?" and: "But who do you say that I am?" (Matthew 16:13, 15). Simon Peter replied to this by saying: "You are the Christ, the Son of the living God" (16:16).

The same challenge was there after His resurrection from the dead. Then the Saviour told Thomas: "Do not be unbelieving, but believing," whereupon Thomas answered: "My Lord and my God!" (John 20:27, 28).

After Christ's ascension into heaven and the day of Pentecost the believers had to come into the open and confess their faith. In Paul's epistle to the Romans we are shown the close relationship between gospel preaching, faith, and confessing faith. He says in 10:8-10: "The Word is near to you, in your mouth and in your heart (that is, the Word of faith which we preach), that, if you confess with your mouth the Lord Jesus and believe in your heart that God has raised Him from the dead, you will be saved. For with the heart one believes unto righteousness, and with the mouth confession is made unto salvation."

"Jesus is Lord," this seems to be an early brief formula in which faith was confessed. We find it also in I Corinthians 12:3, where it says: "no one can say "Jesus is Lord" except by the Holy Spirit."

Fixed formulas

These two places show us how under the guidance of the Holy Spirit faith was soon confessed in fixed formulas of a "Christian" character. Such a fixed formula is also known from Philippians 2:11: "and that every tongue should confess that Jesus Christ is Lord," while the addition of the clause "to the glory of God the Father" suggests its use in the liturgy of the Church.

We can safely presume that in the process which led to expressing faith in fixed formulas the simple ceremonies which accompanied the baptism of adult converts played a role. According to Acts 8:16, 19:5, and I Corinthians 6:11, these people were baptized "in the name of the Lord Jesus Christ" — whereby it is not perfectly clear whether these words served as a baptismal formula different from the one mentioned in the "missionary command" of Matthew 28:19, or whether they were spoken by the baptismal candidates as a credal formula. In Colossians 2:6 the words, "you therefore have received Christ Jesus the Lord" strongly suggest the latter. Anyhow, one of the factors which led to the introduction of fixed formulas was the baptismal ceremony, whereby the converts professed their faith.

Sacred deposit

Another factor is the gospel preaching.

From the gospels we may learn that at various places and under various circumstances the Saviour used the same or similar formulations in His teaching. The two classic examples are "the Sermon on the Mount" — which we find in different forms in Matthew 5-7 and Luke chapter 6 — and the Lord's Prayer — in Matthew 5 and Luke 11.

A comparison of the contents of Paul's epistle to the Ephesians with that to the Colossians shows us that this apostle did the same thing. The term "the apostles' doctrine" in Acts 2:42 clearly suggests that, on the day of Pentecost and after, these men delivered the same message, often in the same or similar terms, adopted from their Master's preaching.

It may be clear that in the course of time a kind of "body of distinct Christian teaching" grew from this preaching. As a "sacred deposit" it had to be transferred to the next generation (II Timothy 2:2). In the New Testament it is introduced by a number of names as e.g. "the gospel," "the truth," "the faith," "deposit," and "the traditions." Therefore it may not be strange to us that in the letter to the Hebrews we read the word "confession" (3:1; 4:14; 10:23).

Faith defended

Another contribution to the fixation of credal formulas was the necessity to defend the truth against heresies. This sounds through the words "he who confesses the Son" in I John 2:23, when the apostle issues a warning against the "lies" of the Antichrist and his followers: "who is a liar but he who denies that Jesus is the Christ" (verse 22). The same in 4:2-3: "By this you know the Spirit of God: Every spirit that confesses that Jesus Christ has come in the flesh is of God, and every spirit that does not confess that Jesus Christ has come in the flesh is not of God. And this is the spirit of the Antichrist." We find something similar in the epistle of Jude, who "found it necessary to write to you exhorting you to contend earnestly for the faith which was once for all delivered to the saints," and then issued a serious warning against some "ungodly men who turn the grace of our God into lewdness and deny the only Lord God and our Lord Jesus Christ."

Liturgy

Again another factor that contributed to the fixation of credal formulas was the development of the liturgy of the Christian Church. This development led to the use of certain words and clauses in liturgical prayers, like "Maranatha" (I Corinthians 16:22), and "come, Lord Jesus" (Revelation 22:20).

It seems as if the apostle Paul reminds the Corinthians of what he transferred to them, an already existing fixed formula, when he wrote: "I delivered to you first of all that which I also received: that Christ died for our sins according to the Scriptures, and that He was buried, and that He rose again on the third day according to the Scriptures . . ." Other credal fragments we may recognize in Romans 4:24-25: "We believe in Him Who raised up Jesus our Lord from the dead, Who was delivered up because of our offenses, and was raised because of our justification," and in I Timothy 2:5-6 where it says: "For there is one God and one Mediator between God and men, the Man Christ Jesus, Who gave Himself a ransom for all," and other places (Romans 1:3-4; 8:34; II Timothy 2:8; I Corinthians 8:6).

The same development even led to the introduction and use of credal hymns, e.g. the hymn called "The Mystery of Godliness:" "He was manifested in the flesh, vindicated in the Spirit, seen by angels, preached among the nations, believed on in the world, taken up in glory" (I Timothy 3:16), and others (Philippians 5:5-11; Ephesians 5:14, the latter most likely being a baptismal song: "Awake, you who sleep, arise from the dead, and Christ will give you light").

Bible and creeds

When in the course of the fifteenth century efforts were undertaken to unite the Eastern and Western Churches, and thereby the Apostles' Creed was mentioned, the delegates of the Greek Orthodox Church are said to have made the remark: "We do not possess it and have never seen it. If it would have existed from the very beginning, the book of Acts would have mentioned it when it reported on the first apostolic synod held at Jerusalem, to which you make an appeal." In other words: these Greek churchmen said something similar to what can be heard every now and then in our own days: The Bible does not contain a creed or confession; therefore we do not want to be bound to such a human document; let us all go back to the Bible, the Bible only! However, these men were wrong, not only in considering the Jerusalem meeting of Acts chapter 15 to be a "synod," but also in this respect that they overlooked what the New Testament tells us about the development which led to confessing faith in fixed formulas and even songs.

When our Churches have adopted some creeds and the Three Forms of Unity — and these documents' contents conform with the teachings of the Holy Scriptures; and we are convinced they are so indeed! — they can rest assured that this has God's approval, Who through His Holy Spirit led the early Church to express her faith in fixed formulas.

3.2 THE APOSTLES' CREED

Baptismal interrogations

According to some ancient manuscripts of the book of Acts — the so-called Western Text — the evangelist Philip, after the Ethiopian eunuch had requested to be baptized, said: "If you believe with all your heart, you may;" whereupon the eunuch would have replied: "I believe that Jesus Christ is the Son of God." We leave undecided the question whether or not all this is an interpolation. For in both cases this text (Acts 8:37) points to what has developed later on into "baptismal interrogations." Before the candidates were baptized they had to respond to certain questions — as is still the case when an adult is baptized.

This process strongly contributed to the developing of the creeds as we know them. Some of these questions have been preserved, e.g. those asked in the Church served by Justin Martyr (appr. 100-165): "Do you believe in the Father and Lord of the universe? Do you believe in Jesus Christ our Saviour, Who was crucified under Pontius Pilate? Do you believe in the Holy Spirit, Who spoke through the prophets?"

Irenaeus (appr. 130-appr. 200) had some similar questions: "Do you believe in God the Father? Do you believe in Jesus Christ, the Son of God,

Who was incarnate, and died, and rose again? Do you believe in the Holy Spirit of God?"

In his "Adversus Haereses" he wrote that, though the Church has been spread all over the world, she has from the apostles and their disciples received faith in one God, the Father, the Almighty; in one Jesus Christ, God's Son, who was incarnate for our salvation; and in the Holy Spirit. She confesses Christ's birth from a virgin, His sufferings, resurrection, and ascension into heaven, and His parousia for the resurrection and judgment of all mankind. The "Rule of Faith" which we receive at baptism is a threefold one: God the Father regenerates us in His grace by His Son through the power of the Holy Spirit. Here the instruction of the baptismal candidates reveals a fragment of the history of the development of our creeds.

We find another illustration of these baptismal interrogations in the "Apostolic Tradition" of Hippolytus of Rome (170-251). They include what we could call a *precursor* of the Apostles' Creed. And because these interrogations were immediately followed by a threefold immersion, we learn at the same time that in its initial stages this creed served as a confession of faith at baptism.

Its text reads as follows:

> The one doing the baptizing lays his hand on him and asks him: "Do you believe in God, the Father almighty?"
> The one being baptized is to answer: "I believe."
> Let him baptize him then a first time, keeping his hand at the person's head. He then asks him: "Do you believe in Jesus Christ, Son of God, born by the Holy Spirit of the Virgin Mary, Who was crucified under Pontius Pilate, Who died, was raised in the third day, living from among the dead, Who ascended to the heavens, Who sits at the right hand of the Father, Who will come to judge the living and the dead?"
> When he has answered: "I believe," he is to baptize him a second time.
> He is to ask him again: "Do you believe in the Holy Spirit, in the holy Church, in the resurrection of the flesh?"
> The one being baptized is to answer: "I believe." Then he baptizes him a third time.

Declaratory forms

This interrogation during the baptismal ceremony presupposes some preceding instruction of the candidates. Already quite early, this instruction seemed to have given rise to a similar development, which resulted in the establishing of a number of declaratory forms of confession. No longer did the baptismal candidates respond in the positive to the questions they were asked and which included a kind of creed, but they themselves recited what they had been taught during the instruction.

In the First Catechesis of Cyrill of Jerusalem, from the fourth century, we find a brief declaratory form. It reads as follows:

> I believe in the Father, in the Son, in the Holy Spirit, and in a single baptism of repentance.

A somewhat longer one is the confession made by the candidate at baptism, which we find in the *Der Balyzeh Papyrus*, which dates from the sixth century but includes some older liturgical material. It reads thus:

> I believe in God, Father almighty, in your only-begotten Son, our Lord, our Lord Jesus Christ, in the Holy Spirit, in the resurrection of the flesh, in the holy catholic Church.

As we can see no distinction was made between: I believe in, and I believe. The present text has the little word "in" where faith is confessed in one of the three divine Persons, but omits it where God's graces are confessed.

It may also be clear that in these credal forms, being either of an interrogatory or of a declaratory character — which differed slightly but not fundamentally in the various local Churches or regions — we find the origin of our creeds, in particular of the Apostles' Creed.

Rule of Faith

We just saw that Irenaeus, in his *Adversus Haereses*, referred to a "Rule of Faith." From it he quoted the following clauses:

> The Church, though dispersed throughout the whole world, even to the ends of the earth, has received from the apostles and their

disciples this faith: (She believes) in one God, the Father almighty, Maker of heaven and earth, and the sea, and all things that are in them; and in one Jesus Christ, the Son of God, Who became incarnate for our salvation; and in the Holy Spirit, Who proclaimed through the prophets the dispensations of God, and the advents, and the birth from a virgin, and the passion, and the resurrection from the dead, and the ascension into heaven in the flesh of the beloved Christ Jesus, our Lord, and His (future) manifestation from heaven in the glory of the Father, "to gather all things in one," and to raise up anew all flesh of the whole human race, in order that to Christ Jesus, our Lord, and God, and Saviour, and King, according to the will of the invisible Father, "every knee should bow, of things in heaven, and things in earth, and things under the earth, and that every tongue should confess" to Him, and that He should execute judgment toward all.

It is really striking that all the New Testament "sacred facts and events" are summed up in the section in which the Holy Spirit is confessed. They were proclaimed by the Holy Spirit. In the days of old the truth and reliability of the Holy Scriptures was not doubted!

At approximately the same time Tertullian (appr. 160-220) also referred to this "Rule of Faith." From his treatise *On the Veiling of Virgins* we quote the following lines, in translation:

> The Rule of Faith which is everywhere the same, and unaltered (. . .) teaches us to believe in one God almighty, Creator of the world, and His Son Jesus Christ, born from the virgin Mary, crucified under Pontius Pilate, raised on the third day, taken up into heaven, now sitting on the Father's right hand, destined to come to judge the living and the dead through the resurrection of the flesh.

So both authors referred to a more or less fixed formula, then existing. More or less fixed, we say, for in spite of Tertullian's assurance that this Rule of Faith was everywhere the same we find some variations in its text. However, we may safely presume that both of them had the *Symbolum Romanum* — or Roman Creed — in mind, or at least a similar formula.

From the Western Church, creeds are known from Aquilea, Milan, Turin, Arles, Toulon, Ravenna, Carthage, Hippo, and Rome. In particular the Roman Creed played a significant role.

Its text is better known to us from a commentary, *Expositio in Symbolum*, written in the year 404 by a certain Rufinus. In his commentary he made a comparison between the *Symbol* of Aquilea in North Italy and the *Symbolum Romanum*. It was shorter than that of today's Apostles' Creed. The words: "He descended into hell" e.g. were missing — later on they may have been adopted from the Creed of Aquilea. Other additions from elsewhere are the clauses "Creator of heaven and earth," "conceived by the Holy Spirit, born of the virgin Mary, suffered, dead," "God almighty," the word "catholic" in "the holy catholic Church," also "communion of saints," and "life everlasting."

Received Text

This development led to the acceptance of what is known as the *Textus Receptus* or Received Text of the Apostles' Creed. This text is certainly not older than the close of the fifth century or the beginning of the sixth century.

The oldest known copies are found in a *Psalterium Graecus Gregorii Magni* from the eighth or ninth century, first published in the year 1647, containing the text in Latin as well as in Greek; and in a booklet written by a certain Priminius, founder and abbot of the monastery of Reichenau (758), containing the Latin text.

In the year 813 Emperor Charlemagne — who was very active in Church affairs — made it the standard form of the creed in his empire, compelling his subjects to learn it by heart.

Initially the Church of Rome refused to adopt it, using the Nicene Creed instead. However, in the year 1014 it accepted the Apostles' Creed.

The Reformation did not change this. On the contrary, the Reformers strongly upheld it, returning to its Scriptural interpretation.

The inclusion of the word "Amen" in the Received Text is doubtful.

Our Churches

From the very beginning our churches have accepted the Three Forms of Unity as their subordinate standards. Their first synods, that of Armadale 1954 and Homewood of the same year, clearly expressed this.

In one of these Forms, the Belgic Confession of Faith, it says: "we willingly receive the three creeds of the Apostles, of Nicea, and of Athanasius" (Article 9). Together with these Forms the three creeds, as summarising the biblical doctrine, are the foundation on which the life of the local congregations and that of both federations of churches rests.

It is no wonder, then, that in both countries the question was raised: Which English version shall we adopt? Usually it was included in another question: How can we obtain a faithful English translation of the doctrinal and liturgical writings, which we took with us when we migrated from The Netherlands?

This led to the respective first synods appointing committees for this purpose. Being aware of the need of uniformity the Australian Synod of 1954 charged its deputies to seek co-operation with their Canadian colleagues.

At the next synod in Canada, that of Homewood-Carman 1958, it was decided to recommend the text of the Heidelberg Catechism and the Canons of Dort as published in the *Psalter Hymnal* of the Christian Reformed Church. As for the Belgic Confession of Faith a report could be expected in the near future. The creeds were not separately mentioned. However, the text of the Apostles' Creed is included in Lord's Day 7 of the Heidelberg Catechism. Therefore the Synod's decision meant that the version of this creed as found in the *Psalter Hymnal* was recommended for use in the Churches. Without a formal synodical decision the Australian churches adopted the same practice.

When in the year 1961 the first, provisional, edition of the *Book of Praise* was published, it appeared that from the creeds and confessions only the Heidelberg Catechism, in the *Psalter Hymnal* version, was included, complete with the historical introduction taken from the same book. (The text of the creeds and confessions as printed in the *Psalter Hymnal* is an even older one, for in her turn the Christian Reformed Church "borrowed" them from the church book of the Reformed Church of America).

The Australian Synod of Albany 1962 was the first one to make separate mention of the creeds. It charged its deputies to contact the Canadian committee amongst others on the English version of the "ecumenical creeds." This may have resulted in the 1965 edition of the *Book of Praise* containing, apart from the text of the Three Forms of Unity, that of the three creeds — again in the *Psalter Hymnal* version, together with their "historical introductions." Anyhow, this publication was a matter of fact.

Therefore it was superfluous for the Orangeville 1968 Synod, to "set as target for the presentation of a complete *Book of Praise* the year in which the next General Synod will be convened" and to give the committee the mandate "to make sure that the Creeds (. . .) are included in the next edition of the *Book of Praise*."

At the New Westminster 1971 Synod no complete book could be presented. Its predecessor appeared to be too optimistic, not sufficiently realizing the enormous task laid on the shoulders of the committee members. Therefore "New Westminster" was wise enough to appoint a separate committee "for the Second Half of the Church Book." This committee also had the mandate "to scrutinize the text of the creeds (and introductions) as to correctness of translation."

A more or less complete edition — the Church Order was not included — was published in the year 1972. However, it still contained the same unscrutinized texts of the creeds and confessions. So the work had to go on. Even the Toronto 1974 Synod had to reappoint the same committee, charging it with virtually the same mandate. But with the apparent aim to speed proceedings up it appointed a special committee for the Heidelberg Catechism.

"Coaldale 1977" even enlarged the number of committees which were working on the respective sections of the *Book of Praise*: a third one was added for the Belgic Confession of Faith and the Canons of Dort, and a fourth one for the revision of the text of the liturgical forms.

One of these committees presented the General Synod of Smithville 1980 with a proposed revised text of the Apostles' Creed. With some amendments Synod adopted this version.

Some further amendments were made at the Cloverdale 1983 Synod: the name "Maker" in the first Article was replaced by "Creator"; "His only Son" was enlarged into "His only-begotten Son;" the words "and" before "born" and "He" before "suffered" were deleted; between "catholic" and "Church" the word "Christian" was inserted; and at the end "Amen" was added.

Synod Lincoln 1992 adopted a revised Preface to the Apostles' Creed, which since then has been inserted in the 1993 edition of the *Book of Praise*.

In Australia the Launceston 1985 Synod decided to provisionally adopt the texts of the three ecumenical creeds. The deputies concerned reported that they had examined these texts and recommended their adoption. They made, however, a restriction regarding the word "Christian." Synod Albany 1987 decided to adopt these texts, with the exception of the word "Christian" in the Article on the Church — which decision was reaffirmed at the Armadale Synod of 1990, which rejected a request for revision.

Since then the International Conference of Reformed Churches (ICRC) sent to its member churches a report on the text of the ecumenical creeds, called "Credo." It was the fruit of the work of a committee that had been given the mandate "to study the text of the three ecumenical creeds in order to come to a common text that can be recommended to the member churches."

The reason for this was twofold: in the respective member churches various texts are used, whereas in the meantime others had undertaken efforts to come to an internationally accepted English text: the International Consultation Text (ICET) — which did not include the Athanasian Creed because some of the member churches of the World Council of Churches, that was at the background of the ICET, do not accept this creed. The Australian Synod of 1990, held at Armadale decided to appoint deputies to study the "Credo" report.

At the Bedfordale 1992 Synod the recommendation of these deputies to accept the ICRC texts was adopted, but because deputies had to admit they had not been able to study the matter adequately, Synod appointed new deputies to study the proposed texts in depth and report to following Synod.

Then a humorous misinterpretation was made. Whereas the subject of the desired "in depth study" was meant to be the ICRC texts — which at certain points deviated from the ICET — deputies appeared to have studied the latter. Part of the blame for this rests on Synod 1992, which in its Considerations mentioned both ICT (ICET is a more common abbreviation) and the ICRC texts. This is why deputies more or less duplicated the work done within the ICRC.

The same mistake was made by the 1994 Byford Synod, which decided "to send the International Consultation Text of the three ecumenical creeds along with the completed deputies" report to the churches to see whether any of the churches wish to place them on the agenda of the following synod."

This misinterpretation may mean the end of the recommended ICRC texts as far as the Australian churches are concerned.

Christian

This word in the Apostles' Creed requires our special attention, because of the different practices between the Canadian Churches and the Australian Churches.

As far as both Church groups are concerned its story starts with the 1972 edition of the *Book of Praise*. It appeared that one of the members of the Committee on the Church Book had unintentionally, and to his later regret, inserted the word "Christian" wherever the text of the Apostles' Creed was quoted — with the exception of the hymn version (then Hymn 45). The Committee on the Second Half of the Church Book correctly drew Synod's attention to the fact that the correction of the text of the creeds belonged to their task and not to that of the Committee on the Church Book. Synod agreed with this and added to the mandate of the latter "to remove the word "Christian" from the Apostles' Creed, Article IX."

One of the consequences of this decision was that the special committee for the Heidelberg Catechism, appointed by the same synod, in its report to the 1977 General Synod, left the word "Christian" out in Lord's Days 7 and 21; and neither the text proposed by the committee appointed by "Coaldale 1977" nor that adopted by the General Synod of Smithville 1980 included that word.

However, at the Cloverdale 1983 Synod there were a few requests for revision, which were granted. The main ground for this synod's decision was its opinion that by removing the word "Christian" a change in policy had been made. This policy, then, was considered to be included in previous synods' declarations that the Dutch text of the Heidelberg Catechism was to be "the authentic text for the time being," and that Synod 1974 referred the committee concerned to the original German text, both having the word "Christian." It seems to this present writer that these "previous Synods" did not have in mind such a literal translation of the Three Forms of Unity, that, as far as the "ecumenical creeds" are concerned, the possibility of basing their English translation on the — original — Received Text would be excluded. For it is remarkable that the early synods of the Canadian Reformed Churches did not even make separate mention of these creeds: they had an English version of the "doctrinal and liturgical forms" in mind. And when the Synod of the year 1958 spoke of the Dutch text as for the time being authentic (*dat voorlopig alleen de Nederlandse tekst van de Catechismus authentiek is*), it overlooked the fact that no Dutch synod — not even the great Synod of Dordrecht 1618-19 — ever adopted an "authentic text," so that *"de Nederlandse tekst"* (*the* Dutch text) did not exist — until during the 1980s of this century the Dutch sister Churches in their synods accepted such an "authentic" revised text. Besides:

1. What does "authentic" mean? In the course of times it had been used in two different meanings: (a) original; (b) authorized. Most likely this synod used it in the latter sense.
2. The Synod of Dordrecht 1618-19 dealt with the Heidelberg Catechism in its 147th and 148th sessions. At the request of the delegates of the States General its contents were examined and found to be in full harmony with the Word of God. The text, however, was not dealt with.
3. This synod was very reluctant in adopting a fixed text. There were so many variations in the respective publications and editions of the Catechism. Besides, the publishers had large stocks and were not very keen to publish another text. Synod did not adopt, let alone declare "authentic," a certain text.
4. The Regional Synod of South Holland of 1622 stated: The revision of the text of the Heidelberg Catechism is referred to the next National Synod — which was never convened! This confirms that there did not exist an authorized text of the Catechism. The reasons for this statement were: The division into Lord's Days is not the same in all editions; the text must be improved either according to the German or according to the Latin text, because there are considerable differences between these two.

It may further be clear that the Coaldale Synod was incorrect in basing its decision on the 1974 Synod's reference to the German text, because the latter declared that the insertion of the word "Christian" in the 1972 edition of the *Book of Praise* was unauthorized, and this word should be deleted.

In our opinion the Australian Churches took the right course when they based their decision on the Received Text of the Apostles' Creed. Their text is not a double translation — a translation into English of the Dutch (or German) translation of the original Latin — but a single one.

I. C. R. C.

At the International Conference of Reformed Churches held in 1985 at Edinburgh, Scotland, a committee was appointed with the following mandate:

> to study the text of the three ecumenical creeds, in order to come to a common text that can be recommended to the member Churches.

The grounds for this appointment were the following:

> 1. In the respective member Churches some various texts of these creeds are used;
>
> 2. It is desirable that the International Consultation Text of the Apostles' Creed and the Nicene Creed be scrutinized to ascertain whether this text is faithful to the Received Texts of the creeds.

Since the Second Vatican Council in November 1964 authorized services in the vernacular, bringing the exclusive use of Latin to an end, several English language liturgies were introduced within the worldwide body of the Roman Catholic Church. However, many of them showed considerable differences. This caused the Vatican to appoint an International Committee on English in the Liturgy (ICEL), which produced a number of texts in the year 1967.

In 1969 this was followed by the establishing of another body, the International Consultation on English Texts (ICET), based on the World Council of Churches. In the year 1970 it published a booklet entitled *Prayers We Have in Common*, revised and enlarged in 1971, second revised edition in 1975. The ICET texts were accepted in many Churches in the English speaking countries.

In the year 1975 ICET ceased to function, but its ideals and work were taken over by ELLC, which stands for English Language Liturgical Consultation. It co-operates with a similar body within the Church of Rome.

The ICRC committee's task was to scrutinize the ICET texts of the Apostles' Creed and the Nicene Creed, and to study more generally the text of the three ecumenical creeds.

In its report to the 1989 conference, held at Langley, BC, Canada, the committee proposed the recommendation of a text that does not contain the word "Christian." This proposal was based on a study of the Received Text of the Apostles' Creed and its history.

This history reveals that during the Middle Ages, for some unknown reasons, the word "catholic" in certain parts of Europe was replaced by *karstine* or *kersten* in the Middle-Dutch language and by *Christliche* in German, or by similar terms. This was already done in the thirteenth and fourteenth centuries. Martin Luther associated himself with this tradition, abandoning the word *catholicam* because the Church of Rome had monopolized it, and he feared confusion, so replacing it by *Christliche*. In later days he also used a double translation: *heylige gemeyne Christliche Kirche*, which double translation was adopted by the Church of the Palatinate in the Heidelberg Catechism.

We may repeat that the Synod of Dordrecht 1618-19 did not adopt an "authentic text" of the Catechism, so that the double translation of the word *catholicam* was never made the official version. On the contrary, that this synod left the use of different texts to the freedom of the Churches, may be proved by the following facts: At this synod the so-called "Schilders edition" of 1611, published at the instigation of the Regional Synod 1610 of Zeeland, was consulted, which edition did not contain the word "Christian" in Article 9 of the Apostles' Creed. "Dordrecht" also granted the French-speaking Dutch Churches permission to continue using the Geneva Catechism, written by John Calvin in the year 1541, which does not have this word either. For religious instruction of adults and slow learners it recommended a shorter catechism, written by Hermanus Faukelius, the so-called *Kort Begrip* (Compendium), and in the year 1608 adopted by the consistory of the Church at Middelburg, which has as question 40: "What do you believe of the holy catholic Church?" (*Wat gelooft gij van de Heilige Algemeene Kerk?*). This synod, then, did not take a decision regarding the insertion or omission of the word "Christian." So that, when our Churches will adopt an official text it is best that they base it on the Received Text.

This, then, is strongly recommended by the ICRC report, which by the 1989 conference was passed on to the member Churches.

This recommended text reads as follows:

I   1   I believe in God the Father almighty,
          Creator of heaven and earth;

II 2 And in Jesus Christ,
       His only Son, our Lord;
    3 Who was conceived by the Holy Spirit,
       born of the virgin Mary;
    4 suffered under Pontius Pilate,
       was crucified, dead, and buried,
       He descended into hell;
    5 on the third day He arose from the dead;
    6 He ascended into heaven,
       and is seated at the right hand of God the
       Father almighty;
    7 from there He will come to judge the living and the dead.
III 8 I believe in the Holy Spirit;
    9 the holy catholic Church,
       the communion of saints;
   10 the forgiveness of sins;
   11 the resurrection of the body;
   12 and the life everlasting.

The word "Amen" has been omitted because it is doubtful in the Received Text.

3.3 THE NICENE CREED

Nicea, 325

The history of the Eastern Church shows us a more intense struggle against heresies than that of the Western Church. This caused her to formulate the truth over against these false teachings in a number of creeds. In particular the biblical doctrine of God the Son and God the Holy Spirit was attacked by the heretics.

These creeds were adopted at a number of "ecumenical councils." The first one was that of Nicea, held there in the year 325. It had to deal with the false teachings of Arius, who, under the influence of a pagan philosophy denied that Christ is really God in the same sense as the Father is God. He was just another creature, inferior and subject to the Father.

This Council issued the so-called *Nicaenum*. This is not the same as the Nicene Creed. It was based on the local creed of Jerusalem — most likely

from the hand of Cyrill, the well known bishop of Jerusalem. It was extended by a number of phrases in which Arius' heresies were rejected. Its text reads, in translation, as follows:
> We believe in one God, the Father, almighty,
>   Maker of all things visible and invisible;
> And in one Lord Jesus Christ, the Son of God,
>   begotten from the Father, only-begotten, that is,
>   from the substance of the Father,
>   God from God, light from light,
>   true God from true God,
>   begotten, not made,
>   of one substance with the Father,
>   through Whom all things came into being,
>   things in heaven and things on earth,
>   Who because of us men and because of our salvation
>   came down and became incarnate,
>   becoming man,
>   suffered,
>   and rose again on the third day,
>   ascended into the heavens,
>   will come to judge the living and the dead.
> And in the Holy Spirit.

Those who would not accept this doctrine were condemned by the following Canon 1, containing an "anathema:"
> But as for those who say, there was a time when He was not, and, before being born He was not, and that He came into existence out of nothing, or those who assert that the Son of God is of a different hypostasis or substance, or is subject to alteration or change — they are anathematized by the catholic and apostolic Church.

Constantinople

Arius' heresy gained new strength after some time. It was supported by some of the emperors.

Another heresy that gained influence was that of Apollinaris, who taught that the human soul in Christ was replaced by the divine Reason.

This made it necessary for the Church to reaffirm the biblical doctrine expressed in the *Nicaenum*.

A third heresy that arose in the same period of time was that of the people who considered the Holy Spirit to be subordinate to the Father and the Son, not being a Person in the same sense as the Father and the Son are. Some names in this context are: Eunomius, and the Macedonians or Pneumatomachians.

The Second Ecumenical Council held at Constantinople in the year 381 indeed reaffirmed the doctrine of the *Nicaenum*.

Scholars, however, are divided on a number of questions. For example: Did the Council issue another creed? For in its records no proof of the promulgation of such a creed can be found. Another possibility is that it adopted an already existing formula. And a third one is that the one that today is called the Nicene Creed — or: *Nicaeno-Constantinopolitanum* — is an extension of the *Nicaenum* of 325, some clauses on the Holy Spirit having been added.

Acceptance

The first one to make mention of the new creed was the Council of Chalcedon, held in 451. There a deacon of the Constantinople Church read it as the "creed of the 150 fathers." It was accepted as being in accordance with the Bible, together with the *Nicaenum*, the "creed of the 318 fathers."

Perhaps already before "Chalcedon" it was used at Constantinople as a baptismal confession. Later on it replaced the many local creeds in the Eastern Church. It is still part of the catechisms of the Greek and Russian Orthodox Churches.

In the Western Church the Third Council of Toledo, 589, gave permission to sing this creed. Without consulting the Eastern Church it also added a few clauses. One of them is the so-called *Filioque*, the clause in which the Holy Spirit is confessed as proceeding not only from the Father but also from the Son. This *Filioque* was one of the reasons for the split between the Western Church and the Eastern Church. Efforts to heal it, undertaken in 1247 and 1439, were not successful.

It took a long time before this creed was officially adopted in the Western Church. This was finally done by Pope Benedict VIII, under pressure from Emperor Henry II. Since then it is used in the liturgy of the Mass.

This may explain the fact that the Lutheran Churches and the Church of England also use the Nicene Creed. The Calvinist Reformation showed preference for the Apostles' Creed. Not the Nicene Creed, but the Apostles' Creed is explained in the Heidelberg Catechism and incorporated in the liturgy of the Lord's Supper. Only every now and then the Apostles' Creed is replaced by the Nicene Creed in the afternoon worship services.

Our Churches

The story of the Nicene Creed in our Churches is almost the same as that of the Apostles' Creed.

In the respective editions of the *Book of Praise* it appeared in the *Psalter Hymnal* version, but together with the other creeds it was to be scrutinized by the committees appointed for this purpose. It received separate mention after the text of the Apostles' Creed had been adopted. The General Synod Burlington 1986 gave mandate to the relevant committee "to see to the linguistic revision of the Nicene Creed and the Athanasian Creed, and to present a draft of the revision to the Churches no later than one year before the next General Synod and to include this revision in the report to the next General Synod for the final edition of the *Book of Praise*." The 1989 Synod was set as a target date for the final edition.

At the Winnipeg 1989 General Synod, however, it appeared that the committee had not obeyed the target date. The committee was charged to complete the mandate given by the 1986 Synod.

Therefore we must come to the conclusion that we are still listening to the *Psalter Hymnal* text whenever the minister in the afternoon services or on festive days replaces the Apostles' Creed by the Nicene Creed.

At the Lincoln 1992 General Synod a revised Preface was adopted, which since then has been inserted in the 1993 edition of the *Book of Praise*.

Since the churches had not been sufficiently informed about the proposed changes in the text of the Nicene Creed, Synod mandated a new committee "to resubmit its revision of the Nicene Creed to the Churches, including an explanation of the proposed changes."

This resulted in the General Synod Abbotsford 1995 provisionally adopting another revised edition of the Nicene Creed, requesting the churches to test it and to send their comments (if any) to the Standing Committee of the *Book of Praise* for evaluation.[49]

As for the Australian churches, the above mentioned misunderstanding played a role regarding the recommended ICRC text of the Nicene Creed.

Deputies for the Ecumenical Creeds also provided the 1992 Synod with information about the text of the Nicene Creed as proposed to the next Canadian Synod. It was decided "to retain our present text of the Nicene Creed for the present" — so the presence is really present in Australia! Deputies had to scrutinize the Canadian revised text. One of the grounds for this decision reads as follows: "Since we use the *Book of Praise* in our churches, it would be preferable to have the same text for the Nicene Creed as found therein."

I. C. R. C.

The report of the committee appointed by the Edinburgh 1985 Conference, and passed on to the member Churches by the 1989 Conference, recommends the following translation:

> We believe in one God, the Father almighty,
>   maker of heaven and earth,
>   of all things visible and invisible.
> And in one Lord Jesus Christ,
>   the only-begotten Son of God,
>   begotten from the Father before all ages;
>   God from God, light from light,
>   true God from true God,
>   begotten, not made,
>   of one substance with the Father;
>   by Whom all things were made;
>   Who for us men and for our salvation
>   came down from the heavens
>   and became incarnate by the Holy Spirit from the virgin Mary
>   and was made man,
>   was also crucified for us under Pontius Pilate,
>   suffered death and was buried;

---

[49] *Acts*, Article 44.

and on the third day He arose, according to the Scriptures,
and ascended into the heavens
and is seated at the right hand of the Father,
and will come back with glory to judge the living and the dead;
Whose Kingdom will have no end.
And in the Holy Spirit, the Lord and Giver of life,
Who proceeds from the Father and the Son;
Who with the Father and the Son together is worshipped
and glorified;
Who has spoken through the prophets;
and one holy catholic and apostolic Church;
We acknowledge one baptism for the remission of sins;
We look forward to the resurrection of the dead,
and to the life of the age to come.
Amen.

3.4 THE ATHANASIAN CREED

Name

It is remarkable that — as we have already learned — the Apostles' Creed was not composed by the apostles, neither did the Nicene Creed originate with the Council of Nicea, 325. The same thing must be said of the Athanasian Creed.

From the ninth century it was for some centuries attributed to Athanasius, a deacon and later on bishop of Alexandria, the "champion of orthodoxy." This may have had its basis — or one of its bases — in the fact that its second part is quoted in a manuscript of a sermon on the Incarnation, dating from approximately 730. This manuscript was found at Treves — hence its name "Treves Fragment." Athanasius as an exile has spent some time at Treves.

However, since the middle of the seventeenth century scholars have come to the conclusion that Athanasius cannot be its author. Nowhere in his works is this document found. His contemporaries do not even refer to it. Athanasius wrote in Greek, while this creed was originally in Latin. It shows affinity with other Latin writings, as those of Ambrose and Augustine. Until the eleventh century the Greek Church did not know about its existence, then rejected it or modified it because it contains the *Filioque* clause.

Because of all this it is often called *Quicunque* — after its first word — or the *Symbolum Quicunque*.

Contents

This creed consists of two main parts. The first section is a summary of the biblical doctrine of the Holy Trinity, referring to the "Trinitarian controversy." The second section is a confession of Christ's Incarnation and His two natures, and reminds us of the "Christological controversy." While in the first part a firm stand is taken over against the heresies of Arius, the second part does the same regarding the false teachings of Arius and Apollinaris.

This structure may explain why this creed never gained the same place in Church life as the Apostles' Creed, not even as that of the Nicene Creed. It is too long for frequent liturgical use. Unlike the two other creeds it is not based on the trinitarian baptismal formula.

It starts and finishes with an anathema, a damnatory statement at the address of those who refuse to accept the Scriptural doctrine it confesses.

History

For the first time this creed was quoted in the Canon of the Fourth Council of Toledo, 633. Part of it was also quoted in a manuscript of a sermon found among the works of Augustine in approximately the year 680. As we have already seen, another section is known from the Treves Fragment (eighth century). A complete manuscript is included in the *Codex Ambrosianus*, Milan, from the end of the seventh or the beginning of the eighth century. Commentaries on it were written in the eighth, ninth, and tenth centuries.

Use

In the Eastern Church the Athanasian Creed has never been officially adopted — not even minus the *Filioque* clause — let alone incorporated into its liturgy. It was used for private devotions only — without the words "and from the Son."

During the Middle Ages it was used almost daily by the Western Church in the morning devotions.

Although the Reformers acknowledged it as a faithful confession of the biblical doctrine, it never gained a prominent place in practical Church life. For ages it was sung or recited on several festive days in the Church of England, but not without opposition.

In addition to the Belgic Confession of Faith — in Article 9 — it is mentioned in the Lutheran Augsburg Confession, in the *Formula Concordiae*, in the Church of England's Thirty-Nine Articles, in the Second Helvetic Confession, and the Bohemian Confession.

This creed has not been translated by the International Consultation on English Texts (ICET). This is understandable considering this body's affiliation with the World Council of Churches, in which the Eastern Orthodox Churches play a prominent role. In its translation of the Nicene Creed the *Filioque* "has been put in brackets as indicating that some churches may include the words and other churches may not. It was not considered to be within the province of this Consultation to make recommendations as to its excision or retention." While for this organization the *Filioque* is doubtful in the Nicene Creed, it cannot deny its legal historical place in the Athanasian Creed. This may explain why ICET did not translate this creed.

Our Churches

From its 1965 edition till the Revised Edition of 1984 the *Book or Praise* has contained the Athanasian Creed in its *Psalter Hymnal* version. This will no longer be the case in the "final edition." For the Synod Winnipeg 1989 of the Canadian Reformed Churches adopted "the final text of the Athanasian Creed." This is the text presented in the 1993 edition of the *Book of Praise*. More proof texts have been added in the margin.

In the same edition a revised Preface, which was adopted by the Lincoln 1992 Synod, is printed.

At the Abbotsford 1995 General Synod, the Standing Committee for the Publication of the *Book of Praise* reported that a few typographical errors had slipped into the new printing of the revised edition, which must be corrected in a future printing.

The 1990 Synod of the Australian Churches was apparently not informed about the decision to adopt, "the final text of the Athanasian Creed," so that no action could be taken in this respect.

At the 1992 Synod deputies for relations with other churches, who had received the "Credo" report, recommended the ICRC text, but since they had not been able to study the matter adequately, new deputies were mandated "to study the proposed texts in depth." Their report to the 1994 Synod included a recommended text which differed at a few points from the Canadian (Revised) text, because the ICRC text or the present text was considered to be better. However, Synod decided to accept the Canadian text of the Athanasian Creed, the reason for this being that the differences between this text and the text recommended by deputies "are of a minor nature, and not of sufficient importance to warrant a departure from the text as found in the *Book of Praise*," which text has been included in the 1993 edition.

I. C. R. C.

The Edinburgh 1985 International Conference of Reformed Churches, in its mandate for the committee on the three ecumenical creeds, correctly used the name "Received Texts" for the Apostles' Creed and the Nicene Creed only. The Latin original of the Athanasian Creed — in the reconstruction by J.N.D. Kelly which was used by the Canadian deputies — does not carry that name.

In its report "Credo" the committee recommended a new English translation, which was sent by the 1989 Conference to the member churches.

The fact that both the Canadian and the Australian churches have adopted a slightly different text, makes it pointless to print the ICRC-recommended text here.

3.5 THE BELGIC CONFESSION OF FAITH

Name and character

The origin of the Belgic Confession of Faith lies in what at that time was called the Southern Netherlands, now known as Belgium.

It was written after the example of the French Confession of Faith and is partly based on it. In the year 1557 this French Confession, which was written by John Calvin, was adopted by the Reformed Churches in France. As a writing in defence of the Reformed faith it was sent to King Henry

II. Guido de Brès wanted to follow this example for his own country. Therefore he wrote a draft which he sent to Geneva in the year 1559. But for the sake of the unity of Reformed believers John Calvin urged the believers in the French speaking part of the Southern Netherlands to adopt the French Confession. This was not done, apparently because the Churches in The Netherlands were more strongly involved in a struggle against the Anabaptists, who were not sufficiently dealt with in the French Confession. So De Brès published his own work, and made arrangements that King Philip II of Spain, Lord of The Netherlands, would receive a copy.

This was done because this king had assumed leadership of the Counter-Reformation, which resulted in heavy persecutions. The Reformed were in danger of being identified with the Anabaptists, who did not acknowledge any authority of non-Anabaptists. And therefore the Reformed believers could easily be considered as rebels. This is why in the night of November 1 and 2, 1561, a parcel was thrown over the outer-wall of the governor's castle at Doornik, with the purpose that the governess, Margareth of Parma, the king's sister, would read its contents and pass them on to the king.

The document enclosed — now known as the Belgic Confession of Faith or *Confessio Belgica* — carried as a motto the words of I Peter 3:15, "Always be prepared to make a defence to any one who calls you to account for the hope that is in you." This document was not only accompanied by a letter to the royal commission, appointed by the governess, but its text was also preceded by a long letter to the king, in which he was respectfully invited to no longer listen to the many false accusations made against the Reformed belief, but to judge it with the help of this confession, to which the many Reformed people, if necessary, would subscribe with their own blood.

Soon afterwards this document became the official confession of the Dutch Churches, and in this way a Form in which their unity of faith was expressed.

Author

Its author, Guido de Brès, was born at Mons in 1522. His parents were Roman Catholic. By an intense reading of the Bible — which was strictly forbidden by the government — he was converted to the truth of God's Word.

Soon afterwards he had to flee to England. There he joined the London Church of Reformed refugees. The years of his stay in that congregation (1547-1552) were of great significance for his work as a minister of the Word of later date.

Back in his homeland he became a traveling minister, making his headquarters in Lille (Rijssel). There he wrote a booklet against the errors of the Roman Catholic Church and the false teachings and practices of the Anabaptists, entitled *The Staff of Christian Faith*.

When heavy persecutions broke out, he had to flee again. At Frankfurt he met John à Lasco, well known to him from his stay in London — and most likely also John Calvin. Soon afterwards he went, via Lausanne, to Geneva, where he studied under Calvin and Theodore Beza.

After his return in the year 1559 he settled at Doornik. There he married Catharine Ramon. At the same time he acted as a minister-at-large, preaching also in Valenciennes and Lille under the pseudonym Jerome.

At Doornik some members of the congregation organized, against his will, *chanteries*, public Psalm singing, in imitation of these at Paris two years ago. This caused the governess to appoint three commissioners. Many arrests were made. The commissioners laid hands on an anonymous booklet, containing a confession of faith and a letter to King Philip II — the confession written by Guido de Brès in his study, a little garden house. He consulted other ministers, such as A. de Saravia, H. Moded, and Chr. Fabricius of Antwerp.

De Brès, who at that time was in hiding, did not know that the commissioners already had knowledge of his booklet, so that the action of the night of November 1 was superfluous.

Soon afterwards his study was discovered, and 240 copies of his confession, his library, and some important documents were found. He himself escaped to the North of France, where he ministered at Amiens, Dieppe, and Sedan. From Sedan the Reformed Count of Bouillon sent him to a conference in the year 1564. The aim of this conference was to establish unity between the Lutherans and the Reformed. Prior to this conference — which was not successful — he had a meeting with Prince William of Orange (William the Silent) who was very interested in this matter.

In 1566, after a brief stay at Antwerp, he went to Valenciennes, which was won for the Reformation. However, Spanish troops laid siege to the city and conquered it after some months. Soon afterwards De Brès was captured. Together with some fellow ministers he was hanged on May 31, 1567.

Adopted

De Brès' booklet was soon adopted by the Churches as their confession of faith. Even in the year 1561 it was already known as the *Confession d'Anvers* (Antwerp). A synod, held at Antwerp in 1566, decided that it must be read at the beginning of every synod, as a testimony of the unity of faith, and for eventual correction and improvement. The same synod made some improvements indeed.

In the year 1568 the Convention of Wesel stated, it should be subscribed to by ministers at their ordination — a rule which since then was repeated by several synods, and which is still in force.

At the first real synod, that of Emden 1571, all the members declared their full agreement with the contents of this confession, and with that expressed the unity of faith among the Dutch Churches.

At the Provincial Synod of South Holland, held at The Hague in the year 1583, a Dutch translation, made by Arent Cornelissen in 1566, was read and subscribed to by all delegates.

In the first decades of the seventeenth century the Arminians expressed their objections against the contents of the confession, claiming that there was no fixed text and it had no official authority. Over against this the Provincial Synod of Zeeland of 1610, held at Veere, decided to publish a new edition, which appeared in 1611, the well known "Schilders edition."

This edition was used at the great Synod of Dordrecht 1618-19, which in its 146th session of April 30, 1619, read and approved the contents of the Confession as being in full harmony with the Holy Scriptures. On May 24, in its 173rd session, the Synod adopted slightly amended French and Dutch texts.

The General Synod 1905 of the Dutch Churches, in response to a gravamen, decided to delete a few lines in Article 36, dealing with the duties of the government.

The General Synod Arnhem 1983 adopted a modernized text. Its successor of Heemse 1984-85 deleted the so-called Comma Johanneum (I John 5:7b-8a) in Article 9.

Our Churches

At their very first synods, of Armadale and Homewood respectively, both held in 1954, the Australian and Canadian/American Churches accepted the Three Forms of Unity as their subordinate standards. They appointed deputies, and charged them to look for a faithful English version. This led to the recommendation to make use for the time being of the text printed in the Christian Reformed *Psalter Hymnal*, which in its turn was taken from the one authorized by the Reformed (Dutch) Church in America, although with Bible quotations taken from the American Standard Version and some words modernized (e.g. "has" instead of "hath").

This version of the Belgic Confession of Faith was printed in the *Book of Praise* for the first time in its 1965 edition, together with its historical introduction.

As we have already seen, efforts undertaken to come to an early publication of a complete *Book of Praise* were not very successful. Initially too much work was put into the hands of too small a number of deputies. Since the general Synods of New Westminster 1971 and Toronto 1974 it was possible to hasten the pace at which preparations were made because a number of separate committees for the respective parts of the Church book were appointed. The result was that the General Synod Cloverdale 1983 was able to adopt provisionally a more modern English version of the creeds and confessions. They were included in the 1984 edition of the *Book of Praise*. The Synod of Burlington 1986 adopted the definite texts, while that of Winnipeg 1989 charged the committee concerned to add proposed Scripture references to the text, and to update its Preface. It also accepted a few proposed changes in the text of the Confession.

The fruit of the committee's endeavours can be found in the 1993 edition of the *Book of Praise*.

Synod Lincoln 1993 declared that the Scripture references to be included in this edition are "not forming an integral part of the Belgic Confession." As for the Australian Churches, the deputies appointed for this purpose examined the text proposed by their Canadian counterparts, sending the outcome of their investigations to them and to their own synods. The final result was that in their Synod of Launceston 1985 the Australian Churches provisionally, and in that of Albany 1987 definitely, adopted the text as printed in the 1984 edition.

3.6 THE HEIDELBERG CATECHISM

Catechisms

If we had lived in Charlemagne's empire, we would, already at an early age, have known the Ten Commandments and the Lord's Prayer by heart. For this mighty man insisted that all of his subjects should learn these texts.

His decree heralded the beginning of a new period in the history of the Western Church. Since then these texts, and also the Apostles' Creed, were explained by the priests. This was particularly the case in the so-called "Preaching Services" (*Predigtdienst* or *Pronaus*), which were arranged in certain parts of medieval Germany, Switzerland, and France. Later on its liturgy had some influence on many Churches of the Reformation.

The Ten Commandments were given special attention since auricular confession was made compulsory in the year 1215. They were extensively explained, together with the so-called mortal sins. Similar long explanations were given of the Lord's Prayer and the Creed.

The leaders of the Great Reformation associated themselves with this tradition. This may explain the fact that many of them produced one or more catechisms, containing an elaboration on the four "texts:" the Ten Commandments, the Lord's Prayer, the words of institution of the two sacraments, and the Apostles' Creed.

Martin Luther of Wittenberg, Leo Judae and Ulrich Zwingli of Zurich, Oecolampadius of Basel, John Calvin of Geneva, John à Lasco, and Marten Micron of London, all wrote one or more catechisms.

Our Heidelberg Catechism, then, is one of a long list, although it has become one of the best known catechisms.

The Palatinate

"The Heidelberg Catechism," this is the name by which we know our little book of religious instruction. Heidelberg was the capital city of an electorate called the Palatinate. Sometimes the booklet is also called the Palatine Catechism.

This part of what is today's Germany was ruled by an elector. Some electors were followers of Martin Luther, including Frederick II and Otto Henry, the predecessors of the man who took the initiative for compiling the Heidelberg Catechism, Frederick III. It was no wonder that Martin

Luther's Shorter Catechism was used in the schools of this tiny state during their days.

However, other catechisms were used. This arose from the fact that in a religious respect there was in those days much confusion and strife among the "Protestants." The Lutherans were divided among themselves: there were some extremists, but also followers of the moderate Philip Melanchthon. There were also Zwinglians, and Calvinists. The particular point of disunity was the question: How is Christ present in the Lord's Supper? Is He present at all?

This confusion caused elector Frederick III to make arrangements for the compiling of one single catechism, to be used in the Churches and the schools. He himself had become a Calvinist, even some fifteen years ago, before he succeeded elector Otto Henry.

The task was given to Zacharias Ursinus, professor of dogmatics at the Heidelberg University from the autumn of 1561. He was at that time 28 years old, and had studied at Wittenberg under Philip Melanchthon, being as moderate a Calvinist as his teacher was a Lutheran.

Ursinus produced a Larger Catechism and an extract from it, his Shorter Catechism, both written in Latin. He consulted for this work the catechisms written by Judae, Calvin, and à Lasco.

A kind of a committee, consisting of the theological faculty of the University and some prominent ministers, supervised the manuscript of the booklet which was based on these two writings and was to become the catechism of the Palatinate. Another professor, Caspar Olevianus, even two years younger than Ursinus, being Frederick's main adviser in ecclesiastical affairs, must have played a significant role in this respect, although it is not known exactly what he has contributed to the final result.

In the month of January 1563 a synod was convened for the purpose of scrutinising and formally adopting the new catechism. After deliberations, which took more than a week, it gave its approval on January 17. Two days later the elector wrote the Preface to the booklet, which was published in the month of February under the — translated from the German — title of *Catechism or Christian Instruction, as conducted in the Churches and Schools of the Electorate Palatinate*.

The contents appeared to have avoided making extreme statements at certain points, attempting thus to reconcile different opinions among the Protestants — with the exception of the doctrine of the Lord's Supper, for at this point the extreme teachings of some Lutherans were clearly rejected.

Editions

The first edition was soon sold out. A second and third were to follow in the same year. In the second edition a new question and answer was inserted, on the papal mass — now Question and Answer 80. In the third edition it was added that the mass is basically "an accursed idolatry," most likely in response to the Council of Trent's statement that every one who adhered to the Reformed belief regarding the Lord's Supper was accursed.

The year 1563 saw even a fourth edition, which in this respect was different from the previous ones that therein the Catechism was incorporated into a complete Church Order. The Heidelberg Order differed from our current Church Order in so far as the texts of the Catechism and of the liturgical forms were included. It had less of the appearance of a "code book." Another difference, and improvement, was that the Catechism was divided into 52 Lord's Days. This was done because, according to the accepted order in the Churches of the Palatinate, the afternoon service had the character of a catechism class and catechism-preaching combined. The Catechism had to be preached on annually. In addition, the text of the Catechism had to be read in Church, this reading was to be completed every ninth Sunday, while on the tenth Sunday a number of Bible texts was read. This was added to the Catechism, and in it everyone's daily duties are explained. These consisted mainly of parts of Ephesians 5 and Colossians 3.

Translations

In the same year, 1563, the Catechism was translated into Latin and Saxonian. In the course of the same and following centuries Greek, Hungarian, Polish, Indian, Chinese, Japanese, Indonesian, and other translations followed.

We read about the Heidelberg Catechism: "It has the pentecostal gift of tongues in a rare degree. It is stated that, next to the Bible, the *Imitation of Christ* by Thomas a Kempis, and Bunyan's *Pilgrim's Progress*, no book has been more frequently translated, more widely circulated and used."[50]

---

[50] Philip Schaff, *Creeds and Confessions*, Grand Rapids, 1877/1990, Volume 1, 536.

Dutch

We will deal with the Dutch translations separately.

Two of them were published in the year in which the first four German editions appeared. The first one was made at Emden, at that time a Reformed stronghold.

The second one is the better known version, and is from the hand of Petrus Dathenus, at that time a minister of the congregation of Dutch refugees. In the previous year they had been welcomed into the Palatinate by Frederick, and were allowed to settle at Frankenthal.

After his return to The Netherlands Dathenus had his translation printed together with his metrical version of the book of Psalms, which appeared in 1566.

That it began to play a significant role in the life of the Dutch Churches immediately after its publication may be proved by the fact that in the same year Petrus Gabriel began to preach on the Catechism in his Amsterdam congregation.

Two years later the Convention of Wesel, chaired by Dathenus, stated that candidates to the ministry of the Word could not be ordained unless it was clear that their beliefs were in full accordance with the contents of the Heidelberg Catechism. Those who had applied for making public profession of faith had to be examined with the help of the Catechism and a brief summary included in the Church Order of Heidelberg. The French-speaking congregations could continue using the Geneva Catechism, while the Dutch-speaking Churches were expected to use the Heidelberg Catechism. However, the Churches were free to use either of them, until the Synod to be convened in the near future had made a decision on this matter.

That synod was held at Emden in 1571. It made the same decision, but allowed the use of other catechisms in the freedom of the Churches. Provincial and national synods held at Dordrecht in 1574 and 1578 respectively, and at Middelburg in 1581, confirmed this. The Acts of "1574" make mention of a Catechism written by Godfried van Wingen, but stated that the Churches should continue using the Heidelberg Catechism. The Synod of The Hague 1586 decided that in the afternoon-service catechism-preaching must take place in such a way that every year a complete series on the 52 Lord's Days would be delivered.

The great Synod of Dordrecht 1618-19, in its 147th and 148th sessions, listened to the reading of the Heidelberg Catechism, and stated that it is a faithful compendium of the doctrine of God's Word. The deputies of the foreign Churches fully participated in this. However, Synod did not adopt a text, most likely because various editions were used in the Churches, and the booksellers were afraid that they would be unable to sell the many copies of the current editions they still had in stock. Although the Acts make no special mention of it, it is very likely that in one of its last sessions Synod appointed a committee for this purpose, and also for the scrutinizing of the liturgical writings. Soon afterwards it became clear that these deputies had not taken any action, so that one of the secretaries, Festus Hommius, took care of it.

However, the provincial synods of South Holland, held during the "twenties, were informed that Hommius had limited his activities to the liturgy, so that the 1622 Synod referred the supervision of the text of the Catechism to the next national synod. The brothers appointed for this purpose were urged to press on with the matter. Their attention was drawn to two special points: In the various editions the division into Lord's Days was not universally the same, and the text should be fixed and improved either according to the Latin or to the German text, which at certain points differed widely. This synod, however, appeared to be too optimistic. For, literally indeed, the "next national synod" would not be held for ages!

Only recently, at the General Synod of our Dutch sister Churches, held at Arnhem in the year 1981, a modernized Dutch translation was adopted as the official text.

English

As for translations into English, they were usually based on the Latin text. We may mention a few of them.

In 1591 an English version was taken into use by the Church of Scotland, "by authority of the king." In the year 1615 another translation was made, "appointed to be printed for use of the Kirk of Edinburgh." In Scotland the "Palatine Catechism" became very popular. It was often bound together with the Book of Common Order and the Psalter. It has served the Scottish Church for many years, until it was superseded, first by Craig's Catechism, then by the Westminster Shorter Catechism.

The Latin version was widely used in grammar schools and at colleges.

America

Along two different paths, and therefore in two different versions, the Heidelberg Catechism reached the American shores. From Holland it crossed the Atlantic, arriving at Manhattan Island together with the first Dutch settlers in the year 1609.

From the Palatinate(!), approximately a century later, it was carried to Pennsylvania and other colonies by migrants who had to flee the Roman Catholic persecutions in that formerly Reformed region.

Since then the Heidelberg Catechism has served the Dutch and German Reformed Churches as an instruction book and as a confession.

In 1771 the Synod of the Reformed Dutch Churches adopted a translation from the hand of Dr. Laidlie, made from the Latin version. For a long time it was used in the Dutch and German Reformed Churches.

In 1873, three hundred years after its first edition, the German Reformed Church — which had assumed a new name in 1869, the "Reformed Church in the United States" — published a three-centenary edition, a so-called *triglot*. It contains the Catechism in three different languages, German, Latin, and English, together with a Historical Introduction.

In the year 1934 this Church merged with the Evangelical Synod of North America, continuing together as the "Evangelical and Reformed Church." Since then it has merged into the United Church of Christ, which has the Heidelberg Catechism as its confession and instruction book. The same can be said of the present Reformed Church in the United States, the sister church of our Dutch sister churches.

The General Assembly of the Presbyterian Church in the United States, held at Philadelphia in 1870, gave formal sanction of the use of the Heidelberg Catechism in any congregation that might desire this. It recognized in the catechism "a valuable Scriptural compendium of Christian doctrine and duty."

Since 1967 the United Presbyterian Church of America recognises it as one of its six "subsidiary standards."

Our Churches

In their early years our own Churches, in Australia as well as in Canada and the United States, used the text of the Catechism as it was printed in the 1934 edition of the *Psalter Hymnal* of the Christian Reformed Church.

In some congregations an older English text was used by some catechism pupils, because it was printed in a separate pocket format, *The Heidelberg Catechism With All the Proof Texts in Full Bible Quotation*. It was an in 1957 photo litho reprinted edition of the Received American Version of 1771, the earlier mentioned English translation from the Latin by Dr. Laidlie. The somewhat old fashioned language — with frequent use of "thy" and "thou" e.g. in Lord's Day 1: "What is thy only comfort in life and death?" — was not too great an obstacle for the students who were familiar with the Authorized or King James Version, then in use in the Churches.

The *Book of Praise* had the *Psalter Hymnal* text from its first edition of 1961 until in the 1984 edition it was replaced by a modern English version, adopted by the General Synod 1983, prepared by a special committee originating with the Toronto 1974 Synod.

The Lincoln 1993 Synod mandated the committee concerned to insert the revised text of the Preface to the Catechism as decided by the Synod Cloverdale 1983. However, the Abbotsford 1995 General Synod decided "not to adopt the historical prefaces of the Heidelberg Catechism and the Canons of Dort and to rescind the decision of Synod 1983, Art. 174, and Synod Lincoln 1992, Art. 64 regarding this matter."[51]

The Australian Churches adopted this text — with the exception of the word "Christian" in Lord's Day 7 and 21 — provisionally at their Synod Launceston 1985 and definitely at the Albany 1987 Synod.

3.7 THE CANONS OF DORT

Complex situation

It may be known: "Dort" stands for "Dordrecht," the city in which in the years 1618 and 1619 a "National Synod" of the Dutch Churches was held. This was virtually an international synod, and therefore had some strong influence on the life of Reformed Churches in several countries. Many "foreign" Churches had sent delegates to this assembly. In the matter that formed the main item on the agenda they were given the right of the floor and voting rights.

---

[51] *Acts*, Article 44.

However, if we would think that "Dort" settled only a doctrinal issue, we do injustice to this important synod. More issues were at stake. It not only made arrangements for a new Bible translation, and settled questions about the baptism of adopted children of pagan background, but it approved the earlier officially accepted Belgic Confession of Faith and the Heidelberg Catechism, apart from compiling the Canons of Dort. It also adopted a new version of the Church Order.

We would be further mistaken if we considered that all these activities and decisions had no relation to each other. Most of them were indeed closely related.

This may become clear if we attempt to gain some insight into the complex situation at the end of the sixteenth and the first decades of the seventeenth century.

The Reformation at stake

That no less than the Reformation was at stake may become clear when we realize that there were a number of men who were, each of them in his own way, a kind of precursor of the Arminians, or who at least prepared the way for Arminianism.

One of these was Dirk Volkertszoon Coornhert (1522-90). Although he had many objections against the Roman Catholic Church, he remained a member of it, just like Desiderius Erasmus who — together with Thomas Erastus — strongly influenced him. He was a man of letters and a politician, secretary of the city of Haarlem.

From Erasmus he took over some humanistic ideas: Lack of insight produces shortcomings in a man's life, but these can be overcome by the use of reason and man's free will.

It is no wonder, then, that he strongly rejected the doctrine of original sin and of predestination as taught by John Calvin and Theodore Beza. He propagated religious tolerance, a "Christendom without divisions." Therefore all human writings such as the confessions should be abolished: the Bible and the Apostles' Creed were sufficient. Discipline was no Church matter. On the contrary, in his opinion the civil magistrate was the final judge in religious matters. He had learned this from Erastus, professor of medicines at the Heidelberg University at the time of the compiling of the Heidelberg Catechism.

From this brief review of his ideas we may learn that several factors played a role, and that they were interlinked. The deepest cause of the growing controversy between the Arminians and the Reformed — also called Remonstrants and Contra-Remonstrants — was that the gospel of free grace and of justification by faith alone was again at stake. The old Roman Catholic semi-pelagian idea of man being "not that bad" led to the denial of the Scriptural doctrine of predestination, and consequently to the rejection of certain parts in the existing confessions, to the request for "religious tolerance," the denial of Church discipline as administered to those who did not agree or live in accordance with the confessions, because this was in conflict with the religious tolerance which must be protected by the civil government. The last mentioned idea was supported by the majority and most prominent members of the Provincial States and for some time also by the Dutch States General. They feared the Church might become "a State within the State."

Therefore it was no wonder that more than once the government rejected the Church Order which was adopted by the respective synods. Efforts were undertaken to replace it by an order compiled by the State.

Taking this complex situation into account we may learn that the Synod of Dordrecht had to settle much more than merely a "doctrinal dispute." The Reformation was at stake, and with that the true gospel, life in covenant communion with the LORD.

Precursors

All this is confirmed when we briefly summarize the ideas of other "precursors" of the Arminians.

Hubert Duifhuis, a former Roman Catholic priest, was another follower of Erasmus. He had ideas similar to those of Coornhert. In his opinion a consistory was not necessary — his Church at Utrecht did not have one! The government had supervision over Church life. He hated the doctrine of predestination, and considered the Apostles' Creed to be sufficient. No other humanly compiled creeds or confessions were needed.

Casper Coolhaes at Leyden, also a former priest, was of the same opinion regarding the government being in charge of Church matters. Therefore he rejected a Church order written by the Churches themselves. He could not accept the binding to confessions. Hating the doctrine of predestination, he taught a kind of general atonement. When charged by his colleague Peter Cornelisz., the Leyden Magistrate put him under its protection.

Hermannus Herberts of Gouda — a former monk and priest — had some strong objections against the Heidelberg Catechism's doctrine of total depravity, because in his opinion a Christian could be perfect in this life. He sometimes refused to preach on the Catechism, and could not accept the doctrine of predestination. Bible study should be free, and not bound to any confession.

These men, together with others, paved the way for what is called Arminianism.

Arminius

Arminianism derives its name from Jacobus Arminius (1560-1609). He was a brilliant student. After his study at the Leyden University he went to Geneva, where he attended the lectures of Theodore Beza.

As a minister at Amsterdam he was requested by his consistory to investigate a response to an attack made by Coornhert on Beza's doctrine of predestination, written by two ministers of the Delft congregation. Studying this matter Arminius came to the conclusion that his own ideas were more in agreement with Coornhert's than with those of his former teacher Beza or his Delft colleagues.

A series of sermons on Paul's epistle to the Romans caused serious disturbance in the Amsterdam congregation. In his sermon on chapter 7 he stated that Paul there records his own experiences as an unregenerated person: a reborn person would not make the statement made by Paul in the second part of this chapter. Here the roots of Arminius' ideas on man's free will are evident. Man's free will was further stressed in his sermons on chapters 8 to 11, while the one on Romans chapter 13 emphasized the civil government's alleged function as the highest authority in ecclesiastical and religious matters.

Therefore it was no wonder that his colleague, Peter Plancius, accused him of Socinianism — a form of Pelagianism, putting strong emphasis on man's reason. However, the Amsterdam magistrate put Arminius under its protection.

When Arminius met Franciscus Junius, professor at Leyden, on the occasion of a wedding, he was able to open a discussion with him in order to have his views on predestination tested by this famous professor. This happened in the year 1597. The discussion was continued afterwards in writing.

In the course of the following year Arminius reviewed a brief treatise on predestination written by William Perkins, a staunch Calvinist at Cambridge. His response to it appeared to be critical to the Calvinistic view of limited atonement, invincible grace, and the perseverance of the saints — issues which were fiercely discussed later on in the controversy between Remonstrants — or Arminians — and Contra Remonstrants, and were settled at the Synod of Dordrecht 1618-19. In Arminius' opinion faith in itself is no fruit of predestination, which thesis includes in a nutshell the Arminian error of predestination on the basis of foreseen faith.

When in the year 1602 Franciscus Junius died as one of the many victims of a pestilence, Arminius was appointed as his successor. The curators of the Leyden University wanted a "moderate" person as the colleague of the outspoken Franciscus Gomarus, since 1594 professor at this institution.

Gomarus raised objections against Arminius' appointment. These were discussed at a conference held at The Hague on May 6, 1603. Having been handicapped by the rule that these objections must be substantiated from Arminius' — scarce — writings, Gomarus had to accept the confirmation of Arminius' appointment, and shortly afterwards had even to confer on him the degree of doctor of theology.

However, soon after Arminius' inauguration new friction arose, when he had some theses on predestination disputed in public by his students. Gomarus soon afterwards responded by having other theses on the same topic disputed.

Rumours on these discussions and friction began to spread soon afterwards. Former students of Arminius propagated his ideas from the pulpit.

Unfortunately the Churches had no say in the affairs of the University. As soon as a request was made from among them that the professors might declare themselves on the doctrinal points under discussion, the curators and the Leyden Magistrate suggested that a national synod would judge them. The States General and Johan van Oldenbarneveldt, since 1586 Advocate-General of Holland and Friesland — he was charged with national and international affairs, so a powerful man! — were finally inclined to give permission for the convening of such a synod, but with the condition that it should put the revision of the Confession on its agenda. It was even suggested that during the Synod the binding character of the Confession should be suspended. At a preparatory conference, held in the year 1607 at The Hague the supporters of Arminius were strongly in favour of this, while his opponents were against it, the latter even requesting the word "revision" should not be used!

At the Provincial Synod of South Holland in the same year objections were raised against Arminius' teachings. This resulted in a "friendly conference" at which he declared that he had some difficulties with certain parts of the Confession, but he would raise them at the proposed national Synod in the context of the revision of the Confession. Gomarus tried to have the issues discussed at this conference, but was not successful because the representatives of the government, in particular van Oldenbarneveldt, drew the conclusion that no fundamentals of the religion were at stake.

Similar conferences were held in the following years, but had the same negative result.

At that time it became clear that Arminius was seriously ill. He died of tuberculosis on October 19, 1609, leaving behind him his wife and nine children, but also a controversy in the Church and the country.

Remonstrants and Contra Remonstrants

After Arminius' death his friend since the days of their common study at Geneva, Johannes Uytenbogaerd, court preacher at The Hague, took over.

On October 14, 1610 he chaired a secret meeting, held at Gouda. At that meeting five articles, also called the "Remonstrance," were compiled and subscribed to by 46 ministers.

After this document the Arminians are also called "Remonstrants." And incorrectly the Canons of Dort, which reject them as errors, are sometimes given the name "Five Articles against the Remonstrants." The name "Five Points of Calvinism" is even worse, because Calvinism covers the doctrine of the whole Bible, so much more than these five points.

The "Remonstrance" can be summarized in the following headings:
1. conditional election; 2. universal atonement; 3. the free will of man; 4. resistible grace; 5. no perseverance of the saints, or: faith that can be lost.

This document was sent to van Oldenbarneveldt, who kept it in his office for a few months as long as he deemed it an unfavourable climate in which it could be forwarded to the States of Holland. These States then took sides with the Arminians by forbidding anyone to contradict the Remonstrance, at the same time refusing permission for the Churches to convene a provincial synod.

This action, as a matter of course, found a favourable reception among the Arminians. Uytenbogaerd showed his appreciation by publishing a pamphlet in which it was repeated that according to him the civil government had the supervision of doctrine and Church life — something against which Festus Hommius, a leading personality among the Contra Remonstrants, strongly protested.

At the end of the year 1610 plans were made for a conference, to be held at The Hague between Remonstrants and Contra Remonstrants, six from each side. This conference was indeed held, on March 10, 1611. During this meeting the so-called "Contra Remonstrance" was read. However, it could not convince the Remonstrants that they were wrong, so no solution was reached.

In the month of February 1612 something of a different nature — although closely related to the doctrinal controversy — happened. The States of Holland, under van Oldenbarneveldt's guidance, issued a Resolution whereby a Church Order drafted by the government was declared operative.

As we have already seen the civil government was very much afraid that the Churches would become "a State within the State." The Arminians were favoured by the magistrates, not only because many of the latter shared their doctrinal convictions, but also because they felt supported by the Remonstrants who had the same Erastian ideas about the relation between Church and State.

In the previous century the governments had refused to grant permission for the introduction of the Church Orders adopted by the Reformed synods. This happened to the Church Order compiled at the Dordrecht Synod of 1574. The States of Holland then drafted their own Order, which, however, was not imposed on the Churches. One of the crucial points was the question who had the right to appoint ministers, the Churches or the government. The same happened to the Church Order of Middelburg 1581. It was rejected by the Provincial States. Van Oldenbarneveldt — who at that time had already played a prominent role — was, together with others, charged to compile a Church Order from the Middelburg Acts. He proposed that an electoral college consisting of four representatives of the government and four delegates of the Churches should be given the right to call and appoint ministers. Other crucial points were the right to depose ministers and discipline ordinary Church members. The result was the so-called State Church Order of 1583, which was, however, not introduced. Neither was the Church Order, adopted by the 1586 The Hague Synod, acceptable to the States. A new draft for a governmental Order was then written by van Oldenbarneveldt and completed in the year 1591. It found strong opposition from the side of the Churches. It is this order that in the year 1612 was declared operative — and confirmed three years later.

As we have already seen, the Arminians closely connected the doctrinal issue with the Church political issue. From their side the Contra Remonstrants did the same. They were of the opinion that there is a firm relationship between a pure *corpus doctrinae* and a Scriptural *corpus disciplinae*, between the doctrine of the Church and upholding it in Church order and discipline.

Conflict

At the instigation of William Louis of Nassau, Stadtholder of the Province of Friesland, another conference was held at Delft on the 26th of February, 1613. Participants were three ministers from each side, Uytenbogaerd and Hommius being their respective main spokesmen. It ended without producing a real solution.

In the meantime unrest grew all over the country, in particular in the provinces of Holland and Utrecht where Arminianism was rather strong.

Then a conflict broke out at The Hague between Uytenbogaerd and his colleague Hendricus Rosaeus, and this resulted in the suspension of Rosaeus. However, many Church members did not recognize this suspension. They established a *dolerende* Church — which literally means: a grieving or mourning Church. Seeing their membership of no less than 1220 they asked for a Church building, the Great Church. This was refused. For some time the members had to walk to the village of Ryswyck for their Church services. After having met at a number of other places, all being too small and inappropriate, they took possession of the Hospital Church, and soon afterwards of the Cloister Church.

It was here that on a certain Sunday, July 23, 1617, they were surprised by the attendance of a prominent person.

Prince Maurice of Orange, who after the murder of "William the Silent" in 1584 had succeeded his father, had for a long time hesitated to take sides. However, under the influence of his cousin William Louis he came to the conclusion that he had to oppose van Oldenbarneveldt — who apparently sought too much power — and to offer his protection to the Contra Remonstrants. At a session of the States of Holland, early 1617, he solemnly declared that he, as the chief commander of the army, would not use his troops against the so-called "schismatics." He assured the meeting that he would keep the oath taken by him in the year 1585, whereby he has sworn to defend the Reformed faith.

This may explain his act of no longer attending the services conducted by his court preacher, Uytenbogaerd — who on Sunday July 16, 1617, in his sermon thundered against the intolerant attitude of the Contra Remonstrants and the convening of a national synod. The next Sunday Maurice joined the "mourning" congregation in the Cloister Church.

Because unrest had broken out simultaneously at several places, for instance at Amsterdam, van Oldenbarneveldt responded by issuing the "Sharp Resolution" on August 4, 1617. It stated that no national synod would be held, and that a special militia (*waardgelders*) could be used by the local authorities to defend the Remonstrants. This was an act whereby the authority of Prince Maurice as the chief commander of the army was denied, and the agreement of the Union of Utrecht — which was so important for the unity of the respective provinces of the Low Lands — was violated. It was a kind of *coup d'etat*.

Maurice reacted by disbanding the special militia at Utrecht, and imprisoning van Oldenbarneveldt.

This created a different atmosphere, wherein the States of Friesland, Groningen, Gelderland, and Zeeland requested the convening of a national synod, to resolve the doctrinal issues and have peace returned in Church life. This request was made in the month of May 1617.

On the eleventh of November of that year the States General made the decision that a national synod would be convened on the first of November 1618. The States of Holland, Utrecht, and Overijssel voted against this, but soon afterwards Prince Maurice convinced Overijssel to tentative agreement with it.

Delegates of the Reformed Churches in other countries were invited to this synod. King James I of England objected against Utrecht as the venue of synod, because of the strong Arminian influence in that city. He recommended Dordrecht, where in the previous century some synods had been held.

Dordrecht 1618-19

The Synod of Dordrecht, which by the States-General was convened on November 1, 1618, was opened on the 13th of that month in the Kloveniersdoelen, a militia building.

It was attended by 84 delegates of the Dutch Churches, 18 commissionaires of the States, some professors of theology representing the Universities or colleges of Leyden, Harderwijk, Middelburg, and Groningen, and a number of delegates from the foreign Churches: England, Emden, Bremen, the Palatinate, Hessen, Nassau, Geneva, Bern, Basel, Zurich, and Schaffhausen. The French delegates were refused permission by their king to leave the country. These foreign Churches had been invited by decree of the States General, "in order that the unity and agreement of religion might be established the better." At this synod much learning was assembled.

This even applies to the Arminians who had been summoned: twelve of the best known and most learned among them were selected to appear at Dordrecht. They were joined by three delegates of the Utrecht Churches, all Arminians, who were replaced by others when the Arminians had to leave the synod.

As members of the *moderamen* the following were chosen: Johannes Bogerman from Leeuwarden, chairman — he was said to have grown "the nicest beard in Europe" — his assessors Jacobus Rolandus from Amsterdam, and Hermanus Faukelius from Middelburg; and Festus Hommius from Leyden and Sebastianus Damman from Zutphen as clerks.

Before they appeared at the Synod the Arminians held a meeting at Rotterdam, where they discussed the tactics to be followed by them. This necessitated the Synod dealing with some other items of the agenda during the first two weeks. Decisions were made on a new Bible translation, on religious instruction in Church, school, and the family, and on baptism of adopted children of pagan background in the Dutch East Indies.

As soon as the Arminians had arrived their spokesman, Simon Episcopius, Arminius' successor at Leyden, made it clear that they considered this synod to be a meeting of equal parties. They did not acknowledge Synod's authority as an ecclesiastical court. In their opinion the representatives of the States and the foreign delegates could give their verdict. Synod, however, wanted to hear the Arminians' objections to the Belgic Confession of Faith. A long debate on this issue followed.

When the doctrinal issue could not be avoided during the debate, the Arminians showed another fruit of their preliminary meeting, for they tried to cause a split among the members of Synod by fiercely attacking the *supralapsarians* among them. They declared themselves only willing to state what they did not believe: the doctrine of eternal reprobation and the above mentioned *supralapsarian* ideas.

As for eternal reprobation, it is remarkable that in the course of time following the Dordrecht Synod and even in the last few decades of our own century, this has been rejected time and again. It appears to be a stumbling block to many.

Regarding the tactics of the Arminians it must be said that there were indeed *supralapsarians* as well as *infralapsarians* among the delegates. The former taught that God, in His eternal counsel, had chosen some and rejected others before His decree to create man, so before the Fall (*lapsus* in Latin), while the *infralapsarians* regarded fallen man as the objects of God's election or reprobation; both parties not strongly enough realizing that we must be careful not to ascribe our human logic to God's divine mind.

When it became clearer and clearer that the Arminians intended to sabotage Synod, and maintained their tactics despite the authorization given to Synod on January 1, 1619 by the States General to act as an ecclesiastical court and solve the Arminian controversy, they were dismissed on January 14.

Synod then decided to judge them from their own writings.

For this purpose the meeting split up into several committees, one consisting of the foreign delegates, another of the Dutch delegates, a third committee consisting of the professors of theology, and the fourth of the *moderamen* members.

The work was carried out very thoroughly. Each of the groups of delegates tabled its own findings — these *sententiae* taking a large number of pages in the Acts of Synod. The outcome was in full accordance with the oath taken on December 7, 1618, whereby all the delegates solemnly declared: "I promise before God, in Whom I believe, and Whom I worship, as being present in this place, and as being the Searcher of all hearts, that during the course of the proceedings of this Synod, which will examine and decide, not only the five points, and all the differences resulting from them, but also any other doctrine, I will use no human writing, but only the Word of God, which is an infallible rule of faith. And during all these discussions, I will only aim at the glory of God, the peace of the Church, and especially the preservation of the purity of doctrine. So help me my Saviour, Jesus Christ! I beseech Him to assist me by His Holy Spirit!"

The contents of this oath may explain why we do not find any quotations in the Canons from the Belgic confession of Faith or the Heidelberg Catechism, although a number of sentences remind us of certain places in the latter. They quote literally from the Bible only, claiming their Scriptural foundation.

The final reading of these *sententiae* was completed on March 21, 1619. However, this did not mean that the Synod could issue its final verdict immediately. The findings of the committees had to be harmonized and summarized in some shorter statements. For this purpose a special committee was appointed on March 25.

On April 16 the reading and discussion of the proposed Canons began. Once more every chapter of the draft that was tabled by this committee was thoroughly discussed in full session. It appeared that the responses to the third and fourth of the "five articles of the Remonstrance" could be combined, so that the headings in the Canons read as follows: Chapter I : Divine election and reprobation; Chapter II : Christ's death and man's redemption through it; Chapter III/IV : The corruption of man, his conversion to God, and the manner in which it occurs; Chapter V : The perseverance of the saints.

Every chapter was followed by a section called "Rejection of Errors," and the whole was introduced by a Preface, and concluded by an Epilogue. In the English-speaking world the "Five Points of Calvinism," incorrectly so called, are sometimes abbreviated as TULIP, which stands for: Total depravity, Unconditional election, Limited atonement, Irresistible (better: Invincible) grace, and Perseverance of the saints.

The final reading of the "Canons of Dort" — "canon" means: rule, standard — took place on April 23. Every Dutch and foreign delegate put his signature to the official document. The text was written in three languages: Latin, the official language of Synod, Dutch, and French.

On the sixth of May the Canons were publicly read and proclaimed in the Great Church of Dordrecht, after an impressive prayer spoken by the president.

Three days later, on Ascension Day, the "international" section of the Synod of Dordrecht was closed.

After reopening, now as a real national synod, the text of the Church Order was revised, a subscription form, including a reference to the Canons, adopted, the Belgic Confession of Faith and the Heidelberg Catechism read and approved, and the text of the former also approved.

After a total of 180 sessions, 154 of which were "international," Synod was closed on May 29, 1619.

After "Dort"

It may be clear that the Synod of Dordrecht did not only settle the doctrinal issue, but it was also of fundamental significance to the relationship between Church and State. The fact that it could adopt a revised text of the Church Order and introduce it in the Churches, is of great importance. On the other hand, the respective territories of Church and State were not yet adequately determined. This may be clear e.g. from the request made to the States General to provide funds for the new Bible translation, which at its completion was officially presented to this body, and as a consequence popularly called *Statenvertaling* — States Version.

Another aspect of the great significance of this synod is that it influenced life in many of the foreign Churches, which had to struggle against the same or similar false teachings. The Canons were officially adopted as binding by the — absent at Dordrecht — Reformed Churches in France, at their Synods of Alais (1620) and Charenton (1623). They strongly influenced the Westminster Confession and Catechisms. Earlier the Presbyterians in England had declared their agreement with the Canons of Dort. However, the Church of England did not express its agreement. The Churches in Switzerland and the Palatinate also stated their approval. In later centuries the Canons were adopted by the Reformed (Dutch) Church in America — although only partly: the Rejection of Errors, the Preface and the Epilogue were omitted — the Churches in South Africa, the Christian Reformed Church in America and others.

As for the Dutch Churches, they required the Arminians to sign a "Deed of Cessation" (*Acte van Stilstand*), whereby they promised to abstain from propagating ideas differing from the Canons. Seventy ministers did so. Two hundred others lost their office, forty of whom were reinstated when finally they subscribed to the adopted confessions.

When Prince Maurice — who died in 1625 — was succeeded by his brother Frederick Henry, the banned Arminians were given permission to return. This was the beginning of a recurring influence on Church life. It may be known that during the nineteenth century in particular, Modernism — a daughter of Arminianism — became dominant in the Church, and that this necessitated many breaking with the apostate Church in the Secession of 1834 and the *Doleantie* ("Grieving" or "Mourning") of 1886 — in both of them the Canons of Dort played their role! After the Churches of the Secession and the *Doleantie* had united in 1892, and the Liberation of the 1940s had taken place, a new type of liberalism or modernism and false tolerance arose in the synodical churches, one of its consequences being that the Canons of Dort were virtually abrogated as far as their doctrine of Rejection is concerned. It even led to the plan to amalgamate with the Dutch Reformed Church (*Nederlands Hervormde Kerk*), which claims to be the "national Church." It justified, apart from other things, the Liberation of the Churches in the 1940s. Our own Churches in Australia, Canada, and the United States, were established by migrants from these Reformed Churches, which are sometimes (unofficially) called the Liberated Churches.

Unfortunately Arminianism gained new influence in the Church of England under Charles I, and later on in Methodist and other Churches, and also in and through the Salvation Army. It appears to be very difficult for man to accept his total depravity, God's free grace, and justification by faith alone. The Canons, summarizing and confessing the biblical doctrine at these points, make man humble before God and very grateful to God. They also keep the preaching of the gospel alive! Therefore it is worthwhile to know the Canons of Dort!

Our Churches

During the fifties, sixties, seventies, and the first years of the eighties of this century, our Churches made use of the text printed in the 1934 edition of the Christian Reformed Church's *Psalter Hymnal*.

The 1984 edition of the *Book of Praise* included a more modern English version, adopted provisionally by the General Synod Cloverdale 1983 of the Canadian Reformed Churches. This edition does not include the Preface to the Canons, in spite of the fact that the same synod decided to have it included.

The Synod of Winnipeg 1989 charged a committee to add Scriptural references to the text of the Canons, and to update the Preface of the confessions and creeds. However, in the latter case by "Preface" is meant the historical introduction supplied by the *Psalter Hymnal*. This confusion requires co-ordination of terms by successive synods.

It is important that the same synod adopted a revised text of the Canons. This revised text was not known when at their Synod of Launceston 1985 the Free Reformed Churches of Australia adopted the 1983 text, be it provisionally. The Albany 1985 Synod made it the Churches' definite text. The Armadale 1990 Synod, however, had to come back from this position because in the meantime the revised Canadian text had reached Australia. Deputies were appointed, who reported favourably to the Bedfordale 1992 Synod. Consequently this Synod decided to "accept the new translation of the Canons of Dort which will appear in the next revision of the *Book of Praise*."

In this "next revision," the 1993 edition, we find a revised Preface, in accordance with a decision made by the Canadian General Synod of 1992. This decision, however, was rescinded by the Abbortsford 1995 General Synod, which decided "not to adopt the historical prefaces of the Heidelberg Catechism and the Canons of Dort."[52]

---

[52] *Acts*, Article 44.

4. ORDERS OF WORSHIP

Suggested only

After the text of the Canons of Dort we find in the *Book of Praise* an "Index of Cross References to the Three Forms of Unity." Apparently it has been inserted "by courtesy of" the Standing Committee for the *Book of Praise*. For we could not find any indication in the respective Acts of synods that authority to do so was given to include this useful item, let alone an official approval of its text.

As for the "Orders of Worship" which then follow, the situation is slightly different. At the instigation of the committee concerned the General Synod Smithville 1980 adopted a recommendation "to include the suggested Orders of Worship in the edition of the *Book of Praise*."[53] The word "suggested" was borrowed from the committee's report, which spoke of "Suggested Orders of Worship," using this term "because Synod should not adopt a specific Order which is mandatory for the Churches."

The Australian Churches were not likely to make any objections against this "policy." For Synod Albany 1956 decided "to rescind the decision of the Synod 1954, Acts, Article 15, regarding the order of the Church services, and decided for the time being not to recommend an order for the Church services." (The Armadale 1954 Synod had decided "that the order of Church services shall be the one that is used in the Reformed Churches in The Netherlands" — so going one bridge too far because in The Netherlands there was at that time only a recommended order, while the word "shall" in the Synod's decision refers to a rule, as the same word does in the Church Order).

At the Albany Synod an order similar to the one that became known as "Kampen 1975" was proposed; however, Synod did not adopt the proposal.

Two proposals

The orders of worship, in the *Book of Praise* introduced as being "in common use," are mainly those recommended by the synods of the Dutch sister Churches, of Middelburg 1933 and Kampen 1975 respectively.

---

[53] *Acts*, Article 122.

Mainly, we may repeat, because in the Middelburg order no proper place is allotted to the administration of the sacraments. Scripture-reading has its place before the first prayer, and it does not mention the possibility of replacing the Apostles' Creed by the Nicene Creed. All these changes and additions cannot be found in the original "Middelburg 1933 order." The name *Offeranden* has been translated by "Offertory," which however reminds us of the term used for part of the papal mass and therefore be replaced by "Offerings."

It may be worthwhile to trace the history of both orders.

History

The "Kampen 1975 order" claims to be virtually the same as the one used by John Calvin.

This is not the place to outline the extent to which Calvin was influenced by the ancient Christian Church and certain ideas developed during the Middle Ages, nor even the impressions made on him by the liturgy followed by Martin Bucer at Strasbourg. We shall limit ourselves to reproducing the order found in Calvin's booklet *La Forme des prieres et chantz ecclesiastiques* from the year 1542. There the order for the morning service was as follows: Votum (Psalm 124:8); Confession of sins, after a brief exhortation; Congregational singing; Salutation, and exhortation to prayer: "The Lord be with you; let us pray to the Lord"; Prayer for illumination by the Holy Spirit before the sermon; Scripture-reading and sermon; Intercessory Prayer, concluded with a paraphrase of the Lord's Prayer; (when the Lord's Supper is celebrated: Prayer for the Lord's Supper, added to the Intercessory Prayer; profession of faith; Words of Institution together with retention and invitation; distribution and communion; thanksgiving); congregational singing; Benediction (from Numbers 6).

This order arrived in The Netherlands together with the Heidelberg Catechism which Petrus Dathenus, when ministering at Frankenthal in the Palatinate, had translated into Dutch. This order was not separately printed in the booklet published in 1566 that contained his metrical version of the Psalms and the liturgical prayers and forms — which were also translated from the Church Order of the Palatinate. However, the notations printed above the text of these prayers and forms referred to an order of service which was virtually the same as John Calvin's order.

Before the Form for Baptism Psalm 124:8 was printed. The Ten Commandments must be read or sung before the prayer for illumination by the Holy Spirit, followed by an exhortation to confess one's sins and the proclamation of God's grace. Immediately before the first prayer the Apostles' Creed was recited. The prayer after the sermon was followed by the Benediction from Numbers 6, after which the minister exhorted the congregation with these words: "Remember the needy," which supposed a door collection.

Remarkable — and important — is the inclusion of a metrical version of a prayer before the sermon, written by John Utenhove of the London Church of Dutch refugees. It confirms that the old Reformed tradition had a brief prayer before the sermon, a prayer for illumination by the Holy Spirit, and that the intercessory prayers followed after the sermon.

The Convention of Wesel 1568 was the first — unofficial — meeting of the Dutch Churches that dealt with the order of service. It was of the opinion that public confession of sins and a prayer for forgiveness were fitting in particular at a special prayer meeting arranged on one of the weekdays, either before or after the sermon. The ordinary prayers — in the Sunday service — had to be adapted to the sermon. To maintain order before the worship service started Scripture reading and Psalm singing should take place.

The so-called "liturgical Synod" of Dordrecht 1574 officially adopted Dathenus' liturgy, the only changes being the inclusion of the Ten Commandments in the afternoon service, and the incorporation of the Apostles' Creed into the prayer after the sermon. This synod left Scripture reading and Psalm singing before the start of the service to the freedom of the Churches. The same applied to the Offerings: they could be taken either during or after the service. The "long prayer" must be shortened. In its original form it was better suited to special days of fasting and prayer. This synod kept silent on the confession of sins and proclamation of grace.

The great Synod of Dordrecht 1618-19 did not make any decisions on the order of service, except that John Utenhove's metrical version of the prayer before the sermon was restored — it had been left out by "Dordrecht 1574" — and that regarding the order to be followed in the Church service book it mentioned: the public prayers first, and then the forms for the sacraments, discipline, and marriage.

However, when in the year 1637 the new Bible translation, initiated by this synod, the *Statenvertaling*, was published, and in certain editions the liturgical writings were included, it appeared that first the liturgical forms had been printed and only then the liturgical prayers. This was an unauthorized initiative of the publishers. Unfortunately this is the order in which the liturgical writings have been arranged in the *Book of Praise*. It is not in full harmony with the requirements of a Reformed Church service book, because we may expect the liturgical prayers to be more frequently used than the liturgical forms, which serve in special services only.

This arrangement may also have contributed to the neglect of these prayer forms: We have seldom heard them from the lips of ministers and "reading-elders!"

Another reason for this neglect is that during the eighteenth and nineteenth centuries the idea was cherished that a "free prayer" more clearly showed the guidance of the Holy Spirit than the use of a prayer form.

During the same centuries Rationalism and Pietism exercised some influence on the order-of-service. The sermon was given most of the attention, the rest of the liturgy being considered as of less importance. Christ's saying of John 4:24 which characterizes a Church service as a worship service, was forgotten. Long sermons were the result, and most of the other elements were transferred to the beginning of the service, and also abbreviated. The administration of baptism, the Offerings, and the "long prayer" were given a place before the sermon. Usually the sermon was interrupted by congregational singing — sometimes even announced as intended to serve the hearers' relaxation — after which "the application" followed — for many people the most, or only, interesting part of the sermon. The unity between Scripture reading and sermon was split up. Consequently most old Church service books did not contain an order of service. They only included the material that could be used — and which was often not used at all!

This was the situation in the Dutch Churches in the early years of the twentieth century, a situation that clearly showed the decay that had crept into the liturgy of the Church.

"Middelburg 1933"

We may be grateful that some people had an eye for this decay. Among them was Abraham Kuyper, who in the year 1911 completed a long series of articles written for his weekly *De Heraut*, and published his book *Onze Eeredienst* (our worship service, our liturgy).

Kuyper made a plea for an order of service of a higher standard. He wanted the element of public confession of sins and proclamation of God's grace — that had disappeared — to return. In his opinion the first prayer must be restored as a prayer for illumination by the Holy Spirit, while the intercessory prayers must be returned to their original place after the sermon.

Some of his former students were strongly stimulated by this publication. Their "Movement of the Younger Ones" (*Beweging der jongeren*) provided a good opportunity to expound their ideas on these and also other aspects of Church life — but we must limit ourselves to the liturgy — in the weekly *De Reformatie*. In its early volumes we find them appealing for more and better expression of worship and adoration, shorter sermons, responses sung more spontaneously, therefore without prior announcement by the minister, the restoring of the Genevan tunes — which were being a-rhythmically sung at that time! — more variety in the order of service, in brief a return to John Calvin's much richer liturgy.

The result was that in the year 1920 the General Synod of Leeuwarden appointed a number of deputies with, among other things, the mandate to draft an order of service.

At the Utrecht 1923 General Synod they proposed the introduction of an order which included a confession of sins and proclamation of forgiveness, then intercessory prayers to be said before the Scripture-reading — which was reconnected to the sermon. The report claimed a return to the order of the seventeenth century and the preservation of the Reformed character of the liturgy — a claim partly incorrect. That the intercessory prayers were introduced before the sermon was a matter of psychology, which was really "in" at that time. It was claimed that the congregation was unable to concentrate during a long prayer after the sermon. Furthermore, the minister was deemed too tired to formulate it, so that, for psychological reasons the second prayer must be kept brief — our own experiences during several decades are entirely different!

The Synod of 1923, however, decided not to make any decision! Too many objections against the report were raised from among the Churches.

The issue of the order of service, together with other aspects of the liturgy — e.g. hymn singing, was dealt with once again at the General Synod held at Middelburg 1933.

The section of the report on the order of service was very brief. Deputies advised Synod to maintain as much as possible "what is customary in our Churches." Therefore they abstained from proposing any radical changes. The result was that Synod recommended what has been known since then as "the order of Middelburg 1933." This is fundamentally the same order as printed under A on pages 581-2 of the *Book of Praise*, except the alterations and additions earlier mentioned.

"Kampen 1975"

We are happy that this was not the end of the story. Since then new interest in our liturgy had been shown. It was discovered that the liturgy of "Middelburg 1933" deviated at some important points from that of the Reformed one which we confess in Lord's Day 38 of the Heidelberg Catechism, that we "diligently attend the Church of God, to hear God's Word, to use the sacraments, to call publicly upon the LORD, and to give Christian offerings for the poor." It is not in harmony with the order of the Ten Commandments and that of the Lord's Prayer either. These both require our attention, obedience, and petitions first of all for God's Name and Kingdom, and only then for our own well being — just as the first "great commandment" is to love God, and the "second like it" to love our neighbour as ourselves.

At the General Synod of Kampen 1975 an excellent report was tabled. It dealt with all sorts of liturgical matters, the order of service included.

It criticized "Middelburg 1933" at the following points:

1. the "long prayer" breaks the unity between Scripture reading and the preaching of God's Word. According to Scriptural data this should be there, and always used to be there in the ancient Church and the days of the Reformation but was lacking before and has been lacking after 1923;

2. "Middelburg 1933" limits the number of prayers to two only, while the Church service book has six; the latter no longer being suitable for "1933;"

3. "Middelburg 1933" shows a lack of esteem for the prayer forms in the Church book. This is the fruit of the influence of English Puritanism, and — via the "Second Reformation" (*Nadere Reformatie*) — of German Pietism;

4. The confession of sins — in the prayer forms — has been pushed into the background; therefore "1933" is *anaemic*, lacking spiritual depth;

5. It is unclear what function in the liturgy the reading of God's Law has — as it has been taken from its reformative relation with the confession of sins;

6. There is no indication of a proper place for the administration of baptism;

7. No arrangements have been made for the administration of the Lord's Supper;

8. Apart from the "long prayer" the Offerings have also been given a wrong place; they belong to the responsory part of the liturgy.

Synod decided to recommend the order proposed in this report as an alternative. Apart from what we noted under the heading "Two Orders," it is the order printed in the *Book of Praise* under B, on pages 582-3.

For many years — even since the "fifties — a similar order has been used by the majority of the Free Reformed Churches of Australia.

5. LITURGICAL WRITINGS

5.1 INTRODUCTION

Liturgy

The word "liturgy" has for us, Reformed people, a double meaning. First of all we understand by it the order of our Church services — which we discussed in the previous chapter. But the same word serves also as an indication of the respective "documents" used for the respective parts of these services.

They are subdivided into liturgical prayers and liturgical forms. We will discuss them in this order. In its 1984 edition the *Book of Praise* has them in the reversed order, which is based on the unauthorized initiative taken by some publishers of the *Statenvertaling* of 1637. The original order is the "natural" one, because we are supposed to use the liturgical prayers more frequently than the liturgical forms which serve in special worship services only. It is to be hoped that in the next edition of the *Book of Praise* the original order will be restored.

History

However, we will first briefly review the history of our Reformed liturgy, and look at the lines along which it has grown into what it is today.

As we have already learned when we dealt with the creeds, the tradition of using fixed formulas and forms for the respective parts of the Church services is rather an old approach. In the Western Church this resulted in the fixed liturgy of the mass, baptism, and other ceremonies. However, since the whole service was held in Latin, and the people began to miss the preaching of God's Word, two kinds of "alternatives" came into being, especially in the Southern part of Germany, across the border in the North-Eastern part of France, and in some regions of Switzerland. Both, the *Predigtdienst* or *Pronaus* and the *Gemeindekommunion* were held in the vernacular. Each of them adopted a particular liturgy.

The *Pronaus* especially has influenced the liturgy of some Churches of the Reformation, as for example Zurich and Strasbourg. The Reformers were no revolutionaries. They tried to maintain and further develop that which in their opinion was good and Scriptural in the medieval Church. Some of them, e.g. Martin Luther, went even too far in this respect by maintaining the mass — though in a "purified" form. However, the Reformation broke with the false doctrine of the Church of Rome and its hierarchy.

This meant that Church life had to be restructured. The preaching of God's Word was restored — and in this respect the *Pronaus* served as an example. The same can be said of the Lord's Supper — which underwent a more thorough purification than the one in the *Gemeindekommunion*, which, over against the mass with its emphasis on the transubstantiation of the elements and its character as a sacrifice, accentuated the idea of the congregation's communion. Baptism and other ceremonies were delivered from their superstitious elements.

All this required new formulas and forms.

Wittenberg, Basel, and Zurich

In the year 1533 Martin Luther wrote his *Taufbuchlein*, a booklet on the sacrament of baptism. It contained a provisional order in the German language. A peculiar element in it was the so-called "Flood Prayer," which is the oldest part in our own Form for the Administration of Holy Baptism, dating back to the Middle Ages.

Leo Judae used this in his baptismal liturgy of the same year. On August 10, 1523 this liturgy was used for the first time by Ulrich Zwingli, Judae's colleague at Zurich. Judae's booklet, however, included more than a baptismal liturgy. It also contained forms for funerals, marriage solemnization, intercessory prayers, and public profession of sins.

As for the Lord's Supper, there is first of all Karlstadt's ceremony, performed by him at a time (1521) which in Luther's opinion was too early. Its participants took the bread and the cup in their own hands — (the celebration "with both elements" was something new). However, this "purified mass" was not celebrated with the help of a fixed form; there was only a kind of a scheme.

We further mention the Basler reformer Johannes Oecolampadius' *Testament Jesu Christ* of the year 1523. It had a form based on the order of the mass. In 1526 he published a booklet containing forms for the administration of the two sacraments and for the visiting of the sick.

Zwingli's *Action oder Bruch des Nachtmals, Gedachtnis oder Danksagung Christ* (1525) broke completely with the idea of a "purified mass."

Transubstantiation of the elements, and the idea of the Lord's Supper as a sacrifice offered to God were rejected. The Lord's Supper was considered to be a memorial meal and a thanksgiving meal (Eucharist, the original Scriptural name) — the last element is often neglected by Zwingli's critics.

In his opinion — the same as Luther's — the intercessory prayers were of great significance. This is why they were given a prominent place in his liturgy. It may be clear that they had no relation with the sacrificial concept of the mass, and thus also had no meritorious application for the dead.

Zwingli's baptismal liturgy appeared to have broken with the medieval practice by no longer using the Vulgate text of the baptismal formula *in nomine* . . . (in the name of . . .), but by returning to the Greek text (into the name of . . .).

Strasbourg

At Strasbourg Theobald Schwarz celebrated a "purified mass" in German on February 16, 1524. This first reformation of the liturgy was followed by Martin Bucer's *Grund und Ursach* of the same year, signed by his colleagues Schwarz, Wolfgang Capito, Matthias Zell, and Caspar Hedio. It contained a kind of liturgical program, dealing with the Lord's Supper, baptism, prayers, congregational singing, and festive days. In 1525 Bucer's liturgy *Von des Herren Nachtmahl oder Mess und dem Predigen* (Of the Lord's Supper or Mass and of the Preaching) was published. Here were some clear influences of Wittenberg and Zurich. Later on some improvements were made: the mass was completely replaced by the Scriptural Lord's Supper, and before the administration of the sacraments the congregation was instructed about their meaning.

John Calvin

When in the year 1537 John Calvin arrived at Geneva, he found there the liturgy written by William Farel in the year 1533, *Maniere et Fasson*. It contained forms for baptism, marriage solemnization, the Lord's Supper, the order of the preaching service, including rules for the prayers, and regulations for the visiting of the sick.

Calvin tried to improve the liturgy, but faced strong opposition from the direction of the magistrates. After having been expelled he arrived finally at Strasbourg. There he became the minister of the French speaking Reformed Church. He adopted the liturgy of the German speaking congregation. However, there were so many amendments and additions that we cannot say that Calvin was dependent on Martin Bucer. In the year 1539 he published a booklet, *Alcuns Pseaumes et Cantiques mys en chant*. The metrical versions of Psalms 113 (by Clement Marot) and 138 (by Calvin himself) and the version of the Song of Simeon (Marot) were meant to be sung during or after the celebration of the Lord's Supper, while the metrical versions of Psalms 25 and the Ten Commandments were most likely used in connection with the confession of sins. This was a fixed liturgical item which had been adopted from the *Pronaus*. In 1540 it was followed by a complete liturgy for the celebration of the Lord's Supper. Up till today a copy of this liturgy has never been found. However, in the year 1542, when in the meantime Calvin had returned to Geneva, a booklet which may be considered as a reprint edited by Pierre Brully, entitled "*La manyere de faire prieres . . .*" (the way in which to say prayers), was published. It contained not only Psalm-versions and hymns, but also prayers for before and after the sermon, and forms for baptism, the Lord's Supper, and marriage solemnization. Calvin himself published in the same year his *La Forme des Prieres at Chantz Ecclesiastiques . . .* The long title also mentions that, apart from prayers and songs, it contained forms for the administration of the sacraments, the solemnization of marriages, and regulations for the visiting of the sick. All this, according to the last line of the title, "in accordance with the tradition of the ancient Church."

London

Another place of significance in the history of our liturgy is the city of London.

Many Reformed people from the Southern parts of The Netherlands, Flanders and the province of Zeeland, found a refuge here, followed later on by French speaking believers from Strasbourg and Wallonia.

In the year 1550 the young King Edward VI, whose protector was his uncle, Edward Seymour, Duke of Somerset, presented them with the former building of the Austin Friars, where they could have their Church services. Here, with some changes, Calvin's liturgy of Strasbourg and Geneva was adopted. Later on it arrived in The Netherlands via Frankenthal in the Palatinate, and from there, after some centuries, in North America and Australia.

Valerandus Pollanus, a Flemish nobleman, arrived in London in 1548 from Strasbourg. Together with Martin Bucer he had been invited to assist

Thomas Cranmer, archbishop of Canterbury, in his efforts to compile a more Reformed Book of Common Prayer. As a superintendent of the Wallonian refugee Church at Glastonbury he wrote his *Liturgia Sacra* (sacred liturgy) in the year 1551. This book meant to inform the king and Church leaders about the liturgy used at Strasbourg, with some additions from the Genevan liturgy. In 1552 this was followed by a Church service book, entitled *L'ordre des prieres et ministere Ecclesiastiques* (the order of prayers and Church ministry).

Pollanus' influence can be noticed in Johannes à Lasco's *Forma ac Ratio*, a booklet he wrote in London, but that could not be published before he arrived at Frankfurt when after the death of King Edward in 1553 persecutions broke out under Mary Tudor.

The same can be said about Marten Micron's *De Christelyke Ordinancien* (Christian Ordinances), printed in 1554, most likely at Emden in East Friesland, the so-called "Geneva of the North."

The London liturgy was strongly based on Calvin's Strasbourg and Genevan liturgy, although there were a few specific points in it, e.g. the tradition to sit at the table during the Lord's Supper — something new in those days — and an addition to the formula of distribution from I Corinthians 10:16, called "The London Appendix."

The Palatinate and Petrus Dathenus

When in the year 1553 the members of the London refugee Church had to flee to the European continent, some of them stayed at Emden, others went to Frankfurt soon afterwards. Their ministers there were Petrus Dathenus and Caspar van der Heyden. It was not strange that for that congregation the London liturgy was introduced (1554).

Because of the intolerant attitude of the Lutherans they had to leave Frankfurt and go to the Palatinate. There a former Augustine monastery at Frankenthal was made available to them.

Now, as a matter of fact, a new Church Order — including the liturgical forms and the Heidelberg Catechism; and so a liturgical and confessional church order at the same time! — was adopted in the year 1563, Dathenus being one of the many theologians who were invited to contribute, under the supervision of Caspar Olevianus. One of the conditions for enjoying the hospitality offered was that the refugees would bind themselves to this Church Order and its liturgy.

When Dathenus and van der Heyden undertook the task of compiling a Church service book in the Dutch language, the result was a liturgy based on both the London and the Heidelberg tradition.

In 1563 a small booklet was published, containing a translation of the Heidelberg Catechism, and a number of prayers: a morning prayer, an evening prayer, prayers before and after meals, a public profession of sins, and prayers for before and after the sermon, including a brief prayer for the latter.

Three years later a complete Dutch service book was printed. It contained Dathenus' version of the Psalms and some hymns; further translations of the Heidelberg Catechism and the liturgical prayers and forms for the administration of the sacraments and for marriage solemnization. These were adopted from the Palatine Church Order; to which a "Brief Examination of Faith" (*Korte Onderzoekinge des Geloofs*) was added. This book may be considered the first complete Reformed Church service book in the Dutch language.[54]

The Netherlands

Dathenus' liturgy found rapid recognition in The Netherlands. Admittedly, in some regions Utenhove's London Psalm version was used for a long time, but Dathenus' version soon started to take precedence, together with the liturgical writings and the translation of the Heidelberg Catechism. Undoubtedly one of the reasons for this was the fact that he and his colleague van der Heyden played a significant role at the ecclesiastical assemblies of those days. Dathenus was the chairman of the — unofficial — Convent of Wesel 1568 and of the National Synod of Dordrecht 1578. Van der Heyden took the same position at the Synod of Emden 1571 and the "liturgical Synod" of Dordrecht 1574.

The last mentioned assembly was of the opinion that the baptismal form and the intercessory prayer after the sermon were too long. Van der Heyden was commissioned to compile shorter forms — which were approved by the Provincial Synod of Rotterdam 1575. In the Form for the Lord's Supper "1574" the "London Appendix" was added to the formula of distribution. It supplied separate questions for parents and witnesses in the baptismal form.

---

[54] The word "complete" in this paragraph refers to the liturgical section of a Reformed Church Service Book.

The Synod of The Hague 1586 added forms for the Ordination or Installation of Office Bearers and for Church Discipline.

The 1610 Provincial Synod of Zeeland appointed a committee — the "Walcheren Committee" — for the supervision and the completion of the liturgy. This committee added a Form for Baptism of Adults, prayers for before and after the ecclesiastical assemblies, and supplied a new text for the Prayer after the Sermon because some intercessory prayers had to be changed in view of the altered political circumstances. Their findings were published in the so-called "Schilders edition" of 1611.

Dordrecht 1618-19 and after

This edition was used at the great Synod of Dordrecht 1618-19.

This synod, after having lasted too long in the opinion of its sponsors, the States General, left no time for a complete overhaul of the liturgy. Therefore, in one of its final sessions, the 178th session of May 28, 1619, it took the following decision: "The Dutch liturgy, containing the public prayers, and the forms for the administration of the sacraments, for Church discipline, ordination or installation of the ministers of the Church, elders and deacons, and marriage solemnization, shall be overseen by the revisers of the brief Acts of Synod or by the Synod's clerks, and be added to the Public Writings." The latter referred to the Creeds, Confessions, and Church Order. In conjunction with the confessions the liturgical prayers and forms are a kind of a testimony, addressing the authorities and the whole nation!

Unfortunately the revisers have never presented a revised text. All that happened was that at a provincial synod, held in the year 1521 at Rotterdam, Festus Hommius read the notes he had made during the National Synod of Dordrecht 1618-19, which he had served as one of its clerks. The meeting decided that every one should use this text. At the same time the other provincial synods were fully informed.

During the last one hundred years

In 1897 a new edition of the confessions and liturgical writings was included in the so-called *Flakkeesche editie*, edited by H.H. Kuyper and F.L. Rutgers. It claimed to contain the text that was authorized — according to them — by the Synod of Dordrecht. This claim, however, was rejected by others, who seem to be correct in this matter. Synod Arnhem

1902 recommended this text for use by the Churches. Subsequent synods, of Utrecht 1923 and Arnhem 1930, made some amendments to it. "1923" added a form for Public Profession of Faith. "1930" added three public admonitions in the Form for Church Discipline, and issued a revised Form for Marriage Confirmation.

After the Liberation of the Churches in the 1940s the General Synods of Hattem 1972-73, Kampen 1975, Groningen-Zuid 1978, Arnhem 1981, and Heemse 1984-85 adopted linguistically renewed texts for most of the liturgical writings, as well as new forms for the Ordination of Missionaries and Marriage Confirmation; further revised texts of other forms, and an Abbreviated Form for the Administration of the Lord's Supper — this last was at the request of Churches which desired to celebrate the Lord's Supper more frequently, although the majority of Churches, if not all of them, use this abbreviated form during the "continuance" in the second service.

Our Churches

Our own Churches in Australia, Canada, and the United States have adopted the Dutch liturgical writings, first of all for their services in the Dutch language, held during the "transition period" of the first few decades of their existence, and soon after this phase for their services in the English language. For the latter the texts in the *Psalter Hymnal* of the Christian Reformed Church were used until they were replaced by the versions in the respective editions of the *Book of Praise*.

The history is briefly as follows:

The first synod of the Canadian Reformed Churches, held in 1954 at Homewood, appointed a committee with the mandate to investigate which English translation of the Liturgical Prayers and Forms could be used. The second synod, of Homewood-Carman 1958, mandated some brothers to present a text of the Liturgical Forms and Prayers including the alterations proposed by the deputies appointed by the previous synod, to the Churches.

"Edmonton 1965" appointed deputies to look for suitable forms for the Excommunication of non-communicant members. The General Synod of Orangeville 1968 adopted the proposed forms for this purpose.

"New Westminster 1971" appointed a separate committee to look at the second half of the Church book. This committee had to propose texts for the Creeds and the Liturgical Forms, new forms included.

At the Toronto 1974 Synod it was agreed that the mandate given to the above mentioned committee was vague. New deputies were appointed with a clearer mandate: they had to scrutinize the texts of the Doctrinal and Liturgical Forms as to correctness of translation from the Dutch version, adopted by the 1954 Synod, the latter to be compared with the original languages. The Heidelberg Catechism was excepted because a separate committee was appointed for that doctrinal standard.

The General Synod of Coaldale 1977 adopted provisionally the English text of the Form for the Ordination of Missionaries — a translation of the text in the Dutch *Gereformeerd Kerkboek* of 1975.

However, a committee for the revision of the Liturgical Forms and the updating of their language, especially of the forms for the Holy Supper and the Marriage Solemnization, was given the mandate to establish the final text of the Form for the Ordination of Missionaries.

At the General Synod of Smithville 1980 the majority of the Liturgical Forms was adopted: the forms for Baptism of Infants and for Adults, that for the Public Profession of Faith, for the Excommunication of communicant members and that for the Excommunication of non-communicant members, the Form for Readmission, the forms for the Ordination/Installation of ministers, elders and deacons, for Marriage Solemnization. The Forms for the Administration of the Lord's Supper, both the "long" and the abbreviated, were adopted provisionally only. As for the prayers, the use of the Lord's Prayer was left to the freedom of the Churches.

"Cloverdale 1983" decided to adopt the text of the Liturgical Writings as they have now been printed in the Revised Edition of the *Book of Praise*. However, the Standing Committee for this publication was charged to scrutinize and correct the text of the entire *Book of Praise* linguistically, wherever necessary, "in order to achieve uniformity with respect to the language and punctuation." This mandate was repeated by the Synod of Burlington 1986. The same Standing Committee was charged by the General Synod of Winnipeg 1989 to add Scriptural references to the Liturgical Forms.

The history of the adoption of the Liturgical Writings by the Free Reformed Churches of Australia is a more simple and brief one.

"Albany 1959" adopted the writings as the Dutch sister Churches had them (N.B.: In the text of the decision concerned the Liturgical Prayers are, correctly, first mentioned; only then the Liturgical Forms!). As for their

English texts, those of the *Psalter Hymnal* could be used, with the exception of the forms for the Public Profession of Faith, the Ordination of elders and deacons, and for Marriage Solemnization — for which special texts were adopted.

The Synods of Albany 1962 and Armadale 1980 charged the deputies concerned to keep in close contact with their Canadian colleagues "in order that there be a consensus of opinion concerning the texts to be included in the complete English Church Book." In this context the Acts of Synod Kelmscott 1983 make mention of amendments proposed by the Australian deputies to the Canadian committee. The same synod recommended use of the prayer section of the *Book of Praise* by the Churches.

At the Launceston 1985 Synod the Liturgical Forms as included in the 1984 edition of the *Book of Praise* were adopted, with the exception of the Abbreviated Form for the Administration of the Lord's Supper, the Forms for the Excommunication of non-communicant members, and that for the Ordination of missionaries — which were only provisionally adopted because Synod wanted deputies to have a closer look at them. However, at the 1987 Synod, held at Albany, it was proposed and decided to finally adopt them.

Only minor linguistic updating has taken place since then. Except for a few Prayers and some sections in the Forms all these writings are the same as those used by our Dutch and South African sister churches.

5.2 LITURGICAL PRAYERS

Prayer forms

Our Reformed Church Service Book contains several prayers. We find them not only in the forms for baptism, the Lord's Supper, and Church discipline, and also in the ordination forms, but there is first of all a special section containing prayers which are intended for use just in "ordinary" Church services.

This raises the question: Is it correct to encourage congregations, families, and individual believers to use fixed forms for their prayers? Is this not a legacy of pre-Reformation days when the Church of Rome made it compulsory for "the clergy" to exclusively use fixed prayer forms?

To provide an answer to these questions, let us first of all turn to John Calvin, and see what he wrote in the "Letter to the Reader" that accompanied his liturgy of 1542, *La Forme des Prieres*.

First he says that there is also a command regarding prayers. Everything should be done in such a way and language that it can be understood by the congregation. Referring to I Corinthians 14:16, he says that otherwise no one can say "Amen" to what he hears. We must realize that the minister leads the congregation in prayer, speaking on behalf of them all. In other words, every one must be able to participate in the prayers.

This element, everyone's participation, has led Calvin to present a number of prayer forms in his liturgy. For every one must know what to say and to do in the Christian assembly.

Martin Luther was perhaps even clearer in this respect. He wrote a "Shorter Catechism," containing a brief and simple explanation of the Ten Commandments, the Apostles' Creed, the Lord's Prayer, the two sacraments, and the keys of the Kingdom of heaven, almost every section beginning with the subtitle containing the words "as a father shall teach this to his family in all simplicity." The father, the "house father," as Luther called him, is the priest and prophet in his own home. Luther strongly emphasized — over against the Church of Rome — the "priesthood of all believers." Well, the whole family must participate in praying the Lord's Prayer, living a life in obedience to the Ten Commandments, and enjoying the sacraments.

A third illustration is that of the Church Order of the Palatinate. This is actually a "liturgical" and "doctrinal" church order because it includes all the liturgical forms and prayers as well as the Heidelberg Catechism and other brief documents of a doctrinal nature. Time and again we read there in the introduction to the prayer forms a verb that can be translated by "to prompt," "to tell them what to say" (in this case: silently, in their hearts). The congregational members were supposed to really join in these prayers.

The Reformers were of the opinion that it was easier for the congregational members to participate in the prayers when these were said according to a fixed form. In the long run they could memorize them.

Of course, they did not make them compulsory — apart from the prayers in the adopted liturgical forms. They did not want to exclude the use of "free prayers." For — once again, over against the Roman Catholic concept of prayer as being of a meritorious character — they put some emphasis on the fact that, according to Scripture, it is the Holy Spirit Who works prayer within our hearts.

This is why we can observe some balance in the statements made by some ecclesiastical bodies.

The Convention of Wesel, 1568, stated that in the prayer services on weekdays free prayers should be said, but at the same time room must be given to every one who wanted (*si volet*) to use the prayer form of the Church of Geneva or of any other Church. As for the ordinary Sunday services it deemed it to be wise when the ministers, after the sermon, would adjust their prayers to the contents of their sermon.

The "liturgical Synod" of Dordrecht 1574 leaned a little more noticeably toward the use of prayer forms, with the addition of what the present situation required. The Provincial Synod of Zeeland, held at Veere in the year 1610, even stipulated that in this instance the approval of the consistory was required.

The great Synod of Dordrecht 1618-19, however, abstained from dealing with requests made by the Provincial Synods of Gelderland, South Holland, and Overijssel for promotion of more unity in Church singing and the use of prayer forms.

The great *canonicus* Gisbertus Voetius was of the opinion that fixed prayer forms might be useful for people who were not yet well trained in Godliness. Such forms could serve their purpose well within the family circle. But the ministers were supposed to be well trained in the Scriptures and therefore should be able to formulate prayers which are in accordance with the Scriptures. Only in exceptional cases should they use prayer forms, e.g. if lack of time prevented them from responsibly formulating their own prayers, and also shortly after the establishment of a Church in a mission field.

Later on the influence of English and Scottish Puritanism and German Pietism brought the prayer forms into disrepute. They were considered as "dead prayers." True prayers were those which were formulated under the immediate and instant guidance of the Holy Spirit.

We can fully understand why the Puritans offered opposition against the ritualism of the compulsory and exclusive use of fixed prayer forms in the Church of England's Book of Common Prayer. However, we cannot agree with those who went to the other extreme of spiritualism. In The Netherlands Jacobus Koelman (1632-95) was its champion. He was not only opposed to the maintaining of "Christian festive days" but also against the use of prayer forms, both of them in his opinion being "noxious roots of papal idolatry." These forms had done considerable damage to the special "prayer gifts." One had to pray from the heart, for only in a "free prayer" life sparkles as it is quickened spontaneously by the Holy Spirit.

Our Churches cannot be blamed for favouring such ideas. Yet it is a matter of fact that the liturgical prayers which we find in our Reformed Church Service Book are hardly ever used in our worship services. During the more than ten years that this present writer has frequently occupied an ordinary pew as a retired minister, he has hardly any recollection of such a use, except when once a minister quoted part of one of these prayers, and a "reading elder" indeed used a prayer form. Others, however, neglect their *Book of Praise* and write out their own prayers. This also is to be regretted when one considers the rich contents of these prayer forms.

It may be made clear: we would like to make a plea for a rehabilitation of our Reformed prayer forms!

Three types of prayers

Moving beyond what we will learn about the story of the third prayer in our *Book of Praise*, we may now already tell our readers that it is known as "the Prayer of Bucer and Calvin."

Its title reads: "A public confession of sins and prayer before the sermon."

Indeed, its main part is a confession of sins. As we will see at a later stage, this part is actually the original prayer.

Then follows a prayer for a right understanding of God's Holy Word as it is preached. This is a later addition.

Finally there is the most recent addition, a prayer of intercession for those who depart from the truth of God's Word.

In its present form this prayer is a combination of what were in earlier days three different types of prayers. We can classify them as:

A. Confessional prayers.
B. Illumination prayers.
C. Intercessory prayers.

Confessional prayers

The prayers of Group A originate from another liturgical element, the public confession of sins, which had its place at the beginning of the Church service, and was followed by a proclamation of God's grace.

The ancient Christian Church had such a confessional prayer in her liturgy, as may be proved by the *Didache* or *The Teachings of the Twelve Apostles*, a document dating back to the first century or of the first half of the second century. We can also mention the *Letter to the Corinthians*, written by Clemens Romanus at the end of the first century, and the liturgical writings of Tertullian (160-220) and Cyprian (who died in 258).

During the Middle Ages this confession of sins was replaced by the private or auricular confession, whereby the priest played a prominent role with the subsequent absolution.

However, since the tenth century we meet the public confession of sins again in the Southern part of Germany, where it was called *Offene Schuld* ("Public" — confession of — "guilt"). It was said — in German — by the priest and repeated by the congregation or responded to with a *Pater Noster*. Its origin was the *Confiteor*, the private confession of the priest, spoken in Latin as a personal preparation for the administration of the mass.

The *Offene Schuld* found its place in the *Pronaus*, the medieval preaching service, a development which was caused by the fact that many people were dissatisfied with the mass, which was held in Latin and, because of its character as a sacrifice, actually a matter involving only the priest.

It is therefore no wonder that we find a number of texts of the *Offene Schuld* in a textbook for the preaching, for liturgy, and for pastoral care, written in the year 1502 by a certain Johann Ulrich Surgant of Basel, entitled *Manuale Curatorum*.

The Reformers have known this book in which the *Pronaus* is described — the *Pronaus* which influenced the Reformed liturgy at Strasbourg and Zurich.

Although Martin Luther maintained the auricular confession, he also reintroduced the public profession of sins and proclamation of God's grace — or absolution. In Zwingli's liturgy the absolution was rather a prayer than a proclamation. Therefore we can say that, at this point, the liturgy was a combination of the *Confiteor* as well as the *Kyrie eleison* — which was already known in the Church of Jerusalem during the fourth century, and in the Middle Ages followed a series of prayers in the first part of the mass.

The same can be said about Bucer's Strasbourg liturgy. In his Psalter of 1537 three different forms of confessional prayers were included.

John Calvin adopted the second one of these three forms for his Genevan liturgy of 1542. From there it has found its way, via the Palatinate and The Netherlands, into our *Book of Praise*.

A number of congregations in The Netherlands wanted to maintain the public confession of sins and the proclamation of God's grace as a separate liturgical element — as, next to the aforementioned prayers, was also done at Strasbourg and Geneva. They made a suggestion to the Synod of Middelburg 1581. However, this synod was of the opinion that both elements were sufficiently honoured in the sermon.

This suggestion made it clear that some congregations followed the practice of the London Church of Reformed refugees, which did indeed have this confession and proclamation as separate liturgical elements.

In spite of some efforts, undertaken by e.g. Abraham Kuyper, to reintroduce these liturgical elements, our Churches and their sister Churches in The Netherlands and South Africa have maintained the form of a prayer, also combined with an illumination prayer and even an intercessory prayer.

From Bucer we are able to understand that we cannot enter into a worship service unless we first of all confess our sins and show repentance and conversion. He used the phrase: First there shall be *metanoia* (conversion) only then we can have *syntaxis* (communion) with God. This was based on Scriptural data: John the Baptist and also our Lord Jesus Christ began their ministry by calling the people to repentance and conversion. The apostle Peter did the same on the day of Pentecost. The Reformers further based their practice on passages as Isaiah 55:6, Psalm 25:6f, Psalm 51 for the confession of sins, and for the proclamation of grace on I John 2:1.

For our own participation in the worship services, and also for the maintaining of a good liturgical order, it may be useful to be well aware of this aspect of the history of our liturgy.

Illumination prayers

As for the illumination prayers the Reformers reverted to the liturgy of the ancient Christian Church.

William Farel, in his *Maniere et Fasson* of 1533, which liturgy was used in the Church of Geneva before it was replaced by John Calvin's liturgy of 1542, went even further back into history. He referred to the prayer spoken by Ezra before the reading of the Scriptures (Nehemiah 8:6, 7).

The synagogue — which most likely came into being in the days of Ezra and Nehemiah or soon afterwards — made this a tradition. Before the

Scripture-reading a prayer was said "for the spirit of wisdom and insight," "for the spirit of knowledge and Godliness;" and on special festive days "for insight and understanding in order that we may comprehend and be able to see the depth of the spirit hidden in God's commandments."

Farel seems to allude to these synagogual prayers in a few lines of his liturgy.

This tradition was adopted by the ancient Christian Church, and is the reason why in the liturgy of bishop Serapion of Tmuis in Egypt (appr. 340) we find this petition: "Send Thy Holy Spirit into our spirit, and grant us the grace of the Holy Spirit so that we may know the divine Scriptures." In a Syrian liturgy we read the following lines: "Grant us, O God, the knowledge of Thy divine Words, and fulfil us with understanding of Thy holy gospel and the riches of Thy divine gifts, and the indwelling of Thy Holy Spirit." Augustine also followed this tradition. He urged the preacher with the words: "Let him pray that God may put a good word into his mouth."

However, in the course of the Middle Ages this prayer of illumination — also called *epiclesis* — was replaced by the so-called *collecta*, which were a kind of prayers that summarized the silent private prayers. Their contents were determined by the "ecclesiastical year." That which in those days was understood by the *epiclesis*, a prayer that the Holy Spirit might transform bread and wine into Christ's body and blood, was abolished because it was presumed that the act of reciting the words of institution would transform the elements.

Nevertheless, the Reformers could still build on a few remnants. The first one was a prayer in the liturgy of the Franciscan Nicolas of Lyra, fourteenth century, wherein God's grace for the preacher as well as the congregation was asked. The other one was the *Pronaus*. In his *Manuale Curatorum* Surgant called the prayer that preceded the Scripture reading and the sermon *invocatio divini auxilii*, the invocation of divine help.

In the *Pronaus* we can observe the restoring of the illumination prayer. However, we must realize that its contents were still fully "Roman Catholic:" it ended in an *Ave Maria*.

The Reformers really restored it, together with the pure preaching of God's Word. This is how we find illumination prayers in the liturgies of Zwingli and Bucer — however, without the name of the Holy Spirit — in Calvin's liturgies of Strasbourg — a petition for guidance by the Holy

Spirit — in the liturgy of Geneva — a prayer for the grace of the Holy Spirit — and in the London liturgy.

The Church of the Palatinate took over "the prayer of Bucer and Calvin" in her Church Order of 1563. However, she added the words that we still find in our *Book of Praise*: "May it please Thee to make us understand Thy holy Word in accordance with Thy holy will . . ."

That is how this illumination prayer arrived — via Dathenus' Church book — in The Netherlands, and from there in our own countries.

It is not the only illumination prayer which we find in the *Book of Praise*. The very first liturgical prayer, called "A General Confession of sins and prayer before the sermon and on days of fasting and prayer" also includes, almost at the end, an illumination prayer; and so does the "Prayer before the explanation of the Catechism."

Apart from a spoken prayer, another was for some centuries included in many editions of the Psalter, namely John Utenhove's "Prayer-Song before the Sermon," which was written by him in London.

Intercessory prayers

We have already learned about a prayer from the third group, the intercessory prayers. It is what we have called the latest addition to "the prayer of Bucer and Calvin." It brings to God's attention "all who depart from Thy truth," asking that they may be brought back to Himself. However, this intercession is made in close connection with the preaching of God's Word, therefore added to the illumination prayer which was an addition to the original confessional prayer.

From the days of old the actual intercessory prayer was given its place after the sermon. In this respect the Reformers returned to the tradition of the ancient Christian Church, the only exception being Ulrich Zwingli, who included this prayer before the sermon. This place in the liturgy is reflected in the order in which the Heidelberg Catechism sums up the elements which, according to the Scriptures, must be included in the worship services: "to hear God's Word, to use the sacraments, to call publicly upon the LORD, and give Christian offerings for the poor" (Lord's Day 38). This was not new, for the same order can be found in the Catechism of Geneva, 1541, in the First Helvetic Confession, 1536, and others. It is the order based on that of God's Law — first love for God, then love for the neighbour — and the Lord's Prayer — first "Thou" and "Thee," only then "us" and "our."

What the Reformers did in this respect was real reformation work, a matter of returning to the practice of the ancient Christian Church which based itself on the Scriptures.

This is why in her prayers we find three different groups of intercessions: first of all for the government — in accordance with I Timothy 2:1-7, then for enemies of the gospel — after Matthew 5:44f — and also for the propagation of the gospel — according to Ephesians 6:19 and others.

We do not always find the intercessory prayers themselves in ancient liturgical texts. Sometimes there are only references to them. In some Churches a deacon announced the prayers while the actual prayers were repeated by a *liturgian*. When this was done in the reversed order, we refer to the "deacons' prayer."

After a few centuries there was, however, a development in the wrong direction. In the Eastern Church the intercessory prayers were repeated in close connection with the Eucharist — the original Lord's Supper slowly deteriorating into the mass. Cyrill of Jerusalem — in the fourth century — was of the opinion that the intercessory prayers would be more effective if they were repeated after the consecration of bread and wine, and that, as a result of Christ being present in the sacrifice, God's heart would be more widely open to them. At the end of the fifth century there was a similar development in the Western Church. Pope Gelasius took the "Prayer of the Faithful" from its traditional place. As a kind of compensation he put it at the beginning of the mass, but at the same time he enlarged it in the eucharistic prayer, the *Canon*. At the end of the sixth century the first, brief, intercessory prayer had already been reduced to a simple and single *Kyrie eleison* (Lord have mercy on us). Intercessions were from then on made in the *Canon* only.

This development went even further. Eventually an intercessory prayer was maintained only in the liturgy of the Good Friday. The Roman mass only retained the word *Oremus* (let us pray), but without a prayer following! What are left in the *Canon* are merely remnants. The idea is that the offering of bread and wine has an atoning power which makes the intercession effective. The concept of the mass as a sacrifice has some far reaching implications for the prayers!

However, during the Middle Ages it appeared that not every one was happy with this situation and development. We have already made several references to the *Pronaus*, the preaching service which came into being next to the mass. Well, already from the tenth century there are indications that intercessory prayers were repeated after the sermon, although their contents were still really "Roman Catholic."

It was genuine reformation when Martin Luther rejected the idea of the meritorious character of the prayers because of their connection with the sacrifice of the mass. According to him there could be no good prayer without any preceding instruction from God's Word. This is why he restored the intercessory prayers and put them back on their original place, after the sermon. Someone called this the most significant liturgical reformation of the sixteenth century.

Zwingli gave the "General Church Prayer" a place before the sermon. He was the only Reformer to do so, the background of this was that he did not restore the original worship service with its two parts, a Word section and a sacrament section. The Lord's Supper was administered only four times a year.

Others, such as Martin Bucer and his Strasbourg colleagues, spoke of a "purified mass," this purification meaning a return to the tradition of the ancient Christian Church. They put the intercessory prayers on their original place, after the sermon, and before the celebration of the Lord's Supper, Bucer's prayer of his 1537 liturgy contained the three above mentioned elements: intercessions for the government, for the enemies of God's Word, and for the propagation of the gospel. His prayer was based directly on Scriptural data.

The same can be said of the prayer in Calvin's liturgy. For in his 1542 liturgy he included a translation of Bucer's intercessory prayer followed by the Lord's Prayer — "the perfect prayer for all the needs of Christendom." This addition was made whenever the Lord's Supper was not celebrated. When the sermon was followed by the administration of the Lord's Supper, the Lord's Prayer was replaced by a petition for a blessed celebration of this sacrament.

John Calvin even had a second intercessory prayer in his 1542 liturgy. It was meant to be used in special weekly services — prayer services — and made intercession for those involved in persecutions, wars, or epidemics, and suchlike.

The Churches of London and the Palatinate had their own texts, though these were in full harmony with John Calvin's prayer. The Church Order of the Palatinate also included a second prayer. It was almost the same as

John Calvin's second prayer. Its original place was, once again, in the weekly prayer-meetings.

This prayer was taken over by Petrus Dathenus, and brought to The Netherlands. It formed the first part of a long prayer "for all the needs of Christendom." Its second part was from the hand of Dathenus himself.

The Dutch Churches adopted it for their liturgy, as soon as they were no longer reluctant to use fixed prayer forms. This happened at the "liturgical Synod" of Dordrecht 1574 — although this synod stated that room must be created for incidental additions. It also made arrangements to have it abbreviated, although many congregations continued to use the longer version. In the course of time a number of changes were made in its text. We hope to come back to them, and also to the reasons behind its minimal use.

At this stage we must say that we regret the fact that many ministers, consistories, and congregations continue to have the "long prayer" before the sermon, contrary to the tradition of the ancient Christian Church and the Reformation.

The first prayer

The origin of this prayer is obscure. Many scholars suppose that Petrus Dathenus was its author.

It is a matter of fact that this prayer was included in his Church book of 1566 under the title "Prayer on Sunday before the sermon." One thing is certain: Dathenus did not borrow it from the Church Order of the Palatinate, for therein we find a different prayer for the same purpose. On the other hand there is some obvious influence from the Palatinate, because in Dathenus' version the prayer did not end with the reciting of the Lord's Prayer, but with the petition: "Wilt Thou also strengthen us in our sincere Christian faith, in order that therein we may daily more and more increase, of which we make confession with mouth and heart, saying: . . . ," after which the Apostles' Creed was recited. In the Form for the Lord's Supper of the Palatinate the first prayer ended in a similar way.

The "liturgical Synod" of 1574 decided that this addition must be omitted. However, in the liturgy edition of 1617 we find these words again.

That it was Dathenus' intention — and that of the Churches which adopted this prayer — to have it repeated at the beginning of the Sunday morning services, may be clear from the following indication in Dathenus'

Church book: "After the congregation of Christ on Sunday morning has read or sung the Ten Commandments, the Church minister shall from them take reason to exhort the congregation to penitence and confession of her transgressions, and to believe the evangelical promises of Christ; both of which he shall support with testimonies from the Scriptures. Then he shall proclaim God's punishment to the impenitent, and to the penitent believers God's grace in Christ. After that he shall pray in the following way: . . ." and then this prayer follows.

It is not known who has changed the title into: "A General Confession of sins and prayer before the sermon and on days of fasting and prayer."

The translation which we find in the *Book of Praise* rests on the one in the *Psalter Hymnal* of the Christian Reformed Church, although, for some unknown reasons, part of a number of sentences have been omitted.

It may be clear that this prayer, which in its shorter second part asks for a blessing upon the sermon, is a combination of a confessional prayer and a prayer for illumination.

The fact that the Lord's Prayer has been made optional in the *Book of Praise* is to be regretted. The Church of later days must have good reasons to alter the prayers which were made by the generations of earlier days.

The "long prayer"

The first pericope of this prayer seems to be a brief repetition of the confession of sins as we found it in the previous prayer. Sins are indeed confessed. But these lines are meant as an introduction to the actual intercessory prayer. Even when intercessions are made we must do this with awareness that we are "unworthy to lift up our eyes toward heaven and present ourselves before Thy face" — as the original text in John Calvin's prayer says. The translation in the *Book of Praise* is not adequate; at this point the *Psalter Hymnal* was better.

We have just referred to John Calvin. The first part of this long prayer has been taken from his liturgy of 1542. This action was taken by the Church of the Palatinate, which in her Church Order had included it as a prayer after the sermon on weekdays. Therein they followed Calvin, who had compiled this prayer for special prayer services on weekdays, in view of pestilences, wars, and other calamities.

The substance of the second — larger — part has been taken from the Palatinate. It is on purpose that we speak of the substance only. For, first of all, the Synod of 1574 was of the opinion that it was too long. Caspar van der Heyden was invited to abbreviate it, and indeed he did this — although many Churches continued to use its longer version.

Furthermore, in the course of time many changes have been made, mainly as a result of the changing political and national scene. The 1564 edition of Dathenus' Church service book contained a prayer for the magistrates of the Palatinate. Soon afterwards, when this prayer was used in The Netherlands, it was replaced by a prayer for "the Royal Majesty of Spain" — who at that time was reigning over the Low Lands as well. In the 1611 edition — the "Schilders edition," so called after its publisher — "the King of Great-Britain" was mentioned, and it is no wonder, for King James, the man of the "King James Version," who later on would send some delegates to the Synod of Dordrecht 1618-19, had some influence in The Netherlands. "1611" was the product of a committee appointed by the Provincial Synod of Zeeland, held at Veere in 1610. This synod charged the committee to add intercessions for widows, orphans, expecting women, mentally ill people, and those who had to travel along dangerous routes. After the Lord's Prayer, the Apostles' Creed had to be included in the context of a petition.

Later on the intercessions for the magistrates were once more changed. They were now made for the Dutch authorities, the States-General, the Prince of Orange, etcetera. However, the Provincial States of Holland and West Friesland insisted that they were to be mentioned first, because they were the most prominent among all the authorities. For some time this was indeed made compulsory, so that the ministers who refused to pray in this order could lose their stipend.

Pietism concentrated on the believer's personal spiritual needs. The Church was considered to be of minor importance. The "needs of Christendom" were neglected. Prayer forms were banned. The same was carried out by Rationalism, because it was of the opinion that even prayers should teach the congregation something, and should therefore briefly repeat the contents of the sermon. All this led to a minimal use of prayer forms like that for "all the needs of Christendom."

In the *Flakkeesche editie* of 1897, by F.L. Rutgers and H.H. Kuyper, the prayer of intercession for the government appears to have been altered once again. The Queen was now mentioned. However, its inclusion in this Church service book had hardly any sense: this prayer was neglected, the ministers preferring to formulate their own prayers and transferring the "long prayer" to the beginning of the service.

The "Middelburg 1933" liturgy, which put the "long prayer" before the sermon, made it almost impossible to use this prayer, because this prayer does not fall into this sequence.

The General Synod of Kampen 1975 recommended an order which is virtually the same as that of the days of the great Reformation. As a result the proper use of this prayer was once again been made possible. However, as long as "Middelburg 1933" is followed and the view taken by many ministers, consistories, and congregations will not change, the "long prayer" with its intercessions will stay where it is and where it does not belong.

Sometimes this particular place of the prayer "before the sermon" is defended with appeal to psychology: the members of the congregation would not be able to concentrate any longer after having heard a sermon. Our own experience and that of others during several decades clearly contradicts this.

Apart from all this: It is not necessary that the "Prayer for all the needs of Christendom" should be used every Sunday. The same can be said of the "free" intercessory prayers: the subjects could be spread over a number of weeks; there is no need for all of them to be included every Sunday!

Returning now to the *Flakkeesche editie* of 1897, it claims to present the "official text," that of the revisers appointed by the Synod of Dordrecht 1618-19. At several points this text deviates considerably from the one printed in most editions which followed "Dathenus." However, since the General Synod of Arnhem 1902 recommended the 1897 text to the Churches, we now find its translation included in the *Book of Praise*, which in turn has taken it from the *Psalter Hymnal* 1934 of the Christian Reformed Church.

Since the linguistic modernization of the Liturgical Writings there are, however, some variations from the text of the *Psalter Hymnal* — which had a faithful translation of the in 1902 recommended text.

Besides, there are some additions. The third and fourth paragraphs on page 643 in the 1984 edition of the *Book of Praise* most likely belong to the "changes" proposed by a committee appointed by the Canadian National Synod of 1958. These paragraphs focus on the mission work, the schools, and other Christian institutes.

Another change may be noted as follows: The petition: "Strengthen us in the true Christian faith, that we may increase daily therein. Of that faith we make confession with mouth and heart, saying: I believe in God the Father, Almighty, etc.," was taken over from the *Psalter Hymnal*. It was maintained up until its 1972 edition and then omitted from the 1984 edition. This omission is in harmony with the text of the sixteenth century, which did not include either this petition or the Creed.

Again we must say that we regret the fact that the reciting of the Lord's Prayer at the conclusion has been made optional: It was always an essential part of this prayer. Let us remember John Calvin's statement that the Lord's Prayer is "the perfect prayer for all the needs of Christendom!"

The "Prayer of Bucer and Calvin"

The third prayer in our *Book of Praise* is often called the "Prayer of Bucer and Calvin." Strictly speaking this name can only be given to the long pericope on page 645. For as soon as it continues with the words: "May it please Thee to make us understand Thy holy Word . . ." we are dealing with an addition made by the Church of the Palatinate. And the very last pericope, "We also beseech Thee, gracious God, to bring back to Thyself in true repentance all who depart from Thy truth . . ." was added at the instigation of the Provincial Synod of Zeeland, held at Veere in the year 1610, which synod wanted to establish unity in the use of liturgical forms, and therefore appointed a committee, which published the so-called "Schilders edition," used at the Synod of Dordrecht 1618-19. They may have followed the example of Ulrich Zwingli in Zurich, who had a similar intercessory petition in one of his liturgical prayers.

However, the original prayer was taken over as a *Confession des peches* by John Calvin in his liturgy of Strasbourg 1538 and Geneva 1542, from Martin Bucer's Church book for the German-speaking Reformed congregation at Strasbourg, which was published in the year 1537. This book contained no less than three confessional prayers. Calvin adopted the second one.

In the first part of this original prayer we can distinguish one of the typical marks of the Strasbourg Reformation. The Church of that city wanted to "purify" the mass. What was deemed to be good in the mass was, in one way or another, preserved. Other elements were deleted. A third group was reformed. This is the case with the Confiteor of the Middle

Ages. This element does not actually belong to the Roman mass because this confession of his unworthiness to celebrate the mass belonged to the private preparations of the priest. This Confiteor was transformed into a congregational prayer.

Another proof of reformation is the fact that, over against the medieval prayers with their invocation of saints, this prayer is of a trinitarian nature: the Father is addressed, a plea is made on the ground of His Son's sufferings, and the grace of the Holy Spirit is sought.

The second part may have appealed to John Calvin especially because for those days it was a "modern" version of the ancient *Kyrie eleison*, which was already known to Chrysostom of Antioch and the Church at Jerusalem of the fourth century. It was based on Psalm 123:3.

The Church of the Palatinate included the whole prayer in her Church Order of 1563. It was introduced by the following sentence: "For the preaching (service) in particular in the morning of Sundays and festive days and of days of prayer, the following prayer shall be said first to the people, in which the Christian congregation is expressly reminded of man's misery, and God's salutary grace is desired, in order that the hearts are prepared to humbleness and the Word of grace is accepted with the stronger desire."

From the Palatinate Dathenus brought it to The Netherlands, and — after some centuries — it arrived from there on the North American continent and in Australia.

Compared with the text in previous editions of the *Book of Praise* the translation has undergone a drastic "modernization." Thereby has a part of the intercessory addition been lost: No longer can we find there the words which refer to the Song of Zacharias: "that we all of one accord may serve Thee in holiness and righteousness all the days of our life." This may arise from the fact that here again the reciting of the Lord's Prayer — as a sort of *Collecta*, a summarising prayer — has been made optional. It would be advisable therefore to entrust an eventual revision of historical documents to persons who have studied the history of liturgy.

This prayer had drawn a great deal of attention. John Knox included it in his work, *The Form of Prayers*, published at Geneva in 1556. This resulted in its being used in Scotland until the new directives of the "Westminster divines" appeared in 1645. It was also included in the "Middelburg liturgy" of the English Puritans under the leadership of Thomas Cartwright, 1586.

It has drawn the attention of many also because of a story in which it is said to have played a prominent role.

During the reign of the young Charles IX of France (1560-74), whose mother, the governess Catharina de Medici, held the actual power, Roman Catholics and Reformed were treated in the same manner. For some time it even seemed that the well known Reformed admiral Caspar de Coligny would be entrusted with the actual political power. An independent national assembly was requested. However, the Roman Catholic clergy were able to prevent all this, and were successful in having a religious colloquium arranged. This colloquium was held at Poissy, near Paris, on September 9, 1561. The spokesman for the Church of Rome was cardinal Guise. The Reformed were reluctant to delegate John Calvin because France was considered to be untrustworthy. Therefore Beza was chosen instead.

The meeting was attended by the king, the queen-mother, many princes, noblemen, cardinals and bishops in full pontificals. Ten ministers, dressed in the simple *robe de Geneve,* bands and gown, and twenty-two congregational members under the guidance of Beza formed the Reformed delegation. They were separated from the others by a screen!

However, a deep impression was made when Beza, before he would deliver his oration, knelt down together with his companions, and, while there was dead silence, said a prayer. It is said that it was the *Confession des peches* from John Calvin's liturgy of 1542, so the "Prayer of Bucer and Calvin."

Some refer to this story as a legend, but indeed, even if it is a legend, it proves that this confessional prayer was held in high esteem.

In their new editions publishers of the Reformed Church service book relegated this prayer to the services on weekdays. This happened in the early years of the seventeenth century. Consequently it was printed under the title, "A brief prayer before the sermon on weekdays." Apart from other considerations this may be the reason why this prayer was rarely used. Its beauty, however, deserves far greater acknowledgment!

The Lord's Prayer is also incorporated as the concluding prayer, since Petrus Dathenus took this part of the liturgy with him to The Netherlands.

A Prayer after the sermon

Once again, in the 1972 edition of the *Book of Praise* we find a translation of this prayer as it was included in the Church Order of the

Palatinate. It was concluded by the reciting of the Lord's Prayer, and a petition for "perseverance and increase in the old true and undoubted Christian faith," which is then confessed with the words of the Apostles' Creed.

The omission of the latter in our present edition may be understandable — although it may be useful to notice that in the Churches of the Reformation the confession of faith was given a place at the end of the service. However, that the Lord's Prayer (again) has been made optional is to be regretted.

In all probability the first sentences have been replaced in the 1984 edition because their formulation and contents were considered to be too negative: "O Lord, Almighty God, we pray that Thy holy Name may not be blasphemed on account of our sins. For we have sinned against Thee in many ways." They have been replaced by a thanksgiving for the sermon — after which the confession of sins is taken up again.

Its formulation leaves room for special intercessory prayers, which may be an addition that originated in The Netherlands. Nevertheless, at the same time it also proves that shortly after the Reformation the Churches in The Netherlands said their intercessory prayers after the sermon, in their proper place.

Prayers concerning the Catechism preaching

Both these prayers originate with Martin Micron's London liturgy, although Petrus Dathenus, who introduced these prayers in The Netherlands, edited them quite heavily.

When we compare the current text — in the 1984 edition of the *Book of Praise* — with the text in previous editions, we reach the conclusion that in the first prayer, for reasons unknown, the words "and Thou wilt succour only those who have a broken and contrite heart and who revere Thy Word" have been omitted. The version of 1972 has "carnal wisdom" instead of "worldly wisdom," and also "that we (. . .) may regulate our lives accordingly" instead of "let ourselves be governed by it." In both cases this provided a more literal translation of the original.

The sentence "Confirm us in our catholic and undoubted Christian faith" is an addition, which we are not able to find anywhere else.

The reciting of the Lord's Prayer has been made optional again. As a result of this the introductory sentence of the original, in the 1972 edition translated: "These things we crave of Thee only for the sake of Christ, Who promised to hear us and also taught us to pray in His Name, saying: . . ." has been deleted.

It is a prayer for and by the whole congregation. This was different in the original of the second prayer, which followed the Catechism-preaching. It concentrated exclusively on the children of the congregation. This may be understandable when one considers the close connection between today's Catechism-preaching and Catechism-class. In the Palatinate, where Petrus Dathenus ministered for some time, these were combined in the afternoon service. The Preface to the Heidelberg Catechism may make this clear, when it says: "Every Sunday afternoon, at a convenient time, Catechism-preaching shall be held, in such a way, that the minister, after congregational singing, first prays the Lord's Prayer, and calls upon God for a right understanding of His Word, and then with a clear voice reads the Ten Commandments to the people. After that he shall interrogate those children who cannot yet learn the questions on which he will preach, and fairly lead them to the text and then to their contents. Then he shall let some of the young people say a number of questions of the Catechism — which for that purpose we have divided into Sundays — namely those that were explained in the previous sermon; which questions they have learned before at school or at home. As soon as some of them have said them in the presence of the congregation, the minister shall simply and briefly explain some of the next questions, so that he shall preach on the complete Catechism at least once every year."

In the meantime the situation has changed. Therefore it is understandable that in our present edition we no longer find the, translated, original text, as it was still in the 1972 edition. Several sentences have been inserted, and these no longer concentrate only on the children and young people in the congregation but include all its members. The current version at its end returns to the text of the original — with the exception, of course, of the Lord's Prayer and its introduction.

The sentence on growing in the knowledge of God's grace in Christ no longer reminds us of the Form for Baptism, as did the line "that they may increasingly grow in Christ, Thy Son . . ." in the original text.

Prayers before and after meals

The two prayers which now follow in the *Book of Praise*, "A Prayer before meals" and "Thanksgiving after meals," seem to be completely out of place in a Church service book. At first glance they have no relation at all with the liturgy of the Church.

However, in the days of the Reformation our forefathers had different ideas about that. According to them these prayers were an essential part of the "home liturgy," the Church giving some assistance to it.

This would be clear immediately if we still had their texts as printed in the 1972 edition of the *Book of Praise*. There they were surrounded by a few Bible sections to be recited by the head of the house.

This has a historical background.

First of all we must go back to the Jewish tradition. One of the earliest indications that such a tradition was developing is I Samuel 9:13, where we are told that already in the days of this prophet it was the custom that at a sacrificial meal no one could start eating before Samuel had blessed the sacrifice.

It will be clear from God's commandment issued in Deuteronomy 8:10 what this blessing means. It says: "When you have eaten and are full, then you shall bless the LORD your God for the good land which He has given you."

At the same time we learn that such a blessing was pronounced before as well as after the meals, and that "blessing the sacrifice" had as it were become an abbreviation of "blessing the LORD for the sacrificial meal."

At a later stage the development had reached such a level that those prayers were given a fixed name, *berakoot*. They consisted of a brief blessing upon the cup and the bread, and of a longer blessing — thanksgiving — after the meal. The latter had four sections. In the first one God was blessed as the King of the Universe, the Creator; in the second He was given thanks for the land of inheritance — in accordance with Deuteronomy 8! — the third part was a prayer for Jerusalem, calling for pity on this city and the sanctuary where God's glory dwells; and the fourth part was a more general blessing — a thanksgiving which referred to the well known words of Psalm 106 and Psalms 136 and other places: "O give thanks to the LORD, for He is good, for His steadfast love endures for ever." (In a German Jewish prayer book from, most likely, the beginning of this century, we found an elaborate prayer, which contained the same four elements, and also a reference to Deuteronomy 8).[55]

---

[55] J. Schwanthaler, *Israelitisches Gebetbuch, hebräisch und deutsch, Elfte Auflage*, Frankfurt am Main.

The Lord Jesus followed this tradition: Before distributing the miraculously multiplied bread and fishes He pronounced a blessing (Matthew 14:19 and 15:36). He did the same in His discourse with the men from Emmaus (Luke 24:30).

In the story of the shipwreck at Malta (Acts 27:35) the apostle Paul gave thanks before he began to eat. He makes allusions to the tradition in Romans 14:6; I Corinthians 10:30; and I Timothy 4:3, 4.

We find a "Christian version" of the Jewish prayer in the *Didache* or *The Teachings of the Twelve Apostles*, from the end of the first century or the early years of the second century. It speaks of "the thanksgiving," to be pronounced over the cup and the broken bread of the *agape*, the love-meal — a common meal of the congregational members whereby the needy were cared for by others who were in better circumstances; it concluded with the celebration of the Lord's Supper (remember the wrong practice in this respect in the Church at Corinth, I Corinthians 10:21).

While this illustration shows us that the ancient Christian Church continued this tradition — and at the same time gave it a richer meaning — regretfully we must add to this that in a later development the blessing of the cup and bread was applied to the elements in the Lord's Supper. This happened at a time when this sacrament used to be called the Eucharist — which is indeed a Scriptural name, the original form for what we called "the thanksgiving" when we referred to the *Didache* — but which was also developed into the mass. The idea was that bread and wine were offered as a sacrifice to God — later on to be identified with Christ's sacrifice on the cross. So the *anaphora* — the sacrificial prayers in the Eucharist — became the most important version of the "Christian" form of the Jewish prayers. Certainly, next to them the Church provided her members with texts for the ordinary meals enjoyed in the family circle, but even these were in the long run more or less connected with the mass. It is no wonder then that in the Middle Ages the fourth petition of the Lord's Prayer was interpreted as referring not only to ordinary bread but also to the sacred bread of the Eucharist, transformed into Christ's body by "transubstantiation."

It was therefore no less than an act of reformation when Martin Luther published his "Shorter Catechism," and had included in it, among others, the appendix, "How a housefather shall teach his family to pray and thank before and after meals." It may be known that Luther put strong emphasis on "the office of all believers," in particular on their priestly office. A housefather is a priest in his own family. In this way, and at this point, Luther freed the people from the power which the clergy had assumed. It was not for nothing that he compared the believers' situation under the priest with Israel's Babylonian captivity.

It is remarkable that in the text of the prayers to be said before and after meals Luther quoted Psalm 145:15 and Psalm 106:1, exactly the same texts which we are able to find in the version of these prayers in the 1972 edition of the *Book of Praise*.

This does not mean that the two prayers under discussion originate from Luther. The second prayer, in its original form, was written by John Calvin. Both prayers have come to us from the Palatinate. They were not included in the Church Order of 1563, but in a booklet that accompanied the first edition of the Heidelberg Catechism, early 1563. As its title tells us — *Christian prayers to be used at home and in Church* — this booklet contains a number of prayers. Petrus Dathenus translated the booklet in the same year, taking it a few years later to The Netherlands. For — while he adopted at least one prayer written by John Calvin — he fully agreed with Martin Luther, who added to his Catechism all sorts of directives for family life, married life, parents, children, widows, magistrates, young people, etcetera, thereby making it clear that he intended his Catechism to be a guideline for the whole of life. Dathenus followed Luther's example when he had his translation of the Heidelberg Catechism accompanied by a Dutch version of the above mentioned booklet. Besides, he had learned this in the Palatinate, where the Heidelberg Catechism — just like Luther's "Shorter Catechism" — was followed by a long series of texts from Holy Scripture, intended to teach "everyone what he has to do in his position and profession."

Taking it altogether, we can say that in the original texts of these prayers, to be used before and after meals, it is possible to see a double reformation. Their contents also refer to Christ, for Whose sake we are so well looked after by our heavenly Father.

This is also why the Lord's Prayer was added to the first prayer, and to the second a reference to the admonition given by our Lord Jesus Christ in Luke 21:3f. Reformation, however, is not the same as revolution. Therefore, as in the Jewish prayers, God's command of Deuteronomy 8:10 is quoted. As was practised in the ancient Christian Church, the Jewish prayers were updated, "reformed" in accordance with the great course which the history of salvation had taken in the coming of the promised

Saviour. There is also a second line of reformation in these prayers. There was a return from the Babylonian captivity of the Church.

All this was expressed in the original texts of these two prayers, still to be found in the *Book of Praise* of 1972. In the 1984 edition the accompanying Scripture references and the Lord's Prayer have been deleted. That is why these prayers appear to be alien in a Church service book. However, by having adopted such prayers, to be included in her service book, the Church thus provides our families with some Scriptural directives for their "home liturgy."

Prayers for the sick and spiritually distressed

In the *Flakkeesche editie* of 1897 by F.L. Rutgers and H.H. Kuyper there is a footnote which says that the second prayer in the oldest editions was printed first, but has never belonged to the official liturgy of the Churches.

This is, of course, a statement based on the opinion of these scholars that there was an "official liturgy" since the Synod of Dordrecht 1618-19 made some arrangements to have it established. We have already dealt with this thesis and denied its correctness. This means, however, that Rutgers and Kuyper have reversed the original order. As we may remember, the General Synod of Arnhem 1902 has recommended the text of the *Flakkeesche editie*, with the result that since then the order has been as we find it in our *Book of Praise*. Besides, our own Churches have adopted both prayers, with the likelihood that they were not even aware of the thesis of these two scholars and their controversy with others. Therefore we will briefly discuss both prayers accepting that they belong to our official liturgical documents. We do so in the order of the *Book of Praise*.

However, there is once again a preliminary question: How have these prayers come to belong to our official Liturgical Writings, since they deal with private visits to the sick and distressed?

We must return to the days of the Reformation for the answer. The Reformers were of the opinion that the people who were sick or in other kinds of misery, had to be faithfully visited. For this purpose they compiled prayer forms which were explained in their liturgical works. William Farel, for example, in his *Maniere et Fasson* of 1533, discussed holy baptism, marriage, the Lord's Supper, the sermon, but also the visiting of the sick. John Calvin, in his *La Forme des Prieres* of 1542, dealt with the same subjects. The visiting of the sick was another point at which life had to undergo reformation. For until then the priest went to see the sick, administering to them the so-called sacraments of auricular confession with its absolution and that of extreme unction — the latter if needed. The Reformers rejected them, replacing them by offering comfort from the Scriptures and a prayer according to James 5:14.

This leads us to the conclusion that the prayers for the sick in our Church service book are products of the Reformation!

That the sick must be comforted not with human inventions, but with the Word of God, was clearly expressed in the introductory words — which unfortunately have been omitted in the *Book of Praise* (they were not included in the Church Order of the Palatinate either) — reading as follows: "After having reminded the sick of God, from Whom illnesses and other kinds of misery come, and of their first cause, sin, which for those who believe in Him has been taken away by Christ, and that therefore all things must be subservient to a sick persons' well being, one shall also pray for him according to James' teaching."

We have already mentioned the name of the Palatinate. This we could do because the first of the two prayers was taken partly from its Church Order by Petrus Dathenus. He did not include the Creed that followed at the end in his own version after an introductory formula.

In the original version of the second prayer this formula and the Apostles' Creed were included — even the 1972 edition of the *Book of Praise* still had them.

This second prayer is in all probability a free composition from the hand of Dathenus, although it is written in the same spirit as the prayers of the Church Order of the Palatinate, which as a second prayer had one for people who were dying.

The language of both prayers is not the same, in translation, as that of the original. In addition to the changes already mentioned we refer to the following illustrations:

The opening sentence of the first prayer did not have, as "1984" reads: "Thou gavest eternal hope and salvation," but is much stronger in the original when it calls God Himself "the eternal salvation of the living and the eternal life of the dying." The order in several sentences has been altered. Older terms such as "our cross" and "tabernacle" have been deleted. The sentence: "We even desire to depart from this weak body," has been treated in the same way. At the end of the first pericope on page

649 it says: "We trust that with body and soul, both in life and death, we belong to Christ," which is much weaker than the original which says: "we have no fear, because we belong to Christ, and therefore shall not perish." There are some changes in the sentences which mention the eyes, the power of speech, and the hearts. The original does not say: "And when our eyes grow dim, let Thy eyes be open toward us," but has a comparison between two kinds of human eyes: "May the eyes of our soul be fastened upon Thee when the eyes of our body become dim." There is a similar approach when the prayer deals with man's heart. The sentence about our hands is an addition, which is also the case with the words: "Deal with us according to Thy promise." And — again! — the Lord's Prayer has been made optional, apparently out of fear that this prayer would be said too frequently — as if all these prayer forms are intended to be used almost weekly or daily!

As for the second prayer, it is understandable that the Creed and its introductory sentence have been deleted. However, we cannot see any reason for leaving out the words of the original by which one confesses: "When we consider how we have hitherto spent our time." In this way the prayer has lost its character as a prayer for terminally ill people in particular. In the original the petition for recovery reads: "lest the evil one think that Thou hast forsaken us," which, in our opinion, is another regrettable omission in the "1984" text. And as for the Lord's Prayer . . . "as already stated!"

Taking all this into consideration we reach the conclusion that there is every reason to ask the question: When do we begin to lack respect for what our forefathers formulated? In concreto: Were all these alterations, additions, and omissions really necessary?

Morning and evening prayers

Already in the *Didache* or *The Teachings of the Twelve Apostles* we begin to hear about prayers said at fixed times of the day. This document mentioned the rule of reciting the Lord's Prayer three times a day. It was in a sense like continuing the Jewish prayer tradition, which bound itself also to some fixed hours. At the same time it was a renewal of the content of these Jewish prayers.

Another continuation and renewal took place in the days of the Reformation of the sixteenth century. This time it concerned the prayer tradition of the Romanized Church. In the course of the ages there had been a development which led to the so-called *officia* and *horae canonicae*, compulsory prayers, as the morning prayer and the evening prayer. Apart from them there were also the "small hours," non-compulsory prayers said at the end of every quarter of the day.

The idea behind it was that every moment of the day must be "consecrated" by prayer, and that every single hour had its own symbolic relation to particular events in sacred history, for example to the respective "stations" in Christ's sufferings. Another idea was that in this way one acts in accordance with what Christ has said: Pray without ceasing. This is why in the literature we find references to Scripture texts such as Luke 18:1; Romans 12:12; Colossians 4:2; I Thessalonians 5:17; and Hebrews 13:15.

It may be clear that the Reformation broke with these ideas and the superstitious interpretation of Scripture texts.

Certainly, Martin Luther maintained the matins and the vespers, but these morning and evening prayers were very simple, as was the accompanying "liturgy:" in the morning the reciting of the Creed and the Lord's Prayer, then a brief thanksgiving for God's protection during the night, and entrusting oneself into God's hands for the day, after which a song followed as for example the metrical version of the Ten Commandments (then it says: "And now, joyfully go to your work!"); in the evening again the reciting of the Creed and the Lord's Prayer, with a similar thanksgiving and petition.

Again we must say that this must be seen in the light of the emphasis Luther placed on the priestly office of all believers. The Appendix to his "Shorter Catechism" — which includes these prayers — has an introductory formula, reading: "How a housefather shall teach his family to pray in the morning and in the evening."

John Calvin also contributed to the liberation of life from the clerical yoke, providing his people with a number of directives for their family devotions. To his Genevan Catechism of 1543 and 1545 he added a series of prayers.

The Church of the Palatinate included some similar prayers in her Church Order, their contents being derived from John Calvin, Marten Micron, and in the evening prayer also from Martin Luther.

They were meant to be used in the very brief daily services which did not last any longer than half an hour. In them there was Scripture reading, and the Lord's Prayer was recited. In the morning the Ten Commandments were read, and in the afternoon the Creed was recited.

Dathenus translated these prayers into Dutch, and included them as an appendix in his Psalm version of 1566, introducing them in The Netherlands.

There the vespers were maintained for a long time in spite of the statement issued by the Synod of Dordrecht 1574 that these services should be abolished. The Synod of The Hague 1586 was of the opinion that they were "useful," and that their abolishment must take place with the consent of the classis and the magistrate.

As for the Morning prayer, the 1972 edition of the *Book of Praise* contained a faithful rendering of the original text. Only the word "Amen" was added to the Ten Commandments! The text of the 1984 edition has some additions to the intercessory prayers in the paragraphs three and four.

The introductory petition to the Ten Commandments and these commandments themselves have been deleted, for the apparent reason that the few people who would consider using this prayer would most likely leave them out.

As for the Evening prayer, in the very first line the name of God, "Light eternal shining in the darkness," has been replaced by "In Whom is no darkness at all." However, if the revisers had consulted older editions they would have learned that there was a marginal reference to II Corinthians 4:6!

At the end two sentences have been added: "Thy steadfast love, O Lord, endures forever. Do not forsake the works of Thy hand;" while, on the other hand, the Lord's Prayer and its introductory formula have been deleted.

Prayers for ecclesiastical assemblies

The first two of these three prayers originate with the "Walcheren Committee," appointed by the Provincial Synod of Zeeland, held at Veere in the year 1610, which synod wanted to promote unity in the use of prayer forms and therefore took the further initiative for completing the prayer book. The fruits of this committee's efforts were published in the "Schilders edition" of 1611, which was used at the Synod of Dordrecht 1618-19.

The "Opening Prayer for the meetings of the deacons' appeared for the first time among the liturgical writings which, together with the current Psalm version, were added to an edition of the New Testament in the then brand new *Statenvertaling*, published by Aert van Ravensteyn in the year 1637. It was written by an unknown author. Only in the year 1930, at the General Synod of Arnhem, was it officially adopted.

There are a number of differences between the text as we find it in the 1984 edition of the *Book of Praise* and the one which was recommended to the Dutch Churches in 1902 and 1930. As explained at an earlier stage, this Dutch text is the one which was produced in the *Flakkeesche editie* by F.L. Rutgers and H.H. Kuyper in 1897. Since their text was based on the "Schilders edition" of 1611, we must come to the conclusion that, as for the first two prayers of this group their text is in harmony with the original.

As a consequence those alterations which are not really necessary must be branded as more or less arbitrary, and therefore rejected.

As for the "Opening Prayer for ecclesiastical assemblies' we mention the following differences:

The words "(to take heed) to ourselves and" can be found in many editions, but were not included in the original.

In the second paragraph the words "after the fashion of the apostolic Churches" have been deleted, as is the case with "agreeably to our office," and "that (. . .) Thou wilt abide in the midst of the present assembly."

The final sentence, "We ask this in the Name of our Lord Jesus Christ, the great Shepherd of the sheep," replaces the original: "This we ask in the Name of Jesus Christ, Thy Son, Who with Thee and the Holy Spirit, the only and true God, is deserving of eternal praise and glory."

The "1972" edition is in these instances better.

In the first line of the "Closing prayer for ecclesiastical assemblies" the words "from our heart" have been omitted. An addition is: "and in ecclesiastical assemblies." "At the close of this present meeting we humbly ask forgiveness for the shortcomings and sins which did not remain hidden from Thy eyes, and we bring thanks for the good we received from Thy fatherly hand" replaces the translation of the original as we find it in "1972," reading: "Thou hast also been present with Thy Holy Spirit in our assembly, guiding our deliberations and decisions according to Thy will, and binding our hearts together in mutual peace and unity." Do we no longer have the courage to pray this?

The sentence which says: "Give perseverance to the overseers and the deacons, that they may be a blessing to Thy people, through the faithful administration of their offices' was already included in the 1972 edition, as it still is in "1984." The *Psalter Hymnal* did not have it, so most likely it was "made in Canada."

We are not, of course, expected to pray for the Dutch authorities of the seventeenth century. Even in The Netherlands the original text, which speaks of "his Excellency and the Lords States and Councillors of these United Lands, as also the honourable Magistrate of this city," would no longer be suitable. Therefore it is understandable that for our own situation this intercessory prayer has been changed, and that the Queen is the first one to be mentioned. "This province" has been left out, so that this petition can be prayed in the United States and Australia as well!

As in the previous prayer the concluding sentence has been abbreviated.

The first sentence of the "Opening prayer for the meetings of the deacons' is a faithful rendering of the original, apart from the omission of the words "for the sake of Jesus Christ" in the petition for the "Spirit of discrimination"; and at the end the omission of the sentence: "May we neither fail to comfort the needy members of Thy dear Son, nor dispense gifts to those who are not in want."

In the second paragraph the words "as Christ's ministers of mercy" are an addition, replacing the deleted line that says: "with true liberality of heart and without difficulty" — which could be read in "1972," but was a weak rendering of the Dutch original.

In the sentence that starts with the words "Give us Thy grace" the slight contrast in the Dutch text is no longer there. In the "1972" it said: "Bestow upon us also the grace we need, not only to relieve want by means of external gifts, but also to instil the comfort of Thy holy Word in hearts afflicted with misery."

The words which then follow, "that they may put their trust in Thee alone," replace the sentence in the original and in the 1972 edition which refers to the Scriptures, and says: "Truly, man lives not by bread alone, but by every Word that proceeds out of Thy mouth."

"In His Name we pray" is another addition.

In conclusion we would like to make a general remark about the text of the Liturgical Prayers in the *Book of Praise* 1984, in particular about the last three prayer forms: We have the impression that the proposed texts of these prayers were never thoroughly scrutinized in the Churches before they were finally adopted by their respective synods. We are afraid that this is symptomatic for their general neglect. Yet we express the hope that we have raised some interest in these forms, often so full of treasures.

5.3 LITURGICAL FORMS
5.3.1 Introduction

It took several ages before our collection of Liturgical Forms was complete. The Psalter which Petrus Dathenus published in 1566 contained only three of them: the forms for infant baptism, for the administration of the Lord's Supper, and for marriage solemnization. The National Synod of The Hague 1586 took the initiative to incorporate forms for the ordination of office-bearers and for excommunication and readmission. The Synod of Dordrecht 1618-19 added a form for the administration of baptism to adults.

The same synod, in one of its final sessions, gave the following order of "the Dutch Liturgy:" "The public prayers and forms for the administration of the sacraments, Church discipline, ordination of ministers, elders, and deacons, and marriage solemnization."

Many editions published in the seventeenth century maintained this "historical order."

Early in the twentieth century (1902) a Form for the Ordination of Missionaries was adopted, which was replaced by the Synod of Hattem 1972-73 with a new form.

"Utrecht 1923" inserted a Form for the Public Profession of Faith. "Sneek 1939" added a Form for Excommunication of non-communicant members, which was amended at the Synod of Groningen-Zuid 1978.

"Hattem 1972-73" accepted an Abbreviated Form for the Celebration of the Lord's Supper.

Finally, the Synod of Kampen 1975 adopted an amended form for marriage solemnization. This was replaced by yet another form at the General Synod of Arnhem 1981.

The current order in which we find all these forms in the *Book of Praise* is: the two baptismal forms, the form for the public profession of faith, both forms for the Lord's Supper, three forms regarding Church discipline, three ordination forms, and the form for marriage solemnization.

In our discussion of the respective forms we will keep this order, which may be regarded as "logical" because our Church service book deals first of all with the sacraments themselves, then with those who are excluded from them or readmitted to them; in the third place with the office-bearers, and finally with the solemnization of marriages which is a more private affair — or perhaps "political," the minister also acting on behalf of the government.

5.3.2 Forms for Baptism

Baptismal history in a nutshell

Apart from the "logical" order in which the liturgical forms have been included in our Church service book, there is also another reason for us to deal first of all with the Form for the Baptism of Infants: In our Churches it is by far the most frequently used form, which is another blessing.

However, before we discuss this form, we will first go briefly through the history of baptism, because without doing so our forms will not appeal to us quite so strongly.

First we would like to emphasize that holy baptism is an institution of Christ Himself. This does not mean that for the Jews of those days baptism was something entirely new. They were familiar with the baptism of converts from among the gentiles, the so-called proselyte baptism.

John the Baptist made it perfectly clear what his baptism meant: he called the people to repentance and baptism, in order that their sins might be washed away. When Christ instituted baptism as a sacrament, He clearly based this washing away of sins on His own blood, shed at Calvary's cross.

The *Didache* or *The Teachings of the Twelve Apostles* is most likely the oldest of all witnesses that baptism was administered in the ancient Christian Church. It even says that it had to be done "into the Name of the Father and the Son and the Holy Spirit" — which, however, does not prove that these words acted as the "baptismal formula," for the same booklet speaks also of "baptizing into the Name of the Lord," Jesus. Another feature is that baptism had to be administered in "running water" — so in a river or near a fountain. It may be interesting to learn that this is the origin of the name "baptismal font," from "fountain."

That the *Didache* was not the only one to emphasize that for baptism running water was required, may be confirmed by Justinus Martyr, born appr. 100, who informs us that the ceremony took place "where there is water." According to him a trinitarian formula was used.

At the end of the second century we can observe a certain development which led to the so-called "catechumenate." The baptismal candidates were given thorough instruction, which later on lasted for no less than two or three years, and ended with a fast of six weeks with the actual ceremony of baptism taking place preferably during the "Easter vigil." This ceremony expanded to a series of rites, as for example the renouncing of Satan, exorcism, anointing, the laying on of hands, the kiss of peace, and the celebration of the Lord's Supper. The pattern for baptism was considered to have been set by the account of Christ being baptized in the river Jordan — here again the figure of running water can be identified — after which the apostles of the future began to follow the Lord: in the same way the baptismal candidates were expected to follow Christ together with the whole congregation.

During the fourth century in the Church of Jerusalem this development led to a number of stages in the preparation of the baptismal candidates. In the so-called pro-catechesis they were informed about the mysteries of the Eucharist — another name for the Lord's Supper, which was gradually influenced by gentile ideas and transformed into something secret. During the actual baptismal catechesis the candidates were taught what constitutes faith with the help of a formula that had much in common with what is now known as the Apostles' Creed — the so-called *traditio symboli*. Exorcism played an important role: the candidates had to get rid of the devil and his influence upon their lives. Finally profession of faith was made, by reciting the Creed — the *redditio symboli*. This instruction took some six to eight weeks. The actual baptism was administered during the Easter night, the underlying idea now being that baptism is a symbol of a believer's dying together with Christ and rising again together with Him. A three-fold immersion was accompanied by a three-fold profession of faith in response to questions asked. The figure three was a reminder of the three days during which the Lord Jesus was in the grave — and not so much a reference to the trinitarian baptismal formula, which again came into use at a later stage. After their baptism the men and women were clothed in white as a symbol of their having entered into a new life. They were given the sign of the cross on their forehead, another anointing took place, and after washing their hands they were received by the congregation with the kiss of peace, and for the first time participated in the celebration of the Eucharist.

The fact that baptism was administered at a fixed time — usually the Easter night, but also at the end of the Easter-cycle and at Pentecost; Augustine, for example, was baptized on Pentecost — was the consequence of the development of the "catechumenate."

Another step in the development was the decline in the number of people who as Jews or gentiles were touched by the gospel and came to faith. Infant baptism took over. No longer could the administration of baptism be restricted to certain fixed dates. The rate of infant mortality was very high. Therefore rules were set for "emergency baptism" and even for "regular" cases. An African synod of 256 gave permission to baptize infants on the second or third day instead of on the eight day. This was adopted from the Jewish date of circumcision. From the thirteenth century on there was even a rule expressed by the phrase "as soon as it is practicable."

Infant baptism was, however, not the only reason. The ideas about the meaning of baptism ran parallel to those in respect of the Lord's Supper. Its administration became more and more a kind of magic act: It was believed to wash away original sin, and, in the case of adults, even of actual sins. This may explain why some people postponed their baptism — Augustine and Emperor Constantine were among them. It may also explain the other extreme, the practice of "emergency baptism."

In addition this meant that the function of the priest became more and more important. As a matter of fact, the rites of adult baptism were simply adopted for infant baptism: the children were supposed to renounce Satan and make public profession of faith — by means of the baptismal witnesses — but the three-fold profession was replaced more and more by the trinitarian baptismal formula, spoken by the celebrant. The activity of the Church and her office was emphasized at the cost of the role played by the baptismal candidate or by the candidate's parents.

In the Middle Ages and the period following all this culminated in the *Rituale Romanum*, the official baptismal liturgy imposed on the Church by Pope Gregory VII (1073-1085) and the Council of Trent (1545-47, 1551-52, 1562-63). The rites of adult baptism with their weeks of fasting, exorcisms, anointings, and other ceremonies were reduced to one single rite, whereby, however, all the elements were maintained. Only recently, at the Second Vatican Council, the whole procedure was adjusted to the real situation: no longer are the infants supposed to profess their faith, but full emphasis is laid on the responsibilities of the parents, while preference is given to the administration of baptism in the midst of the congregation. The Church of Rome has, at least and at last, learned something from the Reformation, although not the fundamentals.

We have just mentioned the Reformation: It may be clear why the Reformers made further strong protest against the doctrine and practice of the Church of Rome as far as baptism is concerned.

Martin Luther was of the opinion that baptism least of all was affected by corruption. He tried to keep as much as possible from the *Rituale Romanum*. Besides, for pedagogical reasons he wanted only a gradual reform of Church life. For him the main point was that baptism would be administered in the vernacular. But he did not want to suggest that he was introducing a new kind of baptism. These are the characteristics of his *Taufbuchlein* (Little Baptismal Booklet) of 1523. In the year 1526, however, some ceremonies were abolished, though not the renouncing of Satan and exorcism.

Leo Judae in Zurich tried to follow a similar line for the same reasons. However, when his booklet on baptism (1523) was replaced by Zwingli's liturgy of 1525, all the old ceremonies were dropped.

In 1524 Martin Bucer at Strasbourg reduced the ritual, concentrating on the main point: the sacrament as a confirmation of the Word, baptism as a sign and seal of the promise of our purification by Christ's blood and Spirit, the responsibility of the parents, and the administration of baptism in the midst of the congregation. With the help of a form, the congregation had to be taught about all these matters. This is what John Calvin adopted for his French-speaking congregation at Strasbourg, and what he introduced in Geneva after his return in 1541. Since then this Reformed baptismal liturgy has spread to the Palatinate, to Scotland, to Hungary, to The Netherlands, also to the North American continent, and to Australia. Our own liturgy is a ripe fruit of the Great Reformation!

The history of the Form for Infant Baptism

We owe the Form for Infant Baptism to Petrus Dathenus, who in the year 1566 included it in his Psalter-edition. This does not mean, however, that he himself wrote it. He partly translated the form used in the Palatinate.

Even the latter was not new. Caspar Olevianus compiled it from the forms of John Calvin, which was used in Geneva, and that of the London Church from the hand of à Lasco and Marten Micron.

Dathenus, however, replaced the questions by his own, which were similar to those used in the Churches of London and Emden.

Tracing the respective parts back to their origin, we obtain the following result: The exposition of the doctrine of holy baptism originates, via Olevianus, from Geneva and London, whereby it is striking that the apologetic sections are from London (the sentence: "if we sometimes, through weakness, fall into sins," and the one about the little children who do not "understand these things"). The call to prayer was taken from the London liturgy. The baptismal prayer came from Zurich. It is called the "Flood Prayer." Originating in the Middle Ages, it is the oldest part of our Liturgical Writings. Also Martin Luther kept it in his own baptismal liturgy. The questions are from the hand of Dathenus, and the thanksgiving prayer comes, via the Palatinate, from the London Church of Reformed refugees.

The Convention of Wesel, 1568, referred to this form, recommending it for use by the Churches.

The Synod of Dordrecht 1574 was of the opinion that it was too long, and decided to have it abbreviated. Caspar van der Heyden was charged with this. The Acts of the next synod of South Holland contain the new text, which was, with some minor changes, adopted by the National Synod of Dordrecht 1578, and published at Antwerp in the year 1580. The Synod of The Hague 1586 slightly revised it.

In spite of this official endorsement of the abbreviated text, the old text was still published in a number of new liturgy-editions, which may be an indication that some Churches continued its use.

In the next paragraph we will print a translation of the original, larger form. In this way we will be able to make a comparison between the old and the new texts. But already we can now say that it is to be regretted that — contrary to the Form for the Lord's Supper — the "words of institution" are no longer quoted.

The original Form

It may be useful to include a translation of the Form for Infant Baptism as Petrus Dathenus had it in his liturgy of 1566.

At this stage we will abstain from commenting on it, because there will be a good opportunity to make some comparisons when we study the current Form.

The Form as it served until replaced by the shorter version, written at the initiative of the "liturgical Synod" of Dordrecht 1574, read as follows:

"By saying that we cannot enter into the Kingdom of God unless we are born again, the Lord Jesus Christ gives us a clear indication of the complete wickedness and corruption of our nature. He thereby admonishes us to humble ourselves before God and to detest ourselves. In this way He makes us desirous of His grace, in order that all wickedness and corruption of our old nature may be washed away and buried by it. For we cannot have part in God's grace unless first of all any confidence in our own strength, our own wisdom and righteousness be taken from our heart, yea, that we damn all that is in us.

After in this way having shown us our misery, He also comforts us by His mercy. He promises us and our children to wash us from all our sins. This means that He will not impute them for the sake of His shed blood and that by His Holy Spirit He will renew us to His image.

In order to confirm such a promise to our weak faith and seal it to our body, He has commanded that we shall be baptized into the Name of God, the Father, the Son, and the Holy Spirit.

Therefore, first, since He wants us to be baptized with water into the Name of the Father, He testifies to us, as with a visible oath, for the whole of our life, that God wants to be our Father as well as the Father of our seed, providing us with all our needs for body and soul, turning all evil to our benefit, because — seeing the covenant which we have with God — no creature can harm us, but they all must be subservient to our salvation.

Second, when we are baptized into the Name of the Son, He promises us that all that the Son of God has done and suffered is our own, so that He is the Saviour of us and our children, anointing us with His saving grace, that by His holy conception, birth, sufferings, and death, He has redeemed us from all impurity and sin, that He has nailed all our corruption on the cross, and has washed it away with His blood and has buried it with Him; and in this way saves us from hellish agony, in order that by His resurrection and ascension He would clothe us with His righteousness, and would now make intercession for us with the heavenly Father, and in the final judgment would present us to the Father in glory and without blemish.

Third, when we are baptized into the Name of the Holy Spirit, we are promised that the Holy Spirit will for ever be the Teacher and Comforter of us and our children, making us true members of Christ's body; in order that we — together with all members of the Christian Church — would have part in Christ and all His goods; so that even the sins and weakness which still remain in us, will no longer be remembered, but that they are more and more mortified, and in us a new life is started, which at last in the blessed resurrection — when this flesh will be conformed to Christ's glorious body — will be perfectly revealed.

However, since in all covenants two parties ally themselves, we, too, from our side promise God the Father, the Son, and the Holy Spirit that we, by His grace, want to hold and confess Him as our only, true, and living God, in our distress call upon Him only, and live as obedient children, as this new birth requires of us, which consists of two parts:

First that, showing true repentance and sorrow because of our sins, we deny our own ingenuity and various lusts, submitting them to God's will, and with our whole heart hate all sins and flee from them. Then also, that we begin to have desire and love to live according to God's Word in all holiness and righteousness.

And if we sometimes through weakness fall into sins, we must not continue lying in them, nor despair, or seek forgiveness of sins in any other way than by Christ, but always be admonished by our baptism to abstain from sin and firmly trust that, for the sake of Christ's shed blood, they never will be remembered before God, because holy baptism is to us an undoubted testimony that we have an eternal covenant with God, and that we have been baptized in the living Fountain of the Father's everlasting mercy and the most holy sufferings and death of Jesus Christ, by the power of the Holy Spirit.

And although our children do not understand the just mentioned causes and mysteries, and much less would be able to confess them, they must not be excluded from baptism. For they have been called by

God to His covenant, which He has established with Abraham — who is a father of all believers — and with his seed, and also with us and our children. "I will," says the LORD, "establish My covenant between Me and you and your descendants after you throughout their generations for an everlasting covenant, to be God to you and to your descendants after you."

Now our Lord Jesus Christ came into this world not in order to diminish this grace of His heavenly Father, but rather to spread this covenant all over the world — which covenant before was enclosed within the people of Israel — and instead of circumcision He has instituted holy baptism as a true sign and seal of this covenant, for us and our children, as the holy apostle Peter expressly teaches in Acts chapter 2, when he says: "Repent, and be baptized every one of you in the name of Jesus Christ for the forgiveness of your sins; and you shall receive the gift of the Holy Spirit. For the promise is to you and to your children and to all that are far off, every one whom the Lord our God calls to Him."

This is how also the Lord Christ Himself commands to bring infants to Him, promising them with words and deeds the Kingdom, as Mark writes in chapter 10: "And they were bringing children to Him that He might touch them; and the disciples rebuked them. But when Jesus saw it, He was indignant, and said to them, "Let the children come to Me, do not hinder them, for to such belongs the Kingdom of heaven. Truly, I say to you, whoever does not receive the Kingdom of God like a child shall not enter it." And He took them in His arms and blessed them, laying His hands upon them."

From these words it is clear that our children too are in God's Kingdom and covenant, and therefore ought to receive baptism as a seal of the covenant, although, seeing their young age, they do not yet understand the mystery of baptism; as also the children were blessed by Jesus Christ Himself with words and deeds; and as in the old Church they were circumcised on the eighth day, although they could not understand or comprehend neither the LORD's blessing nor the mystery of circumcision."

(Apart from some minor changes the prayer that followed, the question, and the thanksgiving were the same as in the present Form).

The structure of the current Form

This is not a commentary on the documents included in our Church service book. Our chief aim is to supply some historical information on them. Nevertheless — also in view of the next section — it will be useful to have a look at its structure.

After its title we can distinguish two parts: a doctrinal and a ritual part.

The former contains "the doctrine of holy baptism." Without mentioning the terms of the Heidelberg Catechism, it explains respectively our sins and misery, our deliverance, and our thankfulness.

First of all it says that baptism shows us that regeneration is necessary for entering into the Kingdom of God: we need the washing away of all our sins, original sin as well as actual sins. Then baptism is introduced as a sign and seal of the promise of the washing away of sins. With a reference to the "words of institution" we are told what each of the Three Persons in the Holy Trinity promises us and seals to us in baptism. In the third place our covenant obligations toward the Triune God are explained. Then follows an exposition of the grounds of infant baptism.

The ritual part contains the baptismal prayer, an admonition at the address of the parents, the questions asked and the parents' answer to them, the actual ceremony of baptism, and a thanksgiving prayer.

Its text

As far as the text of this Form is concerned some particulars of a historical nature are to be reported.

Title

The original title reads — in our translation — "Form for the Administration of Holy Baptism."

Publishers have added the words: "to the children of believers."

In the *Book of Praise* the title simply reads: "Form for the Baptism of Infants."

"In" or "into?"

Former editions of our Church service book had under "Second:" "therefore we are baptized into the Name of God, the Father and the Son and the Holy Spirit." In the latest edition of the *Book of Praise* the name "God" has been deleted. This runs parallel with what happened repeatedly in The Netherlands: Dathenus had this name, but some editions of later days omitted it; and while since the Synod of 1902 the Dutch Churches followed the *Flakkeesche editie* by F.L. Rutgers and H.H. Kuyper — which included this name — they deleted it in their recently revised text. The reason for this may be that immediately afterwards it is explained which promises are given us by, respectively, the Father, the Son, and the Holy Spirit, and that therefore — or even apart from that — the text of Matthew 28:10 followed. However, the longer original version did the same, yet spoke of "God, the Father and the Son and the Holy Spirit." The element of "the Unity in Trinity" (Athanasian Creed) is lost in the present version.

We are happy with the formula "baptized into the Name of . . ." This prevents us from interpreting the baptismal formula as a statement which explains that the celebrant administers this sacrament "on behalf of . . ." as having been authorized by the Triune God. The formula used in the Book of Common Prayer of the Church of England has "In the name of . . ." In this respect it shows another proof of the incomplete reformation of its liturgy, because it still maintains the pre-reformation practice of the Church of Rome, which, using the Vulgate version of Matthew 28:19, baptized *in nomine* ('in the name of . . .') God. Also Leo Judae at Zurich baptized with a similar version (*in dem Namen* . . .), but Ulrich Zwingli reformed the liturgy more thoroughly at this point, returning to the original Greek text of the baptismal formula of Matthew 28.

Indeed, there — and also in other places, as for example Acts 8:16; 19:5; Romans 6:3; I Corinthians 1:13-15; Galatians 3:27 — we read a preposition which indicates a movement or action; it can be translated by "into." Only Acts 2:38 and 10:48 have a different preposition ("on the name of . . ." and "in the name of . . ." respectively).

From all this we may draw the conclusion that it was not Christ's intention to state that the apostles were authorized by the Triune God to baptize converts. Apart from that, this element of authorization is contained in the "missionary command" or "baptismal command" as such, which, besides, makes it clear that He Himself, Christ, gave them this authority.

The preposition used at so many places clearly points to the — new — status of the persons to be baptized: they belong to Jesus Christ, even to the Triune God. This then is further explained when in the Baptismal Form the promises given by the Father, the Son, and the Holy Spirit, are mentioned.

In the 1930s this matter played a role in the life of the Christian Reformed Church in the United States. When this Church adopted the American Standard Version of the Bible it appeared that in the translation of Matthew 28:19 the word "in" (of the AV or KJV) had been replaced by "into." This led to the suggestion that Synod would as yet leave it to the freedom of the Churches to use the word "in" if they preferred this, a suggestion which was not adopted. However, this did not settle the issue. In the official CRC magazine, *The Banner* of September 14, 1939, there was a debate between the Rev. L. Verduin — who preferred "in" — and Professor D.H. Kromminga — a supporter of "into."

In spite of the fact that the Revised Standard Version — recommended in Canada and the U.S.A. and used for the 1984 edition of the *Book of Praise* — has "in" (as has the New International Version), our Forms for Baptism have "into," which indicates the communion with the Triune God into which the covenant of grace has brought the believers and their children.

Two parts

Another point that deserves our attention in the text of the baptismal Forms is the matter of the "two parts."

Following the Dutch sister Churches in their recent linguistic revision of the Forms, our Churches have adopted a text which says: "Third, since every covenant contains two parts, a promise and an obligation . . ."

The old, longer, Form had: "However, since in all covenants two parts ally themselves, we, too from our side promise God the Father, the Son, and the Holy Spirit . . ." This suggests that "parts" in the old Form is meant as "parties." However, the recent addition of the words "a promise and an obligation" clearly interprets the word "parts" in a different way.

Now it is true that the Latin word *pars* can be translated by "party" as well as by "part." The question which term fits in the context of our Baptismal Form can, in our opinion, be settled by the history of its text. The old Form emphasized first the promises of the Father, the Son, and the Holy Spirit, then the promises which "we, too, from our side" make in the covenant communion with the Triune God. However, in the shorter version we no longer read that we, from our side, promise God certain things. The active tense has been replaced by the passive tense: "We are, through baptism, called and obliged by the Lord to a new obedience." The emphasis is no longer on what we do but on what God does in the covenant: He imposes the obligations of the covenant upon us. Therefore we can fully agree with the recent addition of the words "a promise and an obligation."

All this is confirmed by further history. For the old version was not immediately replaced by the present one — without the addition, of course. At the Rotterdam Provincial Synod of 1574 there was a draft which said: "Third, baptism admonishes and obliges us to a new obedience." Already herein the emphasis was no longer on what we from our side promise. For this would not fit in the text of a Form for the Baptism of Infants, who are not yet able to promise anything. A later revision (most likely by the Synod of The Hague, 1586) changed the old version even more radically by putting full emphasis on the fact that — not baptism but — God Himself (though through baptism) puts some obligations on those whom He has taken into His covenant. God is the Active One within the covenant, in both respects, in both "parts," by giving us promises, but also by imposing obligations upon us.

Grounds for infant baptism

As for the grounds of infant baptism it seems as if the reference to the story of Christ blessing little children breaks the reasoning of the paragraph. First we hear that in the old dispensation God commanded that infants be circumcised. A few lines further we read about baptism as replacing circumcision in the new dispensation. Between these two sentences the reference to the story of Christ taking children in His arms and blessing them seems to be an interference. However, what is the real way of reasoning? This, that the children of believers also are in the covenant of grace. This was so during the old dispensation — circumcision being the sign and seal of this covenant. But with the coming of Christ into this world the covenant was not abolished, but continued and enriched, even for our children, as is proven in the story of Mark chapter 10 — the sign and seal (as is explained in the next sentence) now being baptism. The covenant remained, only the token was changed.

This leads to the conclusion that "infants must be baptized as heirs of the Kingdom of God and of His covenant." (The longer version made as it were a shortcut simply by stating that the ground for infant baptism is the fact that "by God they have been called to His covenant").

This "apologetic section" is a nice part of our baptismal Form!

Baptismal Prayer

Turning to the baptismal prayer, we learn from its historical background that, for two different reasons, it is obvious that the reformation of the baptismal ceremony was no revolution or spiritual vandalism. We can observe this in the structure of this prayer, and also in its contents.

As for its structure, it reminds us of the *collecta* in the Roman mass — the summarising, concluding prayer, originally spoken by the priest after the individual believers had silently said their prayers, or after the various common intercessory prayers had been concluded — the Lord's Prayer often serving as a *collecta*.

The way of addressing God in our baptismal Form is fundamentally the same as that in the old *collecta*: God is addressed as "Almighty, eternal God." In the older version of our *Book of Praise* this address is even continued in the same style as these *collecta* did: "Thou Who hast . . ." which has been lost in the present text. An appeal is made to the works done by God in the course of the history of salvation. Then there is a petition. And finally the Lord God is reminded of Christ's position and work as our Mediator, while this is incorporated into a "trinitarian" conclusion. All this is in the style of the *collecta*. An illustration of ancient prayers is the formula "through Jesus Christ, Who together with Thee lives and reigns in the unity of the Holy Spirit: God from eternity unto eternity."

Flood Prayer

The text of the baptismal prayer is the second way in which it is shown that the Reformation did not do away with the good elements in the medieval liturgy.

As we have already stated, it is known as "the Flood Prayer." It is the oldest part of our Liturgical Writings. It originates with the Middle Ages, from where it was maintained by Martin Luther in Wittenberg, and Leo Judae and Ulrich Zwingli in Zurich. From Zurich it came to the Palatinate, Petrus Dathenus translating it for his Dutch congregation from the liturgy of the Palatinate.

Apart from the baptismal formula it is held in common with the Church of Rome, which has also maintained it. There is, however, a difference. The medieval version and that of today's Roman Catholic Church have a third reference to the history of salvation in the so-called "Jordan-typology." Apart from referring to the story of the Flood and that of Israel crossing the Red Sea, it reminded God of the baptism of His Son in the river Jordan. Martin Luther left it in his version of the prayer. Zurich, the Palatinate, and subsequently the Churches in The Netherlands, North-America, Australia, South Africa, and other countries, deleted it.

Lying behind the use of this old prayer there is a typological use of certain events in sacred history, in the instruction of baptismal candidates and the liturgy of baptism in particular. As Martin Luther formulated it, these sacred events of redemptive history were seen as pointing to the future. As for holy baptism his prayer included the following words: "In order that this bath of Thy holy baptism may have some meaning for the future . . ." As "types" these events were not only acknowledged as real historic events, but as it were also foreshadowing future events as well. Already we find this interpretation in the writings of Tertullian (appr. 160-222), with Ambrose of Milan, Cyrill of Jerusalem — in the fourth century — and in the Egyptian liturgy. All sorts of stories in which water played a role were "typologically" interpreted: the Flood, the crossing of the Red Sea, that of the Jordan by Israel and later on by the prophet Elijah. Water was seen in them as a figure of destructive as well as saving power. Other stories are the creation story, in which the Spirit of God was moving over the face of the waters, the waters of Marah, and the story of Naaman being healed by the waters of the river Jordan, having creative and purifying power. It was no wonder that for a long period of time the baptismal font was called "Jordan." Therefore it is remarkable that — whereas the Jordan-typology played a significant role in Luther's liturgy (he also wrote the hymn *Christ, unser Herr, zum Jordan kam*; [Christ, our Lord, came to the Jordan]), and it is still in the Roman Catholic liturgy — it has been deleted in our own baptismal prayer.

The Scriptures themselves have set the pattern. The apostle Peter (I Peter 3:19 - 21) interprets the story of the Flood in a typological way; the apostle Paul (I Corinthians 10:1 - 5) puts that of Israel crossing the Red Sea in this light. Most likely our Reformed forefathers have seen some dangers in extending this kind of biblical interpretation to other stories, for nowhere in Scripture do we find such an interpretation of the other stories mentioned above. Even with respect to the story of Christ being baptized in the Jordan, we cannot find a direct reference of this nature in the apostolic writings. This may have made our Reformers somewhat reluctant in following Martin Luther's example in his Jordan-typology.

In the meantime he formulated the conclusion drawn from these stories in a clearer way than is found in our Form, when he wrote: "by which Thou hast signified baptism" (the current Dutch text has something similar; but this has not been taken over by our Churches in the *Book of Praise*, which still has: "by which baptism was signified").

Him

It was a little humorous when two provincial synods, those of both the Holland provinces, were told in the year 1723 that in several editions the word "Him" in "following Him day by day" was replaced by "them" (in Dutch *hen* instead of *Hem*). Quite seriously they appointed deputies to have this investigated and rectified — which was in perfect harmony with the good Reformed tradition!

Address

As for the address Dathenus had: "Christian brothers" instead of the Palatine "Beloved in Christ the Lord," as some in The Netherlands also had. The Synod of 1578 changed this into "Christian N, who presents this child (or these children) to be baptized," because it created room for the mother in case of the father's absence, or for baptismal witnesses to answer the questions. "1611," however, had: "You, father of this child (or: you fathers of these children)." It is not clear when the old address, "Beloved in Christ the Lord," was reintroduced. It is a more suitable address for the present situation in which usually both parents present their child for baptism. (We will not discussed the question here as to whether this practice conforms with the adopted ancient rule of having our children baptized "as soon as it is practicable," *quamprimum*, as found in our respective Church Orders).

When the Form for Infant Baptism was compiled, the old theory that the water of baptism would wash away original sin and regenerate the candidates was still believed. This may explain the admonition that the parents must not use this sacrament "out of superstition." Here again history makes it clear why this admonition has been inserted.

Questions

As for the questions, in an edition by Marnix van St. Aldegonde each of them was supposed to be answered by "I do."

Questions were not always asked. The Provincial Synod of Edam, North Holland, 1579, made this optional. The Synods of Dordrecht 1574 and 1578, and that of Middelburg 1581 stated, however, that they were compulsory. The Arminians refused to ask them. A Friesland synod, held at Franeker in the year 1609, suggested to replace the asking of questions by "teaching" the parents the same things. But "Joure" 1620 returned to their compulsory character. Still in 1656, however, the magistrate of the city of Groningen even forbade the asking of questions. This was maintained until the French Revolution: only in the year 1804 was the consistory able to reintroduce the questions.

Sanctified in Christ

As for their contents, the words "sanctified in Christ," in the first baptismal question, have caused much confusion in the course of time. It is a kind of summary of what à Lasco had in his London liturgy: "for Christ's sake included in the covenant," of the East Frisian: the child needs, according to the covenant of grace "to be dedicated to God for the forgiveness and mortification of its sins," and of Marten Micron's: "a seed of the covenant in virtue of God's covenant" — the same as in the Canons of Dort I, 17.

However, after Franciscus Gomarus — a theologian well known from the controversy between him and Arminius — had developed his theory of an external and an internal covenant, some ministers changed the first question into: "do you confess that our children (. . .) can be sanctified in Christ," or others: "ought to be sanctified in Christ," because they were of the opinion that the phrase could not be properly applied to all the children since there could be among them children who, when they grew up, would in their behaviour prove that they were unbelievers, and therefore were in "the external covenant" only. In the 1940s this was proclaimed to be the official interpretation by a general synod of the Dutch churches, which was strongly influenced by the teachings of Abraham Kuyper, who took up and further developed this old theory. We may be thankful for having been liberated from this false interpretation of the words "sanctified in Christ" and led back to their real meaning.

Here in this Christian Church

Regarding the second baptismal question history informs us about another controversy. It concerned — and still concerns, because the same issue was taken up again recently — the words "and taught here in this Christian Church."

The original text read: "this doctrine, taught here, and which is further contained in the Old and New Testament, and is summarized in the Articles of the Christian Faith." The abbreviated Form of 1575 had almost the same version as we have today. The trouble was caused by the Synod of Middelburg 1581, which made it optional to use the words "and taught here." This was a matter of trying to meet the reservations held by Roman Catholic and Anabaptist parents who wanted to have their children baptized in a Reformed Church, which at that time was a kind of national Church (Dutch: *volkskerk*). The Provincial States of South Holland were of the opinion that these words had to be deleted because parents could not be compelled to declare their agreement with the Reformed Confession. It was sufficient simply to state their agreement with the doctrine of the Old and the New Testaments and that of the Apostles' Creed. Unfortunately the next National Synod, that of The Hague 1586, did not fully rectify this when it changed the critical words into "and subsequently is taught in the Christian Church." This also is how we find these words in editions published in 1591 and 1611 (the "Schilders edition," consulted at the great Synod of Dordrecht 1618-19). It is to be regretted, for in the Arminian controversy the Remonstrants appealed to this formulation in their desire not to feel too strictly bound to the official doctrinal standards of the Churches. Generally speaking, in this controversy the Reformed view could be recognized by the use of the word "here," and the Arminian view by "and subsequently is taught in the Christian Church." Still after "Dort" the Provincial Synod of Friesland, held at Joure in 1620, maintained the "subsequent-version."

During the Arminian controversy the Reformed ministers of the Amsterdam Church, Plancius and Heydanus, used the version of 1566. This brought them into conflict with the Arminian leaders Uytenbogaerd and

Episcopius, who, on two separate occasions, acting as baptismal witnesses, either declared they had not clearly understood the questions, or had repeated the question with omission of the crucial words. This experience led the Amsterdam ministers to make the use of the words "here" and "in this Church" compulsory.

The Synod of Dordrecht 1618-19, at the request of the Provincial Synod of North Holland, had to deal with the same matter. It is not clear what exactly — if anything — this synod decided. Therefore it is understandable that the Church of The Hague proposed to the Provincial Synod held at Brielle that the next National Synod be invited to create uniformity regarding the second baptismal question. This "next National Synod" was held only after a period of more than two hundred years! However, in the editions of the *Statenvertaling* of 1637, which included the liturgy, a formulation was provided which has served for many years.

The matter was also an issue in the days of the Secession, although from a different angle. Many parents, because of the unscriptural doctrine of their own minister, made conscientious objection to answering in the affirmative the question that "in this Christian Church" the true and complete doctrine of salvation was preached, and therefore travelled to the Rev. Hendrik De Cock at Ulrum to have their children baptized.

Recently voices similar to those heard during the Arminian conflict have been heard in churches that incorrectly lay claim to the name "Reformed." Our own churches first used the 1934 edition of the *Psalter Hymnal* of the Christian Reformed Church, reading: "the doctrine contained in the Old and the New Testament and in the articles of the Christian faith, and which is taught here in this Christian church." In the 1961 edition of the *Book of Praise* this was slightly amended into: "the doctrine which is contained . . ." This version was maintained until the Canadian Reformed Synod of 1980 changed this into "summarized in the Creeds." This was meant to be a "linguistic revision" only, not a "change in meaning."[56] The word "Creeds" must have created some confusion. Therefore the next synod replaced it by "confessions."[57] Requests made at the synods 1986, 1989, and 1992, to return to the original wording, were not acceded to.[58]

---

[56] Synod appointed a committee with the mandate to "update the language of the forms."

[57] *Acts of General Synod 1983*, Article 145.

[58] *Acts of General Synod 1986*, Article 144; *Acts of General Synod 1989*, Article 161; *Acts of General Synod 1992*, Article 121.

This happened despite these synods were reminded of the fact that this original version is in full harmony with what we confess in Lord's Day 7 of our Catechism.[59] This is the more strange when we realize that the Churches of Geneva and the Palatinate included the reading of the Apostles' Creed in the Form, while in the Dutch Churches this was replaced by referring to this creed in the second question. Extending this reference to all the (creeds and) confessions is un-historical and unnecessary.

Parents

Originally the third baptismal question read: "Do you promise and take upon yourself to instruct this child in this doctrine, as soon as it is able to understand, to the utmost of your power?" This formulation was suitable for addressing parents and witnesses alike. However, the Synod of Dordrecht 1578 put strong emphasis on the presence of the father, therefore changing the question into: "Third I ask you, father of this child, whether you promise and intend . . ." while the witnesses were separately addressed.

Some scholars claim that "Dort" 1618-19 reformulated the question as it still reads today. However, this is highly unlikely. We would rather presume that practical Church life has led to the present version.

Thanksgiving Prayer

In the abbreviated form by Caspar van der Heyden the thanksgiving prayer started with the words: "We thank Thee that Thou hast included us and our seed into Thy covenant, and sealest and confirmest the same to our body in holy baptism." Most likely this change was a personal one, not adopted by the Churches, so that we still have the original version.

The history of the Form for Adult Baptism

For more than half a century the Reformed Churches in The Netherlands did not have a common form for the baptism of adults. They used their own local questions.

---

[59] "What, then, must a Christian believe? All that is promised us in the gospel, which the articles of our catholic and undoubted Christian faith teach us in a summary."

When a number of former Anabaptists and Socinians wanted to join the Churches, the matter became urgent. The Synod of North Holland 1580, being confronted with this problem, decided that every local Church would use its own text until a national synod would adopt a form for all the Churches. However, the next national synod, that of The Hague 1586, did not issue such a form.

At the Provincial Synod of North Holland, held in the year 1602 at Hoorn, and that of South Holland, Schiedam, also held in 1602, it was decided to combine efforts to still have such a form compiled. Their deputies tabled a draft at the Synods of 1603 and 1604, held at Brielle and Edam respectively, and it was adopted by them. They sent copies to the other provincial synods, of which Gelderland introduced it in the year 1606 and Friesland in 1608 — the latter adopting it "for those who, by the neglect or a different religious conviction of their parents are still unbaptized."

The Provincial Synod of Veere in Zeeland, 1610, decided to amend the form for infant baptism, so that it could serve for the baptism of adults as well. The "Schilders edition" of 1611 contained the result of this decision.

The next step was undertaken by the Classis Alkmaar, which wanted uniformity in this respect. The Provincial Synod of North Holland, Enkhuizen 1618, decided to pass the proposal on to the National Synod to be convened at Dordrecht 1618. The South Holland Synod did the same.

In its final sessions "Dort" combined both forms. The first section was taken from the Zeeland form, with a few amendments and additions; the address to the baptismal candidates and the questions are a somewhat longer version of the Holland form.

Recently, in the year 1978, our Dutch sister Churches, at their General Synod of Groningen-Zuid, adopted a linguistically modernized version, which is basic to the translation presented in the *Book of Praise* and adopted by our Churches.

Its text

Here, too, a few particulars can be summed up and shown against their historical background.

Doctrinal part

As said before, the "doctrinal part" of this Form is virtually the same as that of the Form for the Baptism of Infants. This is even obvious when in the "apologetic section" a kind of transfer is made from the grounds of infant baptism to those of adult baptism.

Baptismal Prayer

The baptismal prayer is also an amended version of that in the Form for Infant Baptism.

Questions

The questions are based on Marten Micron's *Eene Korte Onderzoekinge des Geloofs* (A Brief Examination of Faith), which acted as a pattern for the compiling of the Heidelberg Catechism and was printed in the oldest editions of the Dutch Church service book between the Forms for Baptism and for the Lord's Supper (at that time there was no official Form for the Public Profession of Faith, but this booklet acted as such in several Churches). In its own turn this document was an abbreviation and translation of a work from the hand of à Lasco, which was written in Latin.

Compared with the original version there are some minor changes.

Apart from these changes our special attention should be given to the following points:

In the fourth question the original had "all the Articles of the Christian religion." In the current Dutch text this has been interpreted as "the Apostles' Creed," which as an interpretation — not as a modernization — is correct. The text in the *Book of Praise*, however, has — as it is in the Form for Infant Baptism — "confessions," which — as was proved before — is objectionable.

The same question asks in its last line, for a faithful "use of the holy sacraments." Throughout the ages, however, a promise of faithfully participating in the Lord's Supper was asked. This had a historical reason. The Provincial Synod of South Holland, held at Leyden in the year 1572, did not want the local consistories to deny adult baptism to persons who were hesitant to take part in the celebration of the Lord's Supper. It suggested some special instruction and exhortation only. In Friesland the Synod of Leeuwarden 1598 stated that those persons should promise to faithfully participate. To this the Synod of Bolsward 1608 added: if this promise is not given then the persons concerned should be admonished. Nevertheless, for some time this matter remained a difficulty in this province, for example because some consistories refused to solemnize marriages of people who had not been baptized. In Utrecht there was even more serious trouble: the Arminian synod of this province, held in 1612 — which was attended by Uytenbogaerd, one of the prominent Arminians — gave the minister of Kockengen permission to baptize people who were denied baptism elsewhere because they did not promise to attend the celebration of the Lord's Supper. The Synod of Dordrecht 1618-19, being aware of this situation, not only included in the Form the words: "Do you promise to persevere in (. . .) the use of the Lord's Supper," but even stated in Article 59 of its Church Order: "Adults are by baptism ingrafted into the Christian congregation and accepted as members of the congregation, and are therefore also obliged to use the Lord's Supper, which to do they shall promise at their baptism."

As for the fifth question, the positive element of forsaking the world — still in the 1972 version of the *Book of Praise* — is lost, having been replaced by the negative promise "not to love the world and its evil desires." In this respect the Form for the Public Profession of Faith is better, having kept the ancient element of renouncing Satan.

At the end the required promise "to submit cheerfully to all Christian admonition" ("1972" after the original) has been replaced by "to submit willingly to the Christian admonition and discipline of the Church, if it should happen, and may God graciously prevent it, that you become delinquent in doctrine or in conduct" — which has been borrowed from the Form for the Public Profession of Faith and made equal to it because the occasions on which these Forms are used are similar.

5.3.3 FORM FOR THE PUBLIC PROFESSION OF FAITH

A young Form

This is one of the youngest Reformed liturgical Forms. For more than three and a half centuries the Dutch Churches had done without a common Form, when finally they adopted one at their General Synod of Utrecht 1923. Our Churches took it over from them, originally in a literal translation which was published in the 1961 edition of the *Book of Praise*, and later in an amended version, which was adopted by the Synods of Winnipeg 1980 and Launceston 1985 respectively.

Reformation

As we will see below, in the days of the Reformation public profession of faith was made in a different way. Yet the mere fact that young people, who as infants were baptized, made their public profession of faith, was an event of a reformative character. It replaced the so-called Confirmation, whereby the laying on of hands, in particular by the bishop, played an important role because this act was considered to transfer the gift of the Holy Spirit.

Confirmation

In the Church of Rome confirmation is still one of the seven sacraments. This Church teaches that it is the completion of the sacrament of baptism. Originally baptism, confirmation, and the celebration of the Eucharist were one single initiation ceremony for converts. However, since the bishop could not always and everywhere attend the ceremony of baptism, confirmation was — as far as its timing was concerned — separated from it. In the long run it became another sacrament.

For this doctrine and practice the Church of Rome refers to the stories of Acts 8 and 19, where indeed we read about the laying on of hands and the gift of the Holy Spirit as a ceremony separate from baptism. However, it is overlooked that we do not hear of such a special ceremony in other stories. Therefore we must conclude that this "sacrament" is based on a few exceptional cases which cannot be accepted as a common tradition, let alone as an institution of the Lord Jesus Christ.

On the occasion of their confirmation the young persons concerned are expected to do what adult converts did but what infants cannot do at their baptism: renouncing Satan and professing faith by declaring agreement with the Apostles' Creed. Then the laying on of hands follows, and the anointing with *chrisma* as a seal of the gift of the Holy Spirit — which is done by making the sign of the cross, a combination of two ancient rites.

In the course of the Middle Ages more ceremonies were added. This led to expressing in the Preface to the Heidelberg Catechism a condemnation of the confirmation in the following terms: "This institution of Catechism, which had its origin in the command of God Himself, was maintained in the Christian Church until the horrible Satan, through the Antichrist the pope — together with other good institutions — abolished it, replacing it by his greasing and slap in the face and other abominations." John Calvin too mocked at this "sacrament" because its magic was considered to be superior to the instruction of the people. In one of the editions of his Genevan Catechism he wrote in a Letter to the Reader, that the instruction of little children in the Christian doctrine was held in high esteem from the very beginning. However, later on the devil started to rend the church, "and making it a fearful ruin (the marks of which are still visible in most of the world), overthrew this sacred policy, and left nothing behind but certain remnants, which cannot but beget superstition, without any edification. This is "confirmation," as they call it, in which there is nothing but mimicry, and has no foundation."

(Honesty requires to add that in recent times a kind of catechumenate has been reintroduced, so that Roman Catholic boys and girls receive religious instruction with the help of a catechism — which is, of course, Roman Catholic. The doctrine and practice of confirmation, however, remains the same!).

Shorter catechisms

The Reformation restored Scriptural instruction for the young members of the Church. For this purpose not only catechisms but also what are commonly called shorter catechisms were written. The latter served as study guides for the young people and for those who were unable to absorb the contents of the larger catechism. But they had another function as well: they were used to interrogate those who wanted to make profession of their faith and requested admission to the Lord's Supper.

This is why in 1553 John Calvin added to his catechism a document called "The way in which the children shall be interrogated whom one will receive at the table of our Lord Jesus Christ" (*La maniere d'interroguer les enfants qu'on vent recevoir a la cene de nostre Seigneur Iesus Christ*). Marten Micron of the London congregation of Reformed refugees abbreviated and translated à Lasco's Catechism. It served for many years in the Dutch Churches in relation to the public profession of faith. Its title revealed its nature and purpose: "Brief Examination of Faith for those who want to join the congregation" (*Eene Korte Onderzoekinge des geloofs voor hen, die zich tot de gemeente begeven willen*). Also the "Brief Summary of the Christian doctrine, for those who request admission to the Lord's Supper" (*Kort Begrip, of samenvatting van de Christelijke leer, voor hen die toegang vragen tot het heilig avondmaal*) has for many years and in many congregations acted as such.

In Scotland "The Little Catechism" of 1566 and "Craig's Short Catechism" of 1592 were used as a form of examination of children before they were admitted to the Lord's Supper "The Little Catechism" was an adaptation of the third and longer redaction of John Calvin's addition to the Catechism, printed at the end of the Genevan Psalter of 1562. Earlier it was included in the service book of the English congregation at Geneva, "approved by the famous and Godly learned Man, John Calvyn." It was also appended to the 1615 edition of the Palatine (Heidelberg) Catechism.

John Calvin

Martin Luther and Martin Bucer did not break radically with the term "confirmation." At Strasbourg Bucer introduced a ceremony whereby the new communicant members, after having professed their faith, were received by the congregation and "confirmed" with a prayer and the laying on of hands by the minister, who addressed them with the words: "Receive the Holy Spirit that He may preserve and protect you against all evil, as a power and help to all good." But John Calvin caused a complete reformation by reintroducing religious instruction with the help of a catechism. Already in 1536, when for the first time he arrived at Geneva, he did so, in accordance with the ancient Christian Church, which, as he put it, already used catechisms to lead people to their public profession of faith. This is, he wrote, a requirement of the Holy Scriptures, which relate faith to its confession. His stay of a few years at Strasbourg did not influence him with respect to his view on confirmation. After the parents had taught their children — this was in Calvin's opinion their task — and the young people were every now and then tested by their minister, and, if necessary, further instructed, they finally professed their faith before the office bearers. After his return to Geneva in the year 1541, he introduced a public catechesis on Sunday afternoon, during which the Catechism was taught. The ceremony of making profession of faith remained simple: the youngsters concerned had to recite the main points of the Catechism.

In Calvin's thinking there was a close relationship between baptism and profession of faith: At an older age the children had to make a profession which they could not yet make when they were baptized, the reason being that at their baptism they were not "able to understand." In other words, baptism requires a profession of faith, but this has to be postponed because infants have not yet received instruction — a thought which is completely neglected in our own days now that many pleas are made for "children's communion."

Calvin was of the opinion that public profession of faith must be made "as soon as it was practicable" — just like baptism. He appealed on what he considered to be the tradition of the ancient Christian Church: the end of the years of childhood would be the appropriate time, e.g. when the children were ten years old (in London the congregation put the age at fourteen years; even this is in our opinion too early).

Calvin also strongly emphasized the relation between profession of faith and the Lord's Supper. This is why in the Church of Geneva there was an opportunity to make public profession of faith before every celebration of the Lord's Supper. This was not just an individual affair only; it was also aimed at building up the Church.

Calvin did not introduce a separate "examination of the motives." This could easily give the impression that knowledge is of minor importance and that the testing of one's knowledge is a kind of Church exam. On the other hand it must be said that John Calvin was definitely not an intellectualist.

London and the Palatinate

The foundations having been laid by John Calvin, the London congregation of Reformed refugees and the Church of the Palatinate could build on them.

We have already mentioned Marten Micron's *Brief Examination*. It was not only used for the instruction of young people, but — as its title says — in particular for the examination of those who requested admission to the Lord's Supper. Eight days before their public profession of faith the candidates were examined with the help of this booklet. After that they were asked two questions, whether they renounced Satan — in this respect "London" returned to the tradition of the ancient Christian Church — and whether they accepted the supervision of the Church, and, if necessary, Church discipline.

In the Palatinate a preparatory sermon was delivered on the Saturday prior to the Sunday on which the Lord's Supper was administered. Then there was also an opportunity to make public profession of faith by reciting the three main parts of the Catechism and its questions and answers on the Lord's Supper. A kind of public confession of sins and faith followed — which by John Calvin was replaced by home visiting.

The Netherlands

Petrus Dathenus brought the — London-influenced — Palatine liturgy with him when he returned to The Netherlands. But there was also some direct influence from the London liturgy on the Churches of this country.

This was proven when the Convention of Wesel 1568 advised that people who wanted to be admitted to the Lord's Supper would be examined before the whole congregation with the help of Micron's *Shorter Catechism*, together with some parts from the larger Catechism, eight days prior to the celebration of this sacrament. One day before its administration they were expected to declare their agreement with the most important points of faith and their submission to the supervision of the Church, all this in front of the congregation.

Soon afterwards some Churches replaced Micron's *Shorter Catechism* by an abbreviation, the already mentioned "Brief Examination." This was first done by the Church at Brielle and the classis. They brought the matter to the Synod of Dordrecht 1574, which decided that the Heidelberg Catechism should be used for the public instruction and the "Brief Examination" for special cases. The Acts of this synod further state that those who request admission to the Table of the Lord would be examined by the minister and two elders or by two ministers, and that they would be received by the congregation by making public profession of faith and promising submission to discipline, either in the "consistory" or in the "temple." This profession of faith should be made by a simple "I do" (old Dutch: *een ia woort*). It is remarkable that here a double act is mentioned: submitting to the supervision and discipline of the Church is inseparable from the act of professing one's faith.

It does not say that Micron's *Brief Examination* was used during the procedure, but it is very likely that this was done, for already in Dathenus' publication of 1566 its text was printed between the Form for Baptism and that for the Lord's Supper, and some directives for the procedure were added. They read — in our translation — as follows: "All those who want to join the congregation and are desirous to be admitted to the Lord's Supper, shall first from the Word of God be instructed in the main points of the Christian doctrine. In the Churches such a form or manner of instruction shall be maintained as is deemed to be most upbuilding. And when they have fundamentally acknowledged and confessed the main points of the doctrine, one shall ask them whether at any point of the doctrine they have any doubt — in order that they may be satisfied. If they say: Yes indeed, we have, one shall seek to satisfy them from Holy Scripture. However, if they are content, one shall ask them whether they have resolved to remain faithful to the aforesaid doctrine, to forsake the world, and to lead a new Christian life. Finally one shall ask them whether they willingly submit themselves to the Christian discipline. When they have promised this, one shall exhort them to peace, love, and concord with all men, and to make peace if they have anything with anyone else."

After some time it appeared that a number of Churches were no longer happy with Micron's *Brief Examination*. In the year 1607 the consistory of Middelburg declared that an improvement was essential. The ministers were mandated to compile a summary of the Heidelberg Catechism. One of them, Hermanus Faukelius, has the reputation of having written this "Brief Summary" (*Kort Begrip*). In August 1608 it was adopted by the consistory, which from then on used it also for the examination of those who wanted to make public profession of faith. It was included in the "Schilders edition" of 1611, although it was printed after the liturgical writings because not all the Churches had adopted it.

At the Synod of Dordrecht 1618-19 this "Brief Summary" would play a role. This synod had to deal with the methods and material of catechesis. It appointed a committee with the mandate to compile two smaller textbooks next to the Heidelberg Catechism. For very small children a booklet should be written, in some simple questions and answers dealing with the Apostles' Creed, the Ten Commandments, the Lord's Prayer, the words of institution of the sacraments, and with Church discipline. For some older ones an extract from the Heidelberg Catechism must be compiled. The oldest ones should learn the Catechism itself. Hermanus Faukelius was one of the committee members. When the committee tabled its report, it appeared that there was not enough time to deal responsibly with the matter. It seems that only the draft of a booklet for the very young was read in one of the final sessions. It could also be that Synod more or less regretted its own decision, and with second thoughts preferred to have only one single booklet for the religious instruction of the young Church members, the Catechism. The president then advised the replacement of the draft of the second booklet by the "Brief Summary."

Synods — provincial synods, as a matter of fact — of later days recommended the "Brief Summary." The Synod of Leyden 1619, on the other hand, wanted to check the draft of the second booklet just mentioned, proving thereby that not everyone was very enthusiastic about the "Brief

Summary." However, in the liturgy which was printed in the back of the *Statenvertaling*, the new Bible-translation initiated by the Synod of Dordrecht and published in the year 1637, it was printed after the Belgic Confession of Faith, thereby replacing Micron's *Brief Examination*, which had taken this place since Dathenus' Psalter and Liturgy of 1566. The Provincial Synods of Gorinchem 1622 and Rotterdam 1631 stated that apart from the Heidelberg Catechism and the "Brief Summary" no new forms should be adopted — for this was considered to only be in the province of the National Synod.

Since then the text of the "Brief Summary" was followed by the directives of Micron's *Brief Examination*, with a small amendment in the first line, reading: "When those who want to join the congregation have fundamentally acknowledged and confessed these main points, one shall ask them . . ."

It may be clear that many Churches, even ministers, following these directives, compiled their own questions. Others adopted — or amended — a set of questions formulated by Gisbertus Voetius, one of the members of the Synod of Dordrecht 1618-19.

These questions strongly influenced the General Synod of Utrecht 1923, which at last created uniformity by adopting a Form for the Public Profession of Faith, and by deleting the liturgical directives which — via the "Brief Summary" — originate from Marten Micron's *Brief Examination*."

The General Synod of Groningen-Zuid 1978 adopted a modernized version of this Form. The Synod of Heemse 1984-85 decided to include a modernized version of the "Brief Summary" in the Reformed Church service book. The liturgical directives which followed after its text, were, as a matter of course, not included.

Its text

In the 1961 edition of the *Book of Praise* this Form begins with the words: "Beloved in our Lord Jesus Christ, You have appeared here to profess your faith before God and His holy Church" — which was a translation of the Dutch Form. In the 1984 edition, however, the modernized version of this sentence is preceded by another paragraph, containing a thanksgiving for what is going to happen: a public profession of faith. This addition was adopted, apparently at the instigation of the deputies concerned, by the General Synod of Winnipeg 1980.

The contents and formulation of the questions are based on those of Gisbertus Voetius, which were in harmony with the directives in the "Brief Examination" and — after the Synod of Dordrecht 1618-19 — of the "Brief Summary."

Besides, the first question has much in common with the second question in the Form for Infant Baptism and the fourth question in that for Adult Baptism. Since "Winnipeg 1980" added the words "rejecting all heresies and errors conflicting with God's Word," this question runs more strongly parallel with the fourth question in the Form for Adult Baptism.

In the same question the phrase "summarized in the confessions" replaces the former "and in the articles of the Christian faith." For our objections against this alteration we may refer to the remarks made in our exposition of the Form for Infant Baptism.

After having shown the connection between baptism and profession of faith — the latter being an acknowledging of the covenant promises signified and sealed in baptism — the second question asks for a statement which is clearly based on the first and second parts of the Heidelberg Catechism, sin or misery, and deliverance.

The third and fourth questions remind us of the third part of the Catechism, that of gratitude.

The fourth question begins with a new sentence: "do you firmly resolve to commit your whole life to the Lord's service as a living member of His Church?"

Taking the introduction and these four questions together we come to the conclusion that all the elements, which already in the ancient Christian Church played a role, have been included, the profession of a personal bond with Christ through faith, the relation between baptism and confession of faith, the promise to faithfully participate in the celebration of the Lord's Supper, membership of the Church, its privileges and responsibilities, the renouncing of Satan, and the final benediction — as it were replacing the laying on of hands.

To forsake the world

Finally we want to pay some special attention to the requirement of the candidates for public profession to declare that they will forsake the world. This touches the kernel of the whole matter.

The solemn declaration in their "I do" goes back to a very old tradition. At their baptism adult converts in the ancient Christian Church solemnly declared — in the negative — to break with their old master, Satan, and — in the positive — to follow their new Master, Christ. The very moment of their baptism, after they had made a public profession of faith, was considered to be the moment at which they changed masters.

Certain formulas were used, whereby, for example, the candidates declared to renounce the devil, his pomp, his angels and works, or a formula like the following one: "I renounce Satan, all his angels, all his works, his whole service, all his vanities and temptations." Again other formulas summed up Satan's pomp, works, angels, and the world. In the Church of Milan there was even a twofold renouncing in the response to the questions: "Do you renounce the devil and his works?" and "Do you forsake (renounce) the world with all its desires?"

In this context the word *pompa* was often used — still known from the expression "pomp and circumstance." Originally it meant: escort. In ancient Rome e.g., it was used for the escorting of officials as *consules* and *praetores* by *lictores*, or for a triumphal march after a war-time victory. Among Christians the word was used as an indication of the means used by Satan to tempt them. They started to speak of the devil and his angels, works, and pomp — the angels being idols like the German Donar or Wodan, the devil's pomp being the sumptuous life he seemed to guarantee his followers. Later it was used in the figurative sense of splendour, magnificence, pageantry. In the latter sense it was used in the context of one's public profession of faith. For when the persecutions ended and the Western world was christened, with the consequence of infant baptism more frequently being administered than adult baptism, the danger arose of taking things easy and no longer seeing Satan's angels and works, the danger of adopting a sumptuous lifestyle.

In the Eastern as well as the Western Church people who made their profession of faith were required to renounce Satan, together with his angels, works, and pomp. This is still the case in the Orthodox and the Roman Catholic Churches. However, adult baptism and — for the majority — confirmation a number of years after infant baptism — was expanded with all sorts of additional ceremonies, as anointings and exorcisms.

This may be the reason why, in their formulas for the public profession of faith, Reformers like William Farel, Martin Bucer, and John Calvin preferred an expression such as "forsaking the world" above "renouncing Satan." Farel, for instance, had the candidates promise to forsake everything in order to follow Jesus — an expression which was taken over by John Calvin in his baptismal Form of 1543. Bucer abolished the other ceremonies and replaced the renouncing of Satan by a prayer for the mortification of sin, in this way emphasising man's need for regeneration. They were apparently of the opinion that the act of formally renouncing the devil was too close to exorcism, and therefore rather avoided the direct use of such a term.

However, we must not forget that the very idea of having changed masters lies in the background when someone, publicly professing his faith, declares he "forsakes the world." He then declares he belongs to Christ — and not to the evil one — and will follow Him. Therewith he states he is thankful for his deliverance from original as well as actual sins. In this way he fully agrees with the three parts of the Catechism, which at the same time are "the doctrine of holy baptism."

For different purposes Marten Micron included in his marriage solemnization Form an exhortation for the bride to walk "without worldly pride" — an exhortation taken over by the marriage Form in the previous editions of the *Book of Praise* but no longer included in our present Form.

Virtually the same thoughts are behind the thanksgiving prayer in both baptismal Forms, when it says there: "and valiantly fight against and overcome sin, the devil, and his whole dominion."

It may now also be clear that the first pericope in the baptismal Forms, pointing to the necessity of regeneration, is not superfluous. The regeneration everyone needs means: a change of masters.

It is a great moment when a new generation, standing in front of the congregation, with their "I do" declares "to forsake the world," and to be willing to joyfully follow their perfect Saviour. These two simple words, "I do," are their response to what the congregation prayed for them at their baptism. The day on which public profession is made — even by one single person — is a festive day in the great struggle between the Saviour and His great opponent, another foretaste of the final victory.

We can be happy and thankful that we still have the words "to forsake the world" in our Form for the Public Profession of Faith. They clearly mark what is going on when this Form is used!

5.3.4 FORMS FOR THE CELEBRATION OF THE LORD'S SUPPER

The history of the Lord's Supper in a nutshell

According to what we are told in the New Testament the celebration of the Lord's Supper was closely connected with the so-called love-meal, *agape*. By this means the more affluent members of the congregation looked after the needy (Acts 2:42; 4:35; 6:1ff; I Corinthians 11:20-34). This put a strong emphasis on the concept of the Church as a community. At the same time the community with the Lord was expressed as a public profession of faith made in the midst of a pagan or false-religious world (I Corinthians 10:21).

For some time these love-meals, with their climax in the celebration of the Lord's Supper, were maintained. Witness to this is, for example, the *Didache* or *The Teachings of the Twelve Apostles*.

In those days the most frequently used name for the Lord's Supper was "Eucharist," which means: thanksgiving. The early Christians were well aware of this character of the Lord's Supper. This may explain the fact that they also called it — as is done in the *Didache* — an "offering," a kind of climax in their life which was also an offering of thankfulness for their salvation in Christ. At that time this name had nothing to do with the idea of the sacrificial character of the mass of later days.

Both terms, Eucharist and offering, would play a prominent role in the history of the Lord's Supper. The word "Eucharist" was originally the name of the thanksgiving spoken for bread and wine, but soon afterwards it became an indication for the whole service of gratitude and praise. It was more serious, however, when the same name was also given to the elements of bread and wine. The main attention was no longer focused upon the Lord Jesus Christ, to the *anamnese* — the commemoration of His atoning sufferings, death and resurrection — neither to the community-idea, but to these ingredients. Godly men like Cyprian (he died in 258) and Augustine (354-430) urged the people "not to cling with their hearts to the outward symbols of bread and wine, but lift their hearts on high in heaven, where Christ is, at the right hand of His heavenly Father." To Cyprian we owe the so-called *Sursum Corda*. He told the priests to say to the people: "On high your hearts!" whereas the latter were expected to respond with:

"We lift them up to the Lord!" Augustine, in his own days, repeated this: the people should not with deaf ears listen to the cry: "On high the hearts!" In spite of the fact that this *Sursum Corda* became a traditional part of the liturgy of the Lord's Supper, things went in the wrong direction. Slowly and slowly the doctrine of transubstantiation was developed and adopted.

This went together with what happened to the word "offering" or "sacrifice." Hippolytus — who died in 253 and to whom we owe the text of the Eucharist prayer in the Church of Rome at the time of the persecutions, a prayer consisting of a thanksgiving, a reference to the words of institution, the *anamnese*, and the *epiclese* (a prayer for the Holy Spirit) — also used the term "offering." Irenaeus (135-202) did the same. At that time it had not yet the sound and meaning of bread and wine which after consecration were considered to be the body and blood of the Lord Jesus Christ and as such offered to God as a kind of repetition or actualization of Christ's Self-sacrifice at Calvary's cross. However, during the fourth century this became different. The idea of offering one's heart and life was replaced by that of the elements of bread and wine. The fact that soon after Emperor Constantine's conversion Christianity became the official religion of the Roman Empire may have contributed to this process because, generally speaking, real piety was no longer the mark of the average Christian's lifestyle.

All this promoted the idea that, in one way or another, bread and wine were changed into Christ's body and blood. Where as at an early stage it was supposed that this happened by praying for the Holy Spirit — in the *epiclese* — at a later stage it was thought that the mere repetition of the words of institution by the priest resulted in this change.

In this respect the development in the Eastern and Western churches ran parallel in spite of all the further differences. In the Syrian Church the *epiclese* became a prayer for the change of the elements. In Jerusalem this was the same in the days of Cyrill (fourth century). Consequently the Eucharist received the character of a sacrifice. More and more the people abstained from the communion because of what is called "pious fear:" seeing the character of the sacrament they were scared to participate. It was deemed to be sufficient when one could observe the heavenly reality of Christ's body and blood being present. At Constantinople the situation was virtually the same in the days of Chrysostom (347-407). In the long run this ended up in the "sacred liturgy" of the Eastern Orthodox Church.

In the West the process started with Tertullian (appr. 160-220), who taught that in the bread of the Lord's Supper Christ was represented in the midst of the congregation. Cyprian used the term "offering:" wine mixed with water — representing respectively Christ's blood and the congregation — were offered to God just like Christ, at the institution of the Lord's Supper, offered bread and wine to God as a symbol of His imminent sufferings and death.

However, Ambrose (he died in 397) taught that, just like the prophet Elijah's word had power over the rain, Christ's Word is able to change bread and wine. Consecration takes place by repeating the words of institution — a matter of transfiguration, not yet of transubstantiation.

Augustine tried to slow down and reverse this process by teaching that the ingredients were only signs of Christ's body and blood, now being in heaven. He strongly emphasized the above mentioned *Sursum Corda*. Besides, the congregation is also herself Christ's body, offering herself to God in the Lord's Supper.

The development, however, could not be stopped. Since Christianity had become the official religion of the Roman Empire, a number of large Church centres became dominant. Their bishops adopted the imperial court ceremonial, the pope being considered at least to be the emperor's equal. Even the ordinary priests became more powerful. The concept of the Eucharist being a sacrifice offered by the Church to God gained more and more ground. A distinction, even a separation, was made between clergy and laity. Pope Gregory the Great (590-604) put some strong emphasis on the thesis that the Eucharist is a repetition of Christ's sacrifice.

Certainly, not everyone readily agreed with these ideas. This even led to a repeated controversy. Paschasius Radbertus' teachings that after consecration bread and wine are Christ's body and blood were strongly opposed by Hrabanus Maurus and Ratramnus, who taught that the elements remain what they are. Two and a half centuries later, at the end of the eleventh century, the struggle flared up again, when Berengarius of Tours publicly denied that the Eucharist is a sacrifice. In his opinion it was a commemoration of Christ's death, and no more than that. He had to retract that.

This means that the idea of the Lord's Supper being a sacrifice and the doctrine of transubstantiation emerged from the struggle as victors. The latter became an official dogma of the Church of Rome at the Fourth Lateran Council of 1215.

This had some consequences. No longer was participation in the communion essential to obtain a blessing. Small slices of unleavened bread, consecrated wafers, were put on the participant's tongue, for nothing of Christ's body should be lost. The cup was taken by the priest only, for the same reason. A new element in the liturgy — in the meantime called "Mass" — was introduced: the "Elevation" of the consecrated bread and cup. The leftovers were kept in a monstrans.

The Council of Trent (1545-63) confirmed this doctrine, adding anathemas to it. "Trent" was the council of the Counter-Reformation. It tried to protect the mass against the efforts of the Reformers to restore the Scriptural way of celebrating the Lord's Supper as found in the ancient Christian Church.

Even the Reformation was a matter of development. This is not the proper place to describe the various stages in which the Lord's Supper was given back to the Church. That there were differences between the Reformers may be a well known fact. Zwingli and John Calvin were more thorough and consistent in their reformative work than Martin Luther, who, for example, continued to speak of "the Mass," and maintained several elements of the *Missa Romana*. We as Reformed people enjoy the fruits of John Calvin's work in particular. The "final result" of it has been preserved in our Form for the Celebration of the Lord's Supper.

The history of the Form for the celebration of the Lord's Supper

That the reformative work of John Calvin is at the background of our Form may become clear from its history.

It was compiled in the Palatinate by Caspar Olevianus, who not only contributed to the publication of the Heidelberg Catechism but in the same year of its first edition, 1563, was entrusted with the compiling of a Church Order which included all the liturgical writings, prayers as well as forms.

However, the Form for the Lord's Supper was not exclusively Olevianus' work. He borrowed from the Form which John Calvin had written, from the London liturgy as described by Marten Micron, and also from the Lutheran Church Order of Wurttemberg 1536 and 1553 — which was based on that of Brandenburg-Nuremberg 1533. That certain sections of the Wurttemberg Form for the Lord's Supper return in our Form is no wonder. In her "Lutheran period" the Church of the Palatinate had adopted the Wurttemberg Church Order. When she adopted her own Order in 1556, it appeared to be based on that of Wurttemberg. Only at the end of the year 1563 a Church Order was adopted which had a more Calvinistic colour, but some Lutheran influences remained.

The Dutch refugees, under the guidance of Petrus Dathenus, were offered hospitality in the Palatinate on the condition that they would accept the same Church Order. This may explain why Dathenus translated many of the liturgical prayers and forms into Dutch, and soon afterwards took them with him to The Netherlands when he was able to return to his native country. The Dutch Churches took his Psalm version of 1566 into use, together with the liturgical writings added to it. In the course of time only minor alterations were made. The General Synod of Arnhem 1981 adopted a modernized Dutch version. Our Churches in Australia, Canada, and the U.S.A. use the English text as found in the *Book of Praise*.

Its text

After what we have been told in the chapter on the Form for the Public Profession of Faith it may not be strange to hear that in — and since — the "Schilders edition" of 1611 the title read: "Of the holy Supper of the Lord" (*Van het heylighe Avendmael des Heeren*), after which followed: "All these who . . ." (*Alle deghenen die . . .*). These were the directions for the examination of those who requested admission to the Lord's Supper. Since the Dutch Churches in 1923 adopted a Form for the Public Profession of Faith the liturgy books no longer include these directives. The title in the *Book of Praise* reads: "Form for the celebration of the Lord's Supper."

We can distinguish two main parts in the Form: a doctrinal or didactic section, and a ritual section respectively.

In the first section there is a reference to the institution of the sacrament by the Lord Jesus Christ. Two elements in Paul's description of this institution have been lifted out and are further explained: "Do this in remembrance of Me," and "Let a man examine himself." The latter is first elaborated on, for a number of paragraphs on the preparation of the Lord's Supper follow: Those who want to participate are urged to examine themselves with the help of the "three parts" well known from the Heidelberg Catechism. This section ends up in the so-called retention, whereby those who live in sin are warned not to participate, and others — in spite of their weaknesses — are encouraged to participate.

Most of this section goes back to John Calvin's Form. However, whereas it is clear that here the keys of the Kingdom of heaven are used, his formulation — "I hereby excommunicate those who . . ." has not been followed. The formula of retention has been borrowed from Micron's London liturgy.

Of special interest is the "catalogue of sins," or — even better — "sinners catalogue." We will deal with this separately below.

The *anamnesis*, the section that stimulates to indeed "do this" in remembrance of Christ, is from Olevianus himself. John Calvin's Form does not have it. It is clearly a product of the Reformation, because in the mass the *anamnesis*, together with the words of institution — which were supposed to consecrate the elements — was incorporated in the Canon, the Eucharist prayer. No longer is it a prayer but a proclamation of the great promises of the gospel. Here the relation with the gospel preaching — so characteristic of the Reformation — jumps to the fore.

The repetition of the words of institution has also been taken out of the communion prayer. Besides, these words are no longer considered as having consecrating power.

The paragraph which shows us the symbolism in the Lord's Supper is again from the hand of Olevianus. That about our communion with Christ and our communion with one another has been taken from the Wurttemberg Form. The figurative language of the one bread out of many grains and the one wine pressed out of many grapes is meant as an elaboration on what is quoted from I Corinthians 10:17, but is not in perfect harmony with these words of the apostle Paul. This may be the reason for the Dutch Churches having deleted this sentence in their recent revision of the Church service book. It is true, "the one bread" in Paul's saying is meant as an indication of the bread of the Lord's Supper which, according to the previous verse is "a participation in the body of Christ," and not a symbol of the unity of the congregation. Yet the apostle emphasises this unity when he says that "we who are many are one body." Therefore it is no wonder that already in the ancient Christian Church this metaphor was used: as many grains are gathered together, ground, and baked, and become one bread, so are the believers gathered together into one Church, being united with Christ into one body. We find this metaphor in the *Didache*, with Cyprian, Chrysostom, and Augustine. This sentence rests on a tradition in the ancient Christian Church. We can be glad that — unlike in the *Gereformeerd Kerkboek* of the Dutch sister Churches — it has been maintained in the text of the *Book of Praise*.

When the apostle Paul described the words of institution of the Lord's Supper, he added: "For as often as you eat this bread and drink the cup you proclaim the Lord's death until He comes." The last few words, "until He comes," put the celebration of the Lord's Supper in an eschatological perspective. We can be grateful that our Churches followed the example set by the Dutch Churches which on the occasion of their recent revision of the liturgical texts added a paragraph in which these words, "until He comes," are elaborated on. They give the attentive participants a foretaste of the great feast to come.

In the ritual part there is first of all the communion prayer, which, via John Calvin, we owe to the Strasbourg liturgy of Martin Bucer.

The Lord's Prayer, at the end, has from ancient times functioned as a preparatory prayer for the Lord's Supper. We will deal with its history in this function separately.

The words "Who taught us to pray" are a late addition. However, what is of greater importance is that it is to be regretted that in the *Book of Praise* the Lord's Prayer has been printed in brackets. From what we will read later on it may be clear that this shows a lack of "history mindedness," a lack of awareness that we are living in the communion of the Church of the ages. Why should this communion not come into the open by maintaining the good traditions of the Church of earlier days?

This communion prayer is preceded by a brief exhortation. This is another fruit of the Reformation. It replaces the *Offertorium* in the mass, whereby originally the ingredients for the common meal — later on all sorts of gifts, and still later money — were offered as a sacrifice to God. The true sacrifice which pleases God is that of a humble spirit. (We therefore rather abstain from using the word "Offertory" for the Church collections because this term has a certain historical background).

That the congregation professes her faith with the words of the Apostles' Creed in a separate act — and no longer, as was the case in older editions of the *Book of Praise*, in the context of the prayer — is an improvement. The nicest way to do this is to sing or recite it in unison. The Apostles' Creed replaces the Nicene Creed which is used in the

Roman mass, being recited between the Mass of the Catechumens and the Mass of the Faithful. Calvin put the Apostles' Creed at the very beginning, even before the actual Form was read. Its present place, however, is a more natural one: by confessing their faith with the Creed those who will participate in the Lord's Supper solemnly declare that they joyfully believe all that was explained to them in the Form: they indeed proclaim the Lord's death!

Then the *Sursum Corda* follows, of which some particulars were given when we dealt with the history of the Lord's Supper. We may add to this that John Calvin in his "Institutes" (IV 17, 36) refers to a custom in the ancient Christian Church "to call aloud upon the people to raise their hearts."

This element in our Form is another product of the Reformation — which includes a return to the Scriptural doctrine and traditions of the ancient Christian Church — because it replaces the worshipping of the consecrated ingredients. William Farel was the first one to have a *Sursum Corda* in his liturgy, *La Maniere et Fasson* of 1533. Apart from in the liturgy of the celebration of the Lord's Supper, it was also used in other parts of the liturgy. In the French speaking London congregation of refugees the minister invited the members to lift their hearts to God (*Leve le coeur*) before the singing of the Ten Commandments at the beginning of the service. In some Churches, for instance those who followed the East-Frisian liturgy, the words "Lift up your heart to God (or: to heaven)" were heard at the very end, before the Benediction was laid upon the congregation. (We cannot be very enthusiastic about using the *Sursum Corda* at the very beginning of our Church services, as an introduction to the Votum. For the Votum is a statement made on behalf of the congregation, and there is no direct relation between it and the *Sursum Corda*. We further presume that those who have started this new tradition were not aware of what happened in the French congregation of London, but that they introduced it because they have lifted the "announcements on behalf of the consistory" out of the actual liturgy, because they are considered not to fit in the "atmosphere" of the service. However, is there not a "legal" place in the second part of the service, before the intercessory prayer is said, for those announcements which cannot be included in the weekly bulletin? We would like to limit the use of the *Sursum Corda* to the celebration of the Lord's Supper. Using it elsewhere in the liturgy takes something from the impact it makes when it is used in the historical and natural context of the Lord's Supper.)

The formula of distribution has been taken from I Corinthians 10:16. In the original Palatine Form this was done at the advice of Philip Melanchthon. The use of Christ's own words, "This is My body" and "This cup is the new covenant in My blood," would undoubtedly have reminded all who heard them of the controversy between Lutherans and Calvinists, and therefore have damaged the unity of believers which was to be expressed by their common participation in this sacred meal.

The Synod of Emden 1571 allowed freedom in the use of such a formula of distribution, but added that the ministers should steer clear of suggesting a sort of consecration of the ingredients.

The words taken from I Corinthians 10 are followed by what is called the "London Appendix:" "Take, eat, remember and believe," etcetera. This formula was taken over by the Dutch Churches in their Synods of 1574 and 1578, although for some time the opinions continued to differ.

The line which says that during the communion some suitable portions of Scripture may be read and a Psalm or hymn be sung, was a bit more elaborate in older editions. They suggested chapters like Isaiah 53, and John 6, and 13-18. The singing of Psalm 34 was very much loved in the days of old, whereas Psalm 138 was a favourite song in the Church of Geneva.

The Synod of Emden 1571 left it to the freedom of the Churches to read from the Scriptures and sing a Psalm during the celebration of the Lord's Supper. "1574" mentioned I Corinthians 10 as a suitable chapter. Psalm 103 and parts of, respectively, Romans 8 and 5 act as an exhortation to the final thanksgiving prayer. In the Palatinate these two sections were divided by the word "Or" (*Oder*): one could use either the former or the latter. In The Netherlands both have been used from the very beginning.

Elements in the well-structured Post-communion prayer remind us of the liturgies of Strasbourg and Geneva.

As for the Form as a whole the Synod of The Hague 1586 stipulated that, whereas the sermon and the regular prayers must be delivered from the pulpit, the Form for the Lord's Supper shall be read from behind the Table!

The "catalogue of sins"

Dealing with the "catalogue of sins" or "sinners catalogue" separately, as we find it in the preparatory part of the Form for the Lord's Supper, we must first of all realize that it rests on a very old tradition. Already in the ancient Christian Church the example set by the apostle Paul, for example in Galatians 5, was followed. Such lists were used to sum up what were considered as "deadly sins." Tertullian mentioned apostasy or idolatry, murder and adultery as being such "deadly sins." Aurelius Augustine was of the opinion that there were more deadly sins, and therefore referred to the apostle Paul. According to Gregory the Great (330-379) theft, perjury, and desecration of graves also belonged in this category. Ambrose (340-97) added intemperance to this list.

Afterwards we find these lists in the directives for auricular confession, also called "confession mirrors." Since in the year 1254 auricular confession was made compulsory, these deadly sins must be confessed, lest one would die in them and perish forever.

These confessional formulas were also used in the Confiteor, the prayer said by the priest in preparation of the celebration of the mass. Already in the eighth century "catalogues of sins" were included in this prayer. However, at approximately the same time also some shorter formulas in the vernacular were used. This may have been the beginning — or otherwise a stimulant — of their transfer to the so-called *Offene Schuld*, another prayer spoken in preparation for the communion, in which the whole congregation confessed their sins. Here was the influence of Charlemagne, who made all sorts of arrangements to provide religious instruction to his subjects; they all had to know by heart the Ten Commandments, the Lord's Prayer, and the Apostles' Creed. Many of these prayers were in the first person singular, which proves that their formulation had been derived from the directives for auricular confession. It is no wonder therefore that in the prayers of the medieval "Preaching Service" or *Pronaus* (*Predigtdienst*) we sometimes find a long penitential meditation on the Ten Commandments, a "catalogue of sins." In the long run this "Preaching Service" became independent from the mass — to which it was meant originally to be a preparatory service, because many people in the South of Germany, the Eastern part of France, and in the North of Switzerland were no longer happy with the mass, which was celebrated in Latin, being merely a priestly affair which made the presence of the "laity" superfluous.

The Reformers strongly objected against the Roman Catholic compulsion of making a confession and the distinction between deadly sins and non-deadly sins. Nevertheless, Martin Luther maintained the auricular confession. In his directives for it we find a "catalogue of sins," although he was of the opinion that not too much attention should be given to all sorts of sins, because one's desire for absolution was most important.

John Calvin was of the opinion that it is impossible to sum up all our sins. There are, according to Psalm 19, also "hidden sins." Yet we shall know "how great our sins and misery are."

A feature of great significance in the Reformation was the fact that the old Confiteor was made into an essential part of the liturgy — instead of being of a preparatory character. In his liturgy of 1539 Martin Bucer, the Reformer of Strasbourg, included no less than three prayers in which sins were confessed. The second one was adopted by John Calvin for his 1542 liturgy, and has since then been known as "the prayer of Bucer and Calvin." We discussed it in the chapter on "Liturgical Prayers." The third of these prayers included a "catalogue of sinners."

Calvin inserted such a "catalogue" into his Form for the Lord's Supper. He followed therein the example of his older colleague William Farel, and in particular of the Reformer of Basel, John Oecolampadius, who in his Church Order of 1525 had such a catalogue in the context of the liturgy of the Lord's Supper and Church discipline, over against the Roman Catholic practice stating: "Only those shall be banned who are banned by God's Word, for as unhealthy and dead members they defame Christ's body."

Among the sins summed up in Oecolampadius' catalogue there were: the refusal to pay taxes, the refusal to let oneself be convinced from the Word of God in matters of faith, the sins of healthy and strong beggars who by their laziness are a burden on their neighbours, together with slanderers and those who suppress justice. Calvin had also: heretics and those who cling to heretic sects by which they break the unity of the Church, imperious persons, assassins, and gluttonous ones.

The recent revision in the Dutch Churches follows more closely the order of the Ten Commandments — as is also the case in the catalogue of the Form in the *Book of Praise*.

The Lord's Prayer in our Form

Already for a long time the Lord's Prayer as well has served as a preparatory prayer for the celebration of the Lord's Supper.

This was not as yet the case in the *Didache* — which ruled that this prayer must be said at least three times a day at fixed times. Even in Tertullian's commentary on the Lord's Supper, and that of his student Cyprian, it did not act as a communion prayer. However, the fact that both of them interpreted the "daily bread" of the fourth petition as Christ, "the Bread of Life," may have played a role in the process which led to this prayer being used in the context of the Lord's Supper.

We do not know exactly when for the first time the Lord's Prayer was given a place in the liturgy of the Eucharist, but it is certain that in the days of Cyrill of Jerusalem and Chrysostom of Constantinople it served as such. It was the first prayer repeated by adult converts immediately after their baptism and just before their first communion. This is most likely how it became a prayer in preparation of the communion in the Eucharist. For, just like Tertullian and Cyprian, Cyrill interpreted the fourth petition in a sacramental way.

Others, such as Ambrose, emphasized the first and fifth petitions as suitable for the communion preparation. Augustine pointed at the sixth petition because it reminds us of Christ's temptation in the Garden of Gethsemane as part of His sufferings. He gave us a picture of the situation at this point when he said: Almost the whole world finishes the Eucharist with the Lord's Prayer.

In the days of Pope Leo the Great the liturgy was extended: the respective petitions of the Lord's Prayer were paraphrased. Later on these so-called embolisms took the place of the doxology in the Roman Mass. Pope Gregory the Great (appr. 540-604) put the Lord's Prayer immediately before the *fractio panis*, the act of breaking the bread, and in this way connected it with the Eucharist prayer, the "Canon" of later days. He considered the Lord's Prayer to be most suitable for the consecration of the elements.

At a later stage it lost its function as a preparatory prayer for the communion. In the Church of Rome it was as such restored after the Second Vatican Council, held in the middle of this twentieth century. Earlier it was restored in this function by the Reformation. Martin Luther did so because the fifth petition in particular was very suitable as a public confession of sins made before one partook in the communion. Ulrich Zwingli used the Lord's Prayer in his liturgy of the Lord's Supper as a kind of retention formula, because it could prevent unrepentant persons from participating. Oecolampadius at Basel used it before the final admonition regarding participating. In his liturgy it was followed by a confession of sins and the proclamation of forgiveness, after which the communion was held. William Farel emphasized the fifth petition when his communion prayer ended with a confession of sin and the reciting of the Lord's Prayer. John Calvin also gave the Lord's Prayer a place in his Strasbourg liturgy, in this respect following the example of the liturgy of his German speaking colleague, Martin Bucer. He did the same in his Genevan liturgy of 1542, but at Geneva there was also the option of the congregational singing of this prayer. This may have led John Utenhove of the London Church to compose a metrical version of the Lord's Prayer, which for a long time was used in The Netherlands, even separate from the celebration of the Lord's Supper. It may also explain why among our hymns in the *Book of Praise* we have a similar metrical version, which, however, would be too long for use during the celebration of the Lord's Supper.

In the Palatinate it had a place in the Form for the preparation to the Lord's Supper — which preparation was held on the Saturday prior to the Sunday on which it was celebrated — and also in the Form for the administration of this sacrament itself.

Since Petrus Dathenus took this Form with him when he returned to The Netherlands, we owe it to him that the ancient tradition of ending our communion prayer with the words of the Lord's Prayer as a sort of *collecta* has been preserved in our Reformed Churches (that is to say: on condition that the brackets between which this prayer has been put in our *Book of Praise* are presently ignored, and in the next edition removed!). For, the Lord's Prayer is not only a suitable prayer for self-examination, but also — to say it together with Tertullian and Cyprian — because in it the whole gospel has been summarized as in a compendium!

Reformation

In our final attempt to sum up the points at which the reformation of the Lord's Supper is reflected in our Form, we can compile the following list:

- The automatism of the mass, whereby the participation of the congregation is no longer essential, has been replaced by thorough instruction from the Scriptures, taking its starting-point in its institution by Christ.

- Attention is no longer focussed on the elements and what is supposed to happen to them, but on the communion with Christ.

- The commemoration of Christ's sufferings and atoning death in the *anamnesis* is therefore no longer included in the communion prayer, but in the instruction given to the congregation.

- No consecrating power is allotted to the words of institution, but these words of institution are the starting-point of the "didactic part." They are as it were "the text of the sermon."

- No longer is the (optional) preaching as a preparation subservient to the mass, but the Scriptural relation between the preaching of God's Word and the administration of the sacraments has been restored: the gospel promises, proclaimed in the sermon, are signified and sealed in the Lord's Supper. The sacrament is "the visible Word."

- The concept of the Eucharist as a sacrifice offered to God, obvious for example in the *Offertorium*, has been replaced by the sacrifice of a humble spirit, an offering that, according to the Scriptures, pleases God.

- The number of symbolic acts and gestures has been reduced to the essentials. All attention is focussed on the distribution and communion.

- Instead of the "Elevation" of the ingredients and their subsequent being worshipped, the ancient traditions of the Lord's Supper have been restored by the Reformers, e.g. the *Sursum Corda*.

- No longer is the fourth petition of the Lord's Prayer dominant in its sacramental interpretation, or is this prayer included because any of the other petitions was deemed to be suitable as a preparation to the communion, but the whole of this prayer now serves as such.

The Abbreviated Form for the celebration of the Lord's Supper

The subtitle of this Form in the *Book of Praise* reads: "For the Second Service." This is not, however, the original purpose for which it was compiled.

This Form has been taken over from the Dutch sister Churches. In these Churches an early effort was made to adopt a brief Form, but the Synod of 1923 decided not to adopt the draft for a Form "for the second administration of it (the Lord's Supper) on the same day."

Another set of circumstances brought the proposal to the Synod of Bunschoten-Spakenburg 1958-59. An abbreviated Form was desired because some Churches wanted to celebrate the Lord's Supper more frequently. However, Synod was of the opinion that this desire was not sufficiently apparent in the Churches.

From among the Churches a similar request was made at the General Synod of Rotterdam-Delfshaven 1964-65. So many Churches had expressed their support for this proposal that Synod made arrangements to have such an abbreviated Form compiled. A draft was tabled at the Synod of Hattem 1972-73, and provisionally adopted. The Synod of Arnhem 1981 adopted its final text.

Since then our Churches are following the example of the Dutch Churches, which — contrary to its original purpose — use this Form for the "continuation" in the second service!

Almost every part of the longer Form has been abbreviated, which, for example, led to the deletion of the "catalogue of sinners" and of the use of the Lord's Prayer as a communion prayer. The *Sursum Corda* has been maintained.

5.3.5 FORMS FOR EXCOMMUNICATION AND READMISSION

Order

From the days when they were first printed — and this happened in the year 1590 — the Forms for excommunication of communicant members and for readmission have been given a place after the Form for the administration of the Lord's Supper. This is their natural place, because excommunication means exclusion from taking part in the celebration of this sacrament, whereas readmission to the community of the Church includes the right to participate in it.

However, unlike the service book of the Dutch sister Churches, *Gereformeerd Kerkboek* — which makes it the third one in a group of three — the *Book of Praise* has first of all the most recent of these disciplinary Forms, that of the excommunication of non-communicant members. It may have been given this place because baptism precedes the Lord's Supper.

Institution

The adoption and use of these Forms rests on the institution of Church discipline by the Lord Jesus Christ. Our Churches desire to obey His command and exercise the authority, given to them by the Saviour, to bind or loose (Matthew 18:18), to forgive or retain sins (John 20:23).

This was not an entirely new institution. Already the ancient Israelites had to exercise supervision over one another and, if necessary, to admonish one another (Leviticus 19:17). More than once we read about the ban being executed by capital punishment (Leviticus 24:10-23; Joshua 7:25). Even the rule that witnesses must be included in the procedure and the role to be played by special office bearers was not entirely new (Deuteronomy 19:15 and 26:18-29 respectively).

However, our Heidelberg Catechism clearly points to "the command of Christ" (Lord's Day 31, Q&A 84 and 85). This is also the case in our Belgic Confession of Faith (Articles 30 and 32). Obeying this command and honouring the institution of Church discipline is proof of acknowledging Jesus Christ as the only Head of the Church (Article 29 B.C.).

Consequently our Churches have adopted a set of rules for the administration of Church discipline in their Church Orders: the Canadian Churches in Articles 66-73, the Australian Churches in Articles 69-79, whereas the Three Forms are the liturgical expression of this obedience.

This is not the place for an exposition on the purpose and procedure of Church discipline. Our confessional standards and also our Church Orders explain its nature, aim, and methods. It may be clear, however, that Church discipline is to be exercised on doctrine as well as on lifestyle.

Church discipline in history

The ancient Christian Church used to be rather strict in the exercise of Church discipline. One of the problems she was confronted with was the readmission of those who after their baptism — as adults — had committed a serious sin and showed repentance: Could and should they be readmitted? In this context certain sins were mentioned: that of blaspheming God's name and of betraying the Church in days of persecutions. Later on also idolatry, adultery, and murder were added. We may remember the "catalogue of sins (or sinners)" from a previous chapter. The general idea was that readmission could be granted once only.

Soon afterwards this readmission was accompanied by a number of ceremonies, e.g. prostrating in front of an emotional bishop. This led to the introduction of a complete system of penance. The procedure of readmission included four different "steps:" on the first one the penitents had to stay outside the Church doors, while inside the congregation was praying for them; the next step was that they were allowed to come inside and listen to the sermon, but without being permitted to join in the prayers; the third step granted the penitents permission to stay after the departure of the catechumens and listen to the prayers said for them by the congregation; then they were allowed to attend the celebration of the Lord's Supper without, however, taking part in it. After these — long — preparations they were formally readmitted to the community of the Church.

At the end of the third century the figure of the special penitential priest came to the fore. In the long term this resulted in the replacement of the old penitential system by auricular confession. The priest became a kind of mediator between God and man, and the confession itself became a sacrament. The Fourth Lateran Council of 1215 made auricular confession compulsory.

The great principle to which the Reformation returned was that supervision and discipline was a matter for the whole congregation, which had to stand firm for the holiness of her own life and of the Lord's Supper. This was emphasized by John Calvin in particular. His efforts to preserve this holiness by reintroducing Church discipline led to his, and his older colleague William Farel's, expulsion from the city of Geneva in the year 1538. At Strasbourg, however, he was able to reestablish Church discipline. Before every celebration of the Lord's Supper every communicant member had to appear before the minister. People who remained ignorant were given further instruction, others were admonished, troubled ones were comforted, in some cases discipline was applied by denying them admission to the Lord's Supper. Soon after his return to Geneva, on January 2, 1542, Calvin introduced a new Church Order. It ruled that home visits had to be made before every administration of the Supper. Those who had committed a serious sin were denied admission.

Calvin's struggle against the libertine magistrates and others in the city of Geneva was a struggle for the Church's rights to excommunicate hardened sinners. The fact that it was won by him had some wide consequences for other Reformed Churches.

The story of the Forms

Neither at Geneva nor in the London congregation of Reformed refugees or in the Palatinate was a fixed Form for excommunication ever adopted. It took some decades before the Dutch Churches had compiled Forms for excommunication and readmission.

Then something remarkable happened: Whereas these Churches owed their liturgical Forms to the Palatine Churches, the latter adopted the Dutch Forms for Church discipline: They were published in the liturgy which was added to the German Bible translation by Piscator, professor of theology at Herborn.

The Convention of Wesel, 1568, issued some directives for the administration of Church discipline. These were based on Christ's command of Matthew 18. Special emphasis was put on the discipline to be administered upon the ministers of the Word, issuing a catalogue of sins which could not be tolerated as well as a list of sins which requested admonishing but no formal discipline. However, no Form was mentioned or compiled. The same must be said of the Synods of Emden 1571 and Dordrecht 1574 and 1578.

In the year 1681, however, the Synod of Middelburg adopted a Church Order which in Article 62 ruled that excommunication shall take place "according to the form adopted by the congregation." The word "form" does not necessarily refer to a certain liturgical Form for excommunication, because the Latin text speaks of an "order" accepted by the Churches. Anyhow, the Churches in the provinces of Zeeland and South Holland proposed that Synod would compile a Form for excommunication. Synod reacted to this proposal by referring to a certain Form used in the Churches. It even included the full text of this Form in its Acts. Although being considerably shorter than our present Form, it is nevertheless basic to it.

However, this was only an advice, not an adopted rule. Besides, this advice did not include anything about the readmission of penitent sinners. Therefore the National Synod of The Hague 1586 was asked — as its Acts formulate one of the "Particular Questions" — "if it would not be wise to use a fixed Form not only for the explanation (of Church discipline) and excommunication, but also for the acceptance, after confession of sins, of penitents." Unfortunately it is not clear whether Synod itself compiled them or mandated a committee to do so, but two Forms, respectively for excommunication and for readmission, were published in the year 1590. Marten Micron's *Christian Ordinances* served as a pattern.

After almost three and a half centuries the General Synod of Arnhem 1930 added to the first Form three "public admonitions," popularly called "the three steps" — which is an acceptable name if interpreted as indicating that step by step the congregation is more intensely involved in the battle against sin.

As for discipline administered to non-communicant members, this was already under discussion in the sixteenth century, but it was only at the General Synod of Sneek 1939 that a number of directives was adopted. On the other hand, the Synod of Groningen-Zuid 1978 adopted a Form for the excommunication of non-communicant members, preceded by two announcements (this title is a *contradictio in terminis*, but who will come forward with a better one?).

The same 1978 Synod adopted a modernized version of the other two Forms.

Structure

The structure of the two Forms for excommunication is fundamentally the same. First of all they explain why excommunication ought to take place in the case in question, then the official proclamation is made, after which the congregation is admonished and instructed about the Scriptural attitude to be shown to the person concerned, and finally a prayer is said. These Forms are preceded by the necessary public announcements.

As for the Form for readmission, first of all it informs the congregation that the preceding announcement has not resulted in any objections having been brought forward against readmission of the person concerned. A reference is then made to what Christ has taught about excommunication, repentance, and readmission. Then follows public confession of sin and repentance, preceding a solemn proclamation. The person concerned is addressed, so also is the congregation. A thanksgiving prayer concludes the procedure.

5.3.6 FORMS FOR ORDINATION OR INSTALLATION
The offices in Scripture

In this section our Reformed Church service book contains three Forms: the Form for the ordination (or installation) of ministers of the Word, the Form for the ordination (or installation) of missionaries, and the Form for the ordination of elders and deacons.

As for the elders, in the New Testament Church it appeared to be necessary to spread the workload over two different groups: they all had to rule the congregation, but some of them were set apart to labour in preaching and teaching (I Timothy 5:17), now being called ministers of the Word.

Some may trace back to the apostolic office the setting apart of a number of ministers for the preaching of the gospel to those who are outside, these ministers being called missionaries.

As for the deacons, their assignment was also originally a matter of the workload being spread (Acts 6:1-7).

The New Testament mentions some other special officers as well: evangelists (Acts 21:8; Ephesians 4:11; II Timothy 4:5) and prophets (Acts 11:27f; 13:1; 15:32; and other places).

(In the days of the "Church fathers" some widows were given a special position and task in the congregation, the so-called *viduate*. They had to care for the sick, give instruction to women who were interested in the Christian religion, and to assist at the baptism of female converts. This "office" was based on I Timothy 5:9f. John Calvin is said to have made a plea for its reintroduction. In some Dutch congregations it has indeed existed for some time. Also in England and "New England" efforts were made to restore this "office").

All these offices were the gifts of the glorified Jesus Christ, meant "to equip the saints for the work of ministry, for building up the body of Christ" (Ephesians 4:11f).

In our Forms the Scriptural origin of the offices still in existence is explained. The first Form, that of the ordination or installation of ministers, concentrates on the gift of "pastors and teachers." In the Bible we do not read about a direct institution by the Lord Jesus. It says that the apostles appointed elders in every Church, and the Form explains that they did so under the guidance of the Holy Spirit. For the first time we hear about elders in Acts 11:30. Soon afterwards the spreading of the workload, and consequently the distinction, must have been made between ministers (teaching and ruling elders) and elders (ruling elders) (I Timothy 5:17).

The ordination or installation of missionaries is based on the gift of the Holy Spirit, and His command to the Church to set men apart for the spreading of the gospel (Acts 13:2).

As for the offices of the ruling elders, our Form refers first of all to the Old Dispensation, when in the days of Moses the elders of Israel were given the Law to rule the people. The Lord Jesus had this practice continued as it were when He let the apostles appoint elders in every Church.

The office of the deacons also has its roots in the Old Testament, as our Form explains. For "the Lord impressed upon His people Israel the obligation to show mercy to the needy." Even this was fulfilled by the Lord Jesus, not only when He Himself showed mercy by feeding the hungry, healing the sick, and showing compassion to the afflicted, but also by giving deacons to the Church, again under the guidance of the Holy Spirit in that particular situation.

A special point in this context is the ordination of these office bearers. In accordance with an Old Testament tradition (Deuteronomy 34:9), it seems that this ceremony was performed — at least sometimes — by the laying on of hands (I Timothy 4:14; II Timothy 1:6). This is understood by some as the symbolic act of transferring the Holy Spirit — as in the Roman-Catholic "sacraments" of confirmation and the ordination of priests. However, the gift of the Holy Spirit is conditional to being eligible to serve in one of the offices (Acts 6:3, and the prayer in the Form for the ordination of elders and deacons).

The offices in Church history

It was not long before the apostolic word was neglected which says that the offices in the Church are meant to equip the saints and to upbuild the body of Christ. Hierarchy crept slowly into the life of the Church. The *episcopos*, who had been entrusted with "overseeing" the life of the Church and her members, became the "bishop." The development of his position into a monopolistic one ran parallel with the decay in the administration and celebration of the Lord's Supper. As an illustration we refer to Ignatius of Antioch (69-107), who in a letter to the Church of Smyrna wrote: "No one in Church shall do anything without the consent of the bishop. One shall count as valid the celebration of the Eucharist which takes place under the guidance of the bishop or of those to whom he has transferred it. (. . .) Without the bishop('s presence) baptizing or partaking in a love-meal is not allowed."

This development led to the distinction between clergy and laity, to the celibacy of the clergy, and the position of ordinary priests and deacons as assistants of the bishop in the celebration of the mass: a bishop's mass, let alone a papal mass, is superior. From the office of bishop were developed those of the archbishop, of the cardinal, and of the pope. Later on the order was reversed: it was claimed that the pope is Christ's vicar, and the cardinals, archbishops, and bishops derive their authority from him.

The laying on of hands became a sacrament. According to Augustine it was on a level with baptism. In the Church of Rome the administration of this "sacrament" is the prerogative of the bishop.

Over against this the Reformers stated that the ordination of office bearers is not a sacrament but a public ceremony of putting them into their respective offices. The laying on of hands takes place only when a minister is ordained — not installed in a different congregation.

In the Dutch Churches there was even some hesitation introducing this ceremony. The Provincial Synod of Dordrecht 1574 decided against it because of the danger of superstition and of identifying it with the Roman Catholic "sacrament." The next Provincial Synod of South Holland, 1575, was of the opinion that it would be better to refrain from it "in these days," i.e. for the time being. The National Synod of Dordrecht 1578 left it to the discretion of the Churches to choose between the laying on of hands and the giving of "the right hand of communion." "Middelburg 1581" decided in favour of the laying on of hands, which could be done, if necessary, in the consistory or at a classis. The Synod of The Hague 1586 decided to return to the early practice and advice of the Convention of Wesel 1568, which deemed the laying on of hands to be good for the ordination of ministers, and to be optional for elders. The Synod of Emden 1571 was in favour of this ceremony, but with the reservation that it should be performed "without any superstition or necessity," the former pointing to "Rome," the latter stating that the ceremony was not essential.

It may be clear that the Reformed Churches followed the footsteps of John Calvin who restored the office of elders, and reintroduced the "presbyterial system" of Church government. He also reformed the office of the deacons. Every office bearer had to contribute to the equipping of the saints and the upbuilding of the body of Christ. The Reformed concept of the Church offices is anti-hierarchical. All this is clearly expressed in our Forms of ordination or installation.

The story of the Forms

As for the ordination of office bearers Petrus Dathenus could not serve the Dutch Churches by importing something from the Palatinate. The

Church Order of the Church in that country did not contain anything on the ordination of office bearers. It just mentions *Kirchendiener* and *Diaconos*. This means that the Dutch Churches had to find their own ways and means.

During the days of persecution not every congregation had a consistory. Many ministers had not been properly trained, examined, and ordained. However, as soon as it was possible the Churches made all sorts of arrangements to come to an orderly Church life.

The first occasion to do so was the Convention of Wesel, 1568. This meeting did not produce any Form, but issued a number of directives for the ordination of ministers, elders, and deacons. The Synod of Emden 1571 stated that those ministers who refused to be properly ordained as yet, had to be considered and treated as schismatics. Ordination had to take place with prayers and the laying on of hands. At their ordination the elders were instructed in the duties of their office, and had to promise that they would fight against sins like idolatry, blasphemy, heresy, and leading an excessive life.

Even the "liturgical Synod" of Dordrecht 1574 did not produce a Form. A distinction was made between "newcomers" and those who had already served in a different congregation; the former were ordained "with longer admonitions and stipulations," the latter were installed "with shorter admonitions and stipulations." Those who had not been properly ordained must as yet be examined by classis and ordained. This synod also issued some directives for the ordination of elders and deacons. The next synod, that of Dordrecht 1578, and the 1581 Synod, held at Middelburg, confirmed all this. They formulated three questions for the ordination of ministers, based on the work of à Lasco and Micron.

The Synod of The Hague 1586 inserted into its Church Order an article on the calling of ministers who had not yet served before. It mentioned the requirements of election, examination, approbation, and ordination. This ordination should be carried out "with proper stipulations, questions, exhortations, a prayer, and the laying on of hands," all this "according to the appropriate Form." The same reference to a Form is made in the articles on the ordination of elders and deacons. It is not clear whether Synod itself compiled these Forms, or mandated a committee to do so. However, in the year 1590 they were included in the liturgical writings which were printed in the back of the Dutch Bible, and in the next year after the metrical Psalm version by Marnix of St. Aldegonde.

The great National Synod of Dordrecht 1618-19 confirmed all this.

The Churches of the Palatinate and also the Wallonian (French-speaking) Churches in The Netherlands adopted these Forms.

More than three and a half centuries later the General Synod of Hattem 1971-73 added a Form for the ordination or installation of missionaries. Thereby it replaced another Form adopted by the Dutch Churches in the beginning of this century, at the Synod of Arnhem 1902. However, this Form remained almost completely unknown; we have never seen its text included in a Church service book.

The Synod of Kampen 1975 adopted rewritten Forms for the ordination of ministers, elders and deacons, because the Churches were of the opinion that the old Forms showed a number of weaknesses.

Our Churches

Our own Churches have adopted the same Forms in translation. Some paragraphs and sentences have been abbreviated or even omitted. References to Scripture texts have sometimes been changed into full quotations. Most amendments have been made in the Form for the ordination of elders and deacons, in which the Scriptural foundation has been expanded (pages 629 and 631 of the *Book of Praise*). In all these Forms the third and fourth questions of the Dutch original have been combined, and the Lord's Prayer — acting as a *collecta* — has been left out.

5.3.7 FORM FOR THE SOLEMNIZATION OF MARRIAGES

Marriage in history

The Old Testament does not give us any indications of the way in which marriages were solemnized. It seems to be purely a family affair, as confirmed, for example, by the story of Samson's marriage in Judges 4.

The apocryphal book Tobias contains an illustration of how the marriage ceremony took place in the days of the exile and after. It tells us that, after young Tobias had formally requested his uncle Raquel for permission to marry the latter's daughter Sarah, Raquel took her hand and laid it into Tobias' hand, saying: "The God of Abraham, the God of Isaac, the God of Jacob be with you both and may help you, richly blessing you." Then they took a letter and wrote down the marriage-contract. After a meal Sarah's parents led Tobias into their daughter's room (Tobias 7:10-8:1).

Whereas it is not known whether this was a fixed custom among the Jews of those days, this story may explain the original meaning of joining right hands: the father gave away "this woman."

Also the New Testament is silent on the actual marriage ceremony. Neither the story of the marriage feast at Cana (John 2) nor the parable of the ten virgins (Matthew 25), or any other story, gives us the particulars of the way in which marriage formally came into being.

The Christians of the apostolic and post-apostolic era maintained the traditions of their environment. In the centuries of the Roman Empire the rules of law of the empire were obeyed, one of them being that the mutual consent of the two parties was the ground on which a marriage came into existence: this consensus "made" the marriage.

For the believers two other aspects played a role as well. The first one was the biblical concept that "becoming one flesh" was the consummation of marriage, the other that they, as Christians, realized themselves to be under the supervision of the Church. This gave Ignatius of Antioch (early second century) reason to rule that the marriage state should not be entered into without the consent of the bishop.

In the Western Church there were some ancient German influences, for example the tradition that marriages were solemnized in the presence of a few witnesses, and that the father gave away his daughter — the *traditio puellae* — by laying her right hand into that of the bridegroom.

One of the witnesses became a man of significance, seeing his position in the local community: the priest. He soon afterwards took over from the father. At a later stage he was even no longer supposed to be the father's representative but to act on behalf of the Church. This led to the idea that neither the family nor the bridal couple performed the act of "making" a marriage, but that the Church was doing so. This became the official doctrine of the Church under Pope Alexander III (1159-81).

This also led to the reversing of the traditional order whereby first the bridal couple started to live together and on the next day went to the priest to have their marriage blessed by him. From then on the ceremony in Church had to be performed first.

Marriage then became a twofold ceremony. The first part took place outside the Church, in front of the Church doors, whereby the priest, after having heard the solemn vows, pronounced bridegroom and bride husband and wife, at the same time laying their right hands together. Then he led them inside in front of the altar, and celebrated a nuptial mass, which included prayers for the bridal couple and a blessing.

In the meantime marriage had been declared to be a sacrament. This was officially confirmed by the Council of Trent, which in Canon I "on the sacrament of matrimony" stated: "If any one says, that matrimony is not truly and properly one of the seven sacraments of the evangelical law, instituted by Christ the Lord; but that it has been invented by men in the Church; and that it does not confer grace: let him be anathema." This conferring of grace was deemed to be essential because marriage is considered by the Church of Rome as belonging to natural life and therefore affected by sin: also in married life husband and wife need supernatural grace, which is given in a sacrament only.

The same Council of Trent reserved the solemnization of marriages to the Church — on the same ground: that it is a sacrament — rejecting the idea that the civil government had anything to do with it. Canon XII reads: "If any one say, that matrimonial causes do not belong to ecclesiastical judges: let him be anathema."

The Reformation rejected the concept of marriage being a sacrament. However, the solemnization of marriages remained in the hands of the Church, for this reason also that the governments were unwilling to take this ceremony upon themselves.

Martin Luther abolished the Roman nuptial mass, replacing it by Scriptural instruction and a benediction. However, he was of the opinion that marriage had been established just as soon as the persons concerned promised to be faithful to each other — which happened at their "engagement." Therefore it was a "worldly affair," becoming public during the ceremony performed in front of the Church doors.

At Strasbourg John Calvin found the following order: The vows taken by the bridal couple were made public, after which in Church a prayer was said and a blessing laid upon bridegroom and bride, as an "introduction" to their actual married life. John Calvin adopted this concept. In his opinion the government should solemnize and register marriages, and the Church restrict herself to a prayer and a blessing.

In The Netherlands Gisbertus Voetius propagated similar ideas. According to him marriage was a "political" affair, and the Church's role was only that of praying for the newly-wed and laying a blessing upon them.

However, these ideas did not become commonly accepted. On the contrary, the two different acts explained above were amalgamated into one single act: the Church was seen to solemnize marriages.

From the side of the civil government there was no initiative to come to a right understanding of its own position and responsibilities in this respect. This in spite of the efforts undertaken by several synods of the sixteenth century and also by the National Synod of Dordrecht 1618-19, which made it clear that the actual legalizing and registering of marriages was the State's responsibility.

Things changed after the French Revolution. This resulted in a separation of Church and State. Consequently in the province of Holland marriages were solemnized by the government from the year 1795, and this became law for the whole of The Netherlands in 1809.

Since then the Dutch practice is that the official marriage solemnization is performed by the government, after which the so-called "marriage confirmation" in Church follows.

In several countries, however, the government continued to acknowledge the right of the Church to solemnize marriages on their behalf. In this respect the French Revolution did not affect Great Britain, and subsequently its — now former — colonies, the U.S.A., Canada, and Australia!

The history of the Form

Not many people, including many scholars, are aware of the fact that it was not John Calvin but his older colleague and friend William Farel who wrote the first really Reformed Form. Calvin apparently saw no reason for making improvements in it. Therefore he simply adopted the Form which was included in Farel's *Maniere et Fasson* of 1533, and reprinted it literally in his 1542 liturgy, *La Forme des Prieres* . . .

In view of the developments of later days it may be useful to take a bird's eye view of Farel's Form. First of all there is an introduction, which refers to the institution of marriage by God the Creator, rejecting the papal rules regarding dispensation in certain cases of consanguinity, and stipulating that married life should not be entered into without the consent of the parents of both parties: they "give away" their son or daughter. In order to prevent deceit an announcement shall be made to the congregation on two or three successive Sundays, lest there be an objection or obstacle in the meeting of the congregation on the wedding day. Then the actual

Form follows, starting with the well known "Votum" of Psalm 124. The next section contains biblical instruction on God's institution and the married people's responsibilities. After this instruction a ritual section follows, in which the bridal couple is asked first of all whether they desire to live in accordance with what they have just heard, and want the congregation's approval. The bridal couple's vows are then taken, by their answer to the question as to whether they have taken and do take each other as wife or husband and solemnly promise to live in the married state in full obedience to God's Word, His holy gospel. After their affirmative answer the minister pronounces a benediction, wishing them the gift of the Holy Spirit. Some more instruction from the Scriptures follows: the bond of marriage is firm and unbreakable, according to Matthew 19. God Himself has joined the bridal couple together. The ceremony ends with a prayer, from which the "old" Dutch Form — for a number of years also used in our own Churches — has derived several passages, and with another benediction, reading: "Our Lord replenish you with all grace, and grant you a long and holy life in all good things. Go in peace. God be always with you. Amen" — even our current Form has part of this final sentence in common with this ancient Form.

It may be clear, Farel and Calvin really reformed the ceremony: the nuptial mass was replaced by biblical instruction. Important also is that the Church abstained from making an official statement whereby it was declared that bridegroom and bride were pronounced husband and wife. They themselves, and not the Church, "made" their marriage, by taking solemn vows in the meeting of the congregation which acted as witnesses.

Another aspect is the formulation "have taken and take." This refers to respectively the "engagement" when for the first time the two young people promised to love each other, and to the vow taken at this very moment on the wedding day. Later on — for some centuries in the Dutch Churches, and in our own Churches for some decades — this was misinterpreted as applying to what had just happened before the representatives of the government, and to what happens in Church.

As for what follows after the vows have been taken, the reference to Matthew 19, which shows "how firm the bond of marriage is," is intended to underline that the marriage is now indeed a matter of fact.

Although at several places the Form by Farel and Calvin reminds us of the "old" Form which was used for some centuries, it was not integrally adopted by the Dutch Churches — and consequently for some years by our own Churches. For when Petrus Dathenus in the year 1566 was able to publish his Dutch metrical Psalter and liturgy, after Margareth of Parma as the governess on behalf of the Spanish king proclaimed freedom of religion for the Low Countries, it appeared that he had taken with him the Form as used by the Churches of the Palatinate. However, the fact that this Form had some passages in common with Farel's Form, is explained by the influence not only from the former London refugee Church but also from Geneva. Indeed, the Palatine Form is a compilation of elements taken from both the Genevan and the London Forms, with a few "original" additions. The exposition of God's institution is from Farel-Calvin, the reference to the Cana-marriage of John 2 is from Marten Micron. He also provided the explanation of the "purpose" or "causes" of marriage. However, the emphasis put on the necessity of avoiding fornication and adultery is again from the Genevan Form. The section which explains how husband and wife have to behave toward each other is almost wholly Farel-Calvin. The address and the intercessory prayer are a mixture: here Marten Micron had already taken over something from the Genevan Form. The reference to the promise of Psalm 128 is an addition made by the Palatine Churches themselves.

In the original version of the Dutch Form — more on which is given below — the very first sentence started with a reference to all sorts of miserable things that may be experienced in married life. This, too has been derived from the London Form. However, the Palatine Churches took this out of its original context. In the London Form it said: "Since, as a result of sin, usually all kinds of adversity and cross can befall upon married people, the holy married state is in this world held in contempt by many." This clearly pointed to the Roman Catholic doctrine and practice of celibacy. Taking it from its context — even after it was given a different place later on — it unnecessarily gives the Form a somewhat sombre note.

It may be superfluous to refer to some passages which Dathenus deleted from the Palatine Form. No longer was — and is — the congregation called upon as witnesses of the vows taken by the bridal couple. This may have contributed to a shift of emphasis from what the bridal couple are doing to what the minister is doing. This shift is even stronger in our current Form, when — in accordance with the requirements of civil law — the solemn statement is made: "I now pronounce you husband and wife."

This may be too dominant compared with the vows which really "make" the marriage, being taken by the bridal couple.

As for The Netherlands, when in the year 1566 Dathenus could publish his Church service book, his Marriage Form was taken into use without a formal synodical decision. Only later on, at Dordrecht 1574 and 1578, Middelburg 1581, and The Hague 1586, official references to Dathenus' liturgy were made.

At the same time these synods stated that the formal solemnization and registration of marriages was the responsibility of the civil government. They asked for a consultation with the authorities, but without any success. This necessitated the Churches continuing with the current practice, which meant that the official ceremony whereby marriages became legal took place in Church. In the Form this was expressed by the double statement of having taken and taking each other as husband and wife.

The Synod of Dordrecht 1618-19 amended the Form in a few places. Most of them were of minor importance. However, when the phrase "before the Christian congregation" was replaced by "publicly here in Church," it may be that this led to the loss of the idea that the congregation acted as witnesses.

For some centuries the situation remained the same. Even when marriage solemnization before the magistrate was made obligatory in the year 1809, the Form remained the same, complete with the double "have taken and do take." Classis Winschoten in 1816 even proposed to the General Synod that the latter would urge the government to abolish the civil solemnization of marriages and return the ceremony to the Church, but this proposal was not accepted.

As for the twentieth century, in 1935 the General Synod of the *Nederlands Hervormde Kerk* (Dutch Reformed Church) was requested to revise the Form because the Church was no longer living under the persecutions during which the Form was compiled. Only when this Church adopted a new service book, it appeared that a choice could be made from no less than four different Forms.

As for the Reformed Churches, at their General Synod of Leeuwarden 1920 a number of provincial synods made a request for a revision of the Form. They were of the opinion that it no longer applied in a situation where civil marriage solemnization was compulsory, where changes had to be made in view of marriages of older people, and where the "causes" for the institution of marriage by God were not in full conformance with the Bible. Synod appointed some deputies, who tabled a draft at the next synod, that of Utrecht 1923. However, it was not adopted. The General Synod of Groningen 1927 and that of Arnhem 1930 saw the same item on their agenda. The latter adopted another provisional draft of a revised Form and this was made final at the Middelburg 1933 General Synod.

One of the changes must have our special attention. It was made in the announcement, to be made in Church prior to the actual ceremony. From 1566 it included the information that the bridal couple "desires a Christian prayer of the whole congregation." From 1933 this was replaced by the words: "They have requested confirmation (of their marriage) in Church." At the background of this change lies Abraham Kuyper's theory of the "two territories" of "common grace" and "particular grace." The term "marriage confirmation" was reintroduced, in the sense now of confirming, by an official act of the Church in the territory of "particular grace" of what previously had taken place before the magistrate on the territory of "common grace." The civil ceremony was considered for Christians not to constitute a Christian marriage! In our Churches we may be thankful that we no longer have to deal with the exegesis of the term "marriage confirmation."

As for The Netherlands this "problem" was not solved when the General Synod of Hattem 1972-73 was requested to make arrangements for a revision of Article 70 of the Church Order. The Church at Vrouwenpolder was of the opinion that this article was not Scripturally founded when it stated that it was "proper" (*behoorlijk*) that marriages were confirmed in Church. This Church proposed to replace the "confirmation" with a prayer on the Sunday after the marriage ceremony had taken place. Together with this Church Synod was of the opinion that the government did indeed have the responsibility of declaring a marriage constituted, and that the ceremony in Church should not be a kind of repetition. But at the same time she wanted to maintain the special character of the confirmation and its purpose and meaning should be formulated in a clearer and richer way. Deputies were appointed, who reported to the Synod of Kampen 1975 — which adopted a revised Form to be tested by the Churches. One of the changes was that the purpose of marriage was restored into a threefold one: the 1933 Synod had removed the third purpose, taken over from William Farel and John Calvin who had emphasized God's desire that fornication should be prevented. Another change was that a dubious interpretation of Genesis 3:16 — regarding the position of the wife toward her husband — was no longer maintained.

This revised Form was not received enthusiastically in the Churches. Many objections were raised. At the Groningen-Zuid Synod of 1978 the deputies concerned evaluated many of these objections as containing valuable elements. Synod appointed new deputies. Their report was discussed at the General Synod of Arnhem 1981, which resulted in the adoption of a Form which shows considerable improvement in structure, contents, and formulation.

Our Churches

It is remarkable that our own Churches make use of a revised Form that is based virtually on the since replaced Dutch Form from the year 1975.

The story reads as follows: The *Book of Praise* in its editions of 1961 to 1972 contained a translation of the "old" Dutch Form of the year 1933. The Synod of Coaldale 1977 had to discuss a request from among the Churches not only to have the Marriage Form retranslated into present day English, but also to have it revised, and, where necessary and possible, shortened. Criticism had been raised, for example when the Form called it an "ordinance of God" that "the desire of the woman shall be to her husband and that he shall rule over her." This could also be interpreted as a punishment for Eve because she had tempted her husband.

At the next General Synod, that of Smithville 1980, the appointed deputies reported. The discussion resulted in, amongst others, the following consideration: "Synod is now presented with a major revision along the lines of the new form presently in use in our Netherlands sister-churches. Contrary to the present Dutch Form, there is more emphasis in this revision on the seriousness of divorce and the subjection of the wife to the husband." The Recommendation that "Synod decide to adopt the Revised Form for the Solemnization of Marriages, as amended by Synod," was adopted.

However, there are some differences between this Form and the Dutch version which was replaced in 1981. The announcement of 1933 had been restored — as is also the case in the Dutch Churches since 1981 — except, of course, the reference to "marriage confirmation." The reference to the institution of marriage by God is a little longer, consisting of a literal quotation from Scripture. It is strongly emphasized that God hates divorce and immorality. The promise for those who live in the fear of the LORD, taken from Psalm 128, has been formulated in stronger terms. The third purpose of married life — Farel and Calvin's purpose: prevention of fornication — has been deleted. In the vows the word "take" refers to what is happening at the very moment: marriage solemnization. For our situation and according to the requirements of law the statement is added: "I now pronounce you husband and wife." The Lord's Prayer has been made optional.

Solemnization or confirmation?

The history as we have briefly related resulted in the maintaining of the term "confirmation" in the Dutch churches, and in the practice based on the current — but not original — interpretation of this word.

The situation in the migrant Churches of the English speaking countries was originally the same, at any rate as long as worship services in the Dutch language were held. However, in the 1961 edition of the *Book of Praise* the Marriage Form was based on "solemnization": It already included the statement: "I now pronounce you husband and wife." This was not adopted immediately by the Australian Churches. Their 1964 Synod left the choice between solemnization and confirmation, as may be proven by the then adopted text of their Church Order. The 1966 Synod left it to the discretion of the local Churches as to whether the solemnization would take place in a worship service or in a private ceremony — which indicates that solemnization was becoming common practice in these Churches. However, the option of marriage confirmation in a worship service was still kept open in their Church Order, until the latter was revised at the Kelmscott 1983 Synod.

Article 63 of the Canadian Church Order gives the options of marriage solemnization "either in a private ceremony or in a public worship service."

6. CHURCH ORDER

Character and purpose

Our Belgic Confession of Faith, in Articles 27 to 29 having explained what the Church is, continues in Article 30 with a sentence that gives a clear indication of the necessity to have a sound Church Order. It says: "We believe that this true Church must be governed according to the Spiritual order which our Lord has taught in His Word."

At the end the same Article refers to Paul's statement made in I Corinthians 14:40, which says: "Let all things be done decently and in order."

A Church Order moves even more clearly into our field of vision when in Article 32 we read: "We believe that although it is useful and good for those who govern the Church to establish a certain order to maintain the body of the Church, they must at all times watch that they do not deviate from what Christ, our only Master, has commanded." This sentence raises the possibility that even with a Church Order of the highest quality Church leaders may act in a hierarchical way. But in the meantime it maintains: a good Church Order is needed and is beneficial to Church life.

The same thought was expressed when in the year 1561 a document was published for the Reformed Church at Geneva, called *Ordonnances Ecclesiastiques*, ecclesiastical ordinances, a Church Order. In its Introduction it says that: "the doctrine of the holy Gospel of our Lord shall be preserved in its purity, and that the Christian Church be maintained by a sound government and police, and that also the youth be well and faithfully instructed in the things which have to be done (. . .) and which cannot be done without a certain fixed rule and manner, from which everyone can learn the duty of his particular office. Therefore it seemed to be useful that the spiritual government which our Lord has shown us and has instituted by His Word, would be moulded in a good form, so that it would have a place among us and be observed by us."

We are convinced that — though not being perfect — the Church Orders adopted respectively by the Free Reformed Churches of Australia and the Canadian Reformed Churches comply with these Scriptural requirements.

Historical roots

When in our Confession we state that our Lord has taught us a Spiritual order (Article 30) and that we must watch not to deviate from what Christ our Master has commanded (Article 32), we do not mean to say thereby that He has left us a complete Church Order. It is true that He gave some directives for the gospel preaching (Matthew 10:7; 28:19), the administration of the sacraments (Matthew 28:19; I Corinthians 11:24-6), Church discipline (Matthew 18:15-20; John 20:23; I Corinthians 5), and even regarding the preacher's livelihood (Matthew 10:10), but these directives do not constitute a comprehensive Church Order.

When the apostle Paul in I Corinthians 14:40 tells us that all things should be done decently and in order, we are a bit closer to such a document, although this admonition is of a very general, non-specific character. We move still closer to the Pastoral Epistles, I and II Timothy and Titus, sometimes called "an apostolic Church Order."

Such an Order had to "grow," to be developed in the course of time. This was the case in the early centuries of the Christian Church. We can observe the same phenomenon after the Reformation. It had to "grow" from decisions taken by ecclesiastical assemblies in matters with which they were confronted.

Certainly, gifted Church leaders also, together with the documents which they left behind, played a prominent role in this process. The oldest one in this series is the *Didache* or *The Teachings of the Twelve Apostles*, written by an unknown author at the end of the first or the beginning of the second century. (This document has been mentioned more than once already in previous chapters).

A remarkable feature is that the *Didache* begins with an exposition of the doctrine and practice of the "two ways," and that only after this instructive and pastoral section a second part follows on Church life, dealing with topics such as fasting, baptism, prayer, the love-meals and the Lord's Supper, and the offices. As we can see, it is a doctrinal, pastoral, liturgical, as well as Church-political document.

Another document deserving our attention is the *Didascalia Apostolorum*, originating from Syria in the mid third century. It includes parts of the *Didache*, but deals also with the election and ordination of bishops, priests, and deacons, the instruction of the catechumens, the layout of Church buildings, the liturgy, and days of fasting.

The *Didache* was copied in its full extent in the *Apostolic Constitutions* — later on also called *Canones Apostolici*. This document was also written in Syria, although not before the end of the fourth or the beginning of the fifth century. It is attributed to Clemens Romanus. Its first six "books" are based on the *Didascalia Apostolorum*, the seventh is partly an adaptation of the *Didache*, containing a series of prayers, directives for the catechumenate, baptism and confirmation, and songs of praise. The eighth "book," dealing with the election and ordination of bishops, festive days, and morning and evening prayers, reminds us of another important document, Hippolytus' *Apostolic Traditions*, also called the *Egyptian Church Order*, written at Rome in the first half of the third century. It was directed against a renewal movement which was guided by Pope Zefyrinus and Pope Calixtus, pleading for the preservation of the traditional liturgy and the apostolic institutions.

All these documents can be called early Church orders.

At the time when the *Apostolic Constitutions* were written, several synods and councils had already been held or would be convened in the near future. The decisions and acts of these assemblies contributed to the process. Some persons compiled them into collections, as e.g. the *Decretum Gratiani*, in 1143 written by Gratianus, bishop of Bologne.

Under the great popes Gregory IX, Boniface VIII, and Clemens V these collections were considerably enlarged, and the study of "Canon Law" started to flourish.

This can be called a more or less "natural" development. After Emperor Constantine proclaimed Christianity as the official religion of the Roman Empire, the Church had to consider the nature and extent of her position in the midst of the world. This led to the development of the "Canon Law," with its rules and regulations for marriage, hereditary right, Church property, etcetera.

A very important aspect is that Augustine's book *De Civitate Dei* (the City of God) strongly influenced this development: he distinguished between the "divine State," a theocracy, and the worldly kingdoms, the former being supreme. A by-product of this development is the medieval doctrine of the "two swords": the pope is entitled to carry the swords of Church government and civil government. It is no wonder that the final documentation of this development in the *Corpus iuris canonici* of 1483 included rules for taxes and other purely material matters.

The Reformation flatly rejected the claim made by the Church of Rome that it was the supreme power in spiritual as well as material, ecclesiastical as well as civil affairs.

When Martin Luther, on December 10, 1520, burned the papal bull, this document was followed into the fire by a copy of the Canon Law. It was, however, regrettable that he had to request the assistance of the civil rulers of some regions whom he formally appointed as "emergency bishops." In the Lutheran Church Orders, e.g. that of Braunzweig, written by Bugenhagen in 1528, of Nuremberg, from the hand of Osiander (1533), and of Cologne, compiled by Melanchthon, Von Wied, and Bucer (1543), the governing of Church life is left to the civil government, which was in authority of the liturgy, the honoraria of ministers, marriage, Church discipline, schools, the caring for the needy, etcetera.

John Calvin pushed the Canon Law aside, returning to the teachings of the Scriptures. From them he developed the presbyterial-synodical system of Church government. Certainly, the civil government had its task to protect the Church, but it had no authority whatsoever over her life. Church and State each had their own jurisdiction, Christ Jesus is the universal Bishop and the only Head of the Church (Article 31 Belgic Confession).

Later on the relation between Church and State once again became an issue in the controversy between Arminians and Reformed.

As a result of the *Aufklärung* and the French Revolution the separation of Church and State made it impossible to meddle in the other's affairs. The Church was degraded to a "religious association," a "society." Therefore it was very inconsistent that King William I of Orange interfered in the life of the Dutch Churches, as the Seceders of 1834 experienced.

Great Britain was not directly affected by the French Revolution. Consequently the situation in the Church of England remained the same as it was after the days of the Reformation: this Church is still bound to the pre-Reformation Canon Law. The king or queen who is the head of the Church, officially appoints the bishops. On the other hand, the latter are members of the House of Lords, and the primate, the Archbishop of Canterbury, is entrusted with the honour and duty of crowning a new king or queen.

The "dissenters," the "free" Churches, reject all this. This is why they do not experience any interference from the side of the civil government in former colonies — now migrants' countries — as Australia, Canada, and — with a different historical background — the U.S.A.

A Reformed Church Order developed

Unlike our Reformed liturgy, the respective Church Orders of the Free Reformed Churches of Australia and of the Canadian Reformed Churches are not based on what was imported from the Palatinate into The Netherlands. As we saw earlier this German country was originally under the influence of Lutheranism. It had adopted the Lutheran Church Order of Wurttemberg 1536 and 1553, on which its Order of 1556 was also based. Even in the Reformed Church Order of November 1563 there are some Lutheran influences left: e.g. the beautiful answer to Question 1 in the Heidelberg Catechism, repeated in Answer 34, which has been derived from Martin Luther's Shorter Catechism.

It is not incorrect when some call this Order a "liturgical Church Order." It includes all the then existing liturgical Forms, as well as the complete text of the Catechism. In our Reformed Church Orders these texts have not been included but references to them are made.

The Palatine Church Order does not deal with ecclesiastical assemblies. Its main subject are: preaching, baptism, catechesis, the Lord's Supper, discipline, care for the needy, prayers, festive days, marriage, Church singing, dresses, visiting ill people, the dying and prisoners, and funerals.

This meant that the Dutch Churches had to compile their own Order. For this they had the examples of the Church Order of the French Churches, compiled in 1559, and the *Ordonnances Ecclesiastiques* of the Genevan Church from the year 1561.

The first efforts were made at the Convention of Wesel in the year 1568, which was chaired by Petrus Dathenus. John Calvin's influence upon this meeting was clearly noticeable. However, a Church Order in the strict sense of the word was not produced. What this Convention left behind are the Acts or the "Articles of Wesel."

Their subtitle reads: "Some chapters of Articles, which the minister of the Dutch Churches consider to be partly essential, partly useful for the ministry of these Churches." Their respective chapters are: I. Collegia and provincial classes; II. Ministers and doctores; III. Catechesis; IV. Elders; V. Deacons; VI. Sacraments; VII. Marriage; VIII. Discipline.

At their very beginning these Articles refer to I Corinthians 14:40. Strong emphasis is laid on the consensus among the Churches to live in accordance with these Articles: their confederation is a matter of being joined together on a voluntary basis!

Even the first real synod of the Dutch Churches, held in 1571 at Emden, did not produce a Church Order, but the *Acta Synodi Ecclesiarum Belgicarum, quae sub cruce sunt, et per Germaniam et Phrisiam Orientalem dispersae*.[60]

One of the features of this document is that it starts with the fundamental rule that no Church shall lord it over any other Church, and no office bearer shall lord it over any other office bearer.

Another feature is that the members of this synod, at its very beginning, even before the *moderamen* was elected, put their names under the Belgic as well as French Confessions of Faith.

What we could call a Church-Order-in-embryo is not only contained in these Acts but also in an Appendix, in which a number of "Particular Questions" from among the Churches are answered. They deal with: the convening of classes, rules for classes; provincial synods and general synods.

The Provincial Synod of Dordrecht 1574 based its decisions on the Acts of Emden — again called by this synod "Articles" — which were publicly read in its second session.

What we can call almost a real Church Order was produced by the National Synod of Dordrecht 1578. Its Acts were not written in the form of "minutes," but contain decisions made "in view of the general order of the Churches, collected into 102 articles, arranged in chapters according to their contents." These chapters deal with, respectively: I. the ministers of the Word, elders, and deacons; II. the consistory and other ecclesiastical assemblies; III. the schools; IV. the doctrine, sacraments, and ceremonies; V. marriage; VI. admonitions and Church discipline. Then, again, there are some "Particular Questions."

The first synod which provided the Churches with a real Church Order was that of Middelburg 1581. It is also called *Corpus Disciplinae*, opening with an introductory article which is almost literally the same as Article 1 of the Church Order of the Canadian Reformed Churches. It reads as follows: "For the maintenance of good order in the congregation of Christ it is necessary that there be in her offices, assemblies, supervision of doctrine, sacraments and ceremonies and Christian discipline. These matters will be dealt with in the above mentioned order." This Order has a total of

---

[60] Acts of the Synod of the Dutch Churches, "under the cross" — under persecution — and dispersed in Germany and East Friesland.

69 Articles, the final ones dealing with "no lording" (68) and an eventual changing, augmenting, or diminishing of the Order (69).

The Church Order adopted by the Synod of The Hague 1586 was fundamentally the same. It contained 79 Articles, the penultimate article dealing with foreign Churches and the so-called *adiaphora* (items of mediocre significance). Its title was also a bit longer than that of the Order of 1581, reading: "Church Order of the Dutch Reformed Churches" (the Synod of Dordrecht 1618-19 returned to Middelburg's brief name, "Church Order" but the General Synod of Utrecht 1905 restored the somewhat longer title of the 1586 Order).

"Dort" 1618-19 made some minor changes and a number of additions. Since then the Churches in The Netherlands have maintained this "Church Order of Dordrecht" officially, with an interruption between 1816 — when the Church became a "society" with a Constitution and By-Laws (*Algemeen Reglement*) — and 1834 — when the Churches of the Secession returned to the adherence to the Church Order of Dordrecht — as did the Churches of the *Doleantie* ("Grieving" or "Mourning") in 1886.

In spite of what Abraham Kuyper and Frederick L. Rutgers had taught, the Reformed Churches in The Netherlands have been since the 1920s inclined toward a hierarchical interpretation and application of the Church Order. This became the official Order in the early 1940s. In the Liberation of 1944 the Churches returned to the real "Dort."

At the General Synod of Groningen-Zuid 1978 a revised version was adopted, the main changes being of a linguistic character.

Our Churches adopted the "Church Order of Dordrecht" in their own versions.

Church and State

Before we deal with the activities of our own Churches in this field, some additional information must be given on the history of the Church Order.

Earlier in history the relation between Church and State played a significant role, as we have already seen. This was the case in the development which led to the dominating place taken by the so-called Canon Law. The Reformers rejected this claim of the Church of Rome.

However, in the controversy between Arminians and Reformed (or: Remonstrants and Contra-Remonstrants) this relation once again played a prominent role. Many of the Dutch national and provincial leaders were Arminians or sympathized with the tenacious efforts to have a "state" or "political" Church Order introduced.

This had happened already in the year 1576. In spite of the fact that the Provincial Synod of Rotterdam 1575 sent a "remonstrance" to the States of Holland and Zeeland, in which they stated that, according to Article 36 of the Belgic Confession of Faith, Church and State each had their own territory, duties, and means, the States of Holland decided to replace the "Articles of Dordrecht 1574" by their own Church Order. One of the main characteristics of this document was that the magistrate assumed the right to appoint and dismiss ministers of religion. However, the States of Holland were not successful in this respect.

The Church Orders of Dordrecht 1578 and Middelburg 1581 also met with opposition from the side of the government, and could not be introduced (only across the borders, in Nassau, were they introduced). Grand Pensionary Johan van Oldenbarneveldt was mandated to compile an "ecclesiastical and political" Order from the 1581 synodical Acts, to be sent for approval to the States and to be enforced by the Prince of Orange. Some of the crucial points were: the extent of Church discipline, and the authority of the government to appoint and depose ministers of the Word. However, the result of these efforts, the State Order of 1583, was never officially introduced because of the firm stand taken by the Churches, and of the politically unstable situation caused by the assassination of William, Prince of Orange, in the year 1584.

Another effort was made in the year 1591, again undertaken by van Oldenbarneveldt. Strong resistance was offered by the Churches. In the year 1612 this new State Order was reconfirmed and the decision to have it officially introduced made in 1615. Unrest in several places was the result. Many Churches rejected the States' interference with their own affairs. The Churches of the province of North Holland expressed that in their opinion the government assumed authority in Church affairs for no other reason than to build a bridge for the introduction of the new Arminian doctrines.

The arguments used by the States were that they were afraid that the Churches would become "a State within the State," and another papacy with a large number of popes would be established with the Churches meddling in political affairs. They even referred to the Bible: God gave His laws to Israel not through Aaron but through Moses!

Van Oldenbarneveldt was supported by Arminian leaders such as Uytenbogaerd, who taught that the government had been called by God to exercise political as well as ecclesiastical authority.

From both sides appeals were made with reference to prominent Church leaders. The Arminians and politicians referred to Zwingli and Bullinger, the Reformed to Calvin and Beza. The "political" stand was also based on the teachings of Thomas Erastus, professor of medicine at the Heidelberg University, whose thesis that the government had the authority to govern and preserve Church life was attacked by Zacharias Ursinus and Caspar Olevianus.

The same happened in The Netherlands as in "the Heidelberg controversy:" fundamentally the Reformed point of view won the battle. This happened at the Synod of Dordrecht 1618-19, which made some decisions on the so-called patronage right after the foreign delegates had left. This right of the owners of some estates to appoint ministers and supply their livelihood was restricted. The latter was in particular settled when the Church Order — the *Canones*, as Synod called the document — was revised and its Latin, French, and Dutch texts approved.

Certainly, the relation between State and Church was not fully clarified: the delegates of the States General had to give their formal approval to all the decisions made at Dordrecht, the Church Order included; they were also humbly requested to pay the huge bill of synodical expenses. In the year 1637 the Dutch version of the Bible, which was originated at the 1618-19 Synod, was officially presented to the States General, and paid for by them! consequently it is popularly called *Statenvertaling* (States Version).

However, the controversy was settled fundamentally in favour of the Churches.

Our Churches

At their first synod the Free Reformed Churches of Australia adopted the Church Order of Dordrecht, however with the restriction that whenever a consistory was of the opinion that it could not act in full accordance with it, it would consult the sister Churches. This may be understandable for those who realize that the small number of Churches at that time, no more than three, made it impossible, for example, to establish classes.

The 1959 Synod adopted a provisional English version. A revised version was adopted at the 1983 Kelmscott Synod. However, already four years later the 1987 Synod charged deputies to, "on the one hand, scrutinize and improve the language use of the Church Order, and on the other, make use of the Canadian text in so far as possible." These deputies reported to the 1990 Armadale Synod, which appointed new deputies and instructed them to "adopt the Canadian text so that it clearly reflects the specific Australian circumstances." Where there are noteworthy differences deputies must report them to Synod. They had also to "maintain the division of Articles of the Canadian Church Order."

These deputies were confronted with a number of obstacles. They reported that the Canadian Church Order had been subject to a number of revisions. Therefore they had chosen the 1989 version as their starting point, even though Synod 1990 based its instructions on the 1983 version then available. They opted to reinterpret their mandate in the light of the 1987 mandate.

Synod had to admit that "the mandate given by Synod 1990 was too idealistic," and approved the deputies' reinterpretation of their mandate. It decided to provisionally adopt the revised text, because further changes might be needed. New deputies were appointed, who reported to the 1994 Byford Synod, which adopted a revised version.

Since as yet in the Free Reformed Churches of Australia no classes have been formed, provisions have been made whereby each church acts as a "classis church" if needed. Even "second appeal churches" have been appointed, but no mention of them is made in the Church Order.

The Canadian Reformed Churches at their 1954 Synod adopted the Dutch Church Order, but were also aware of certain difficulties in applying it to their own circumstances. Proposals of revision regarding nineteen articles were discussed at the 1958 Synod. Ten years later a committee for revision was appointed, the mandate of which was extended in 1971. At the 1974 Synod a draft of 28 articles was discussed. The newly appointed committee was instructed to consider the contents of a report written by their Dutch colleagues. A new Article, No. 75, on Church property, was added to the existing Order. The Synods of 1977 and 1980 discussed 33 and 22 articles respectively.

The process of revision ended at the Cloverdale Synod of 1983, where a new text was adopted, although the General Synod of Smithville 1986 made changes in Articles 13, 44, and 72.

The General Synod of Lincoln 1992 gave a mandate "to prepare an introduction to the Church Order." Such an introduction was adopted by the General Synod 1995.[61]

Contents

The Australian Church Order is subdivided into the following sections:
Introduction, Article 1.
I   Offices and supervision of doctrine, Articles 2-27.
II Assemblies, Articles 28-50.
III Worship, sacraments and ceremonies, Articles 51-68.
IV Church discipline, Articles 69-79.
Concluding Articles, Articles 80-81.

As for the Canadian Order, the contents are:
I   Introduction, Article 1.
II Offices and supervision of doctrine, Articles 2-28.
III The assemblies, Articles 29-51.
IV Worship, sacraments, and ceremonies, Articles 52-65.
V   Christian discipline, Articles 66-76.

---

[61] *Acts*, Article 44 D.

7. IN CONCLUSION

A unity

Our Reformed Church service book is a unity, a whole. It is not a perfect book. Nevertheless we believe that all the other parts are based on its first section, the most important one of all, the Bible.

In conclusion we may give an impression of this unity. We thereby take the Church Order as our starting point, from there going backwards.

Church Order and liturgy

Unlike the Order of the Palatinate, which included the text of the Heidelberg Catechism and of various liturgical forms, the Australian and Canadian Church Orders cannot be called doctrinal and liturgical orders. Yet the relation with our Reformed liturgy is obvious when a number of Articles refer to our liturgical Forms.

Both the Canadian and the Australian Church Orders refer to "the use of the adopted Forms" for the administration of the sacraments, in respectively Article 56 and Article 51.

The same phrase can be read in Article 54 of the Australian Order, which deals with "Public Profession of Faith." In this context the Canadian Order does not mention the Form concerned.

Ordination Forms for all office bearers are mentioned in Article 3 of both documents.

"With (the use of) the adopted Form" the excommunication of sinners as well as the readmission of those who repent shall take place, according to Articles 74 and 75 of the Australian Church Order. The Canadian Order does not mention the adopted Form for Excommunication, but refers to the Form for Readmission in Article 70.

Forms for the Solemnization of Marriages are to be used according to Article 67 of the Australian Order and Article 63 of the Canadian Church Order.

Church Order and worship orders

As for the orders of worship, no provision has been made regarding them in our Church Orders.

However, the unity of our Church service book is obvious when we compare the "Kampen Order" with what we confess regarding the purpose of attending Church in Lord's Day 38 of the Heidelberg Catechism.

Besides, this order is in harmony with the Scriptures when they teach us that "the first and great commandment" is to love the LORD our God — which includes to worship Him — and that then we have also to pay attention to the well being of our neighbour — to be fulfilled in our worship service in our intercessory prayers and monetary offerings. The Lord's Prayer follows the same order: first "Thy," only then "us" and "ours."

Church Order and Confession

There is a close relation between the Church Order and the Belgic Confession of Faith.

Unlike the *Didache* and some Church Orders from the days of the Reformation — e.g. that of Ulm 1531 (by Oecolampadius and Bucer), that of Bern 1532 (by Capito), and the Order of Strasbourg 1533 (by Bucer and Capito) — the Church Order of Dordrecht in its Australian and Canadian versions does not include a summary of the doctrine. This does not prevent it from being an effective instrument in the preservation of the pure doctrine.

Further, whereas in the service book of the Reformed Churches in France of the sixteenth century, the Church Order was the sequel to the Confession of Faith, its text being printed immediately after the final article of the Confession, this is different in our own Church service book. Nevertheless, the close relation between Church Order and Confession may be obvious from the following illustrations:

Under the caption "Character and purpose" we have already referred to Articles 30-32 of our Confession. The Church Order of Dordrecht is a kind of elaboration on what we confess in these articles, in particular on the sentence in Article 32 which says: "it is useful and good for those who govern the Church to establish a certain order to maintain the body of Christ," and — as far as its fundamentals are concerned — of what it says in Article 31 B.C. that Christ is "the only universal Bishop and the only Head of the Church."

One more illustration: What we confess in Article 36 B.C. regarding the respect required of us for the civil government is repeated in the Articles 27 of the Australian and 28 of the Canadian Church Order.

Church Order and Bible

The whole Church Order is meant to be instrumental in the preservation and continuance of what is most important: the pure doctrine of the Scriptures and the preaching thereof.

Therewith we are back at the first and most significant part of our Church service book, the Bible!

Other Books from Inheritance Publications

Where Everything Points to Him by K. Deddens

The Church of Jesus Christ does not live her life in isolation. Even in her corporate worship, she can be adversely influenced by the surrounding culture. Some ministers come to model themselves — even if only unconsciously — after entertainers. And some of the worshipers seem to think that a worship service is essentially a meeting between *people* in which social and aesthetic norms must prevail. In such a climate it is helpful to be reminded of the principles which have shaped corporate worship . . .   **ISBN 0-921100-39-6 Can.$12.95 U.S.$11.90**

Essays in Reformed Doctrine by J. Faber

A collection of seventeen articles, speeches, and lectures which are of fundamental importance to all Christians.

Cecil Tuininga in *Christian Renewal*: This book is easy reading as far as the English goes. It can, I judge, be read by all with great profit. . . I found the first chapter on "The Significance of Dogmatology for the Training of the Ministry" excellent. The six essays on the Church I found very informative and worth-while. . . What makes this book so valuable is that Dr. Faber deals with all the aspects of the Reformed faith from a strictly biblical and confessional viewpoint.
                  ISBN 0-921100-28-0 Can.$19.95 U.S.$17.90

The Covenantal Gospel by C. Van der Waal

G. Van Rongen in *Una Sancta*: . . . We would like to conclude this review with a quotation from the last lines of this - recommended! - book. They are the following: The Gospel is covenantal in every respect. If things go wrong in the churches, ask whether the covenant is indeed preached and understood.

If missionary work is superficial, ask whether the covenant is taken into account. . . If sects and movements multiply, undoubtedly they speak of the covenant in a strange way, or ignore it deliberately. . . It must be proclaimed. Evangelical = Covenantal.
                  ISBN 0-921100-19-1 Can.$17.95 U.S.$16.20

Covenant and Election by Dr. J. Van Genderen

Even though we are familiar with the biblical promises which are also prophecies and recognize them as flowing out of the covenant the Lord made with us, we should not simply view the promise as a prediction of what the Lord is sure to do regardless of how we react to it, but rather as a promise which requires faith on our part. Basically the content of the covenant is this: I am your God and you are My people. This promise never loses its meaning. It even takes on an ever richer meaning for the believer.

But the promise needs to be appropriated. When we in faith accept the promise and the salvation offered in it, we say "amen" to God's "yea" (2 Corinthians 1:20). This is to the honour of God. Faith is worked by the Holy Spirit. The promise takes that into account. As the Form for Baptism puts it: "The Holy Spirit applies to us that which we have in Christ." The demand which goes together with the promise is a demand of the covenant and is as such preceded, followed, borne and surrounded by the promise. It is therefore a gracious demand: the gracious command to believe and obey. What the Lord asks from us He is willing to give us.

All the commands and prohibitions of the Decalogue flow out of the covenant relation: "I am the Lord your God." That is the prologue to the entire law (Calvin). God thereby declares that He is the God of the Church. In light of these words the Reformer of Geneva expounds both the Ten Commandments as well as the summary of the law. For Calvin the law is the law of the covenant of grace. It is a confirmation of the covenant made with Abraham. Even though the law serves to bring out transgressions (Galatians 3:19) it is clothed with the covenant of grace (the covenant of God's gracious acceptance).   **ISBN 0-921100-60-4 Can.$11.95 U.S.$10.90**

Schilder's Struggle for the Unity of the Church by **Rudolf Van Reest**

Klaas Schilder (1890-1952) is remembered both for his courageous stand in opposition to Nazism, which led to his imprisonment three months after the Nazis overran the Netherlands in 1940, and for his role in the Church struggle in the Netherlands, which culminated in 1944 with the suspension of scores of office-bearers and the formation of the liberated Reformed Churches.

Thomas Vanden Heuvel in *The Outlook* of December 1990: I strongly recommend this book for everyone interested in the preservation of and propagation of the Reformed faith.

ISBN 0-921100-23-X Can.$29.95 U.S.$26.60

Proceedings of The International Conference of Reformed Churches
September 1-9, 1993 Zwolle, The Netherlands

Included are the conference papers which were delivered for the general public in the evening sessions.

Section I—Minutes of the Conference
Section II—Speeches and Reports
Section III—Conference Papers

    The Wrath of God as an Essential Part of Mission - C.J. Haak 91
    Prophecy Today? - Norris Wilson 116
    Catechism Preaching (Part 1) - N.H. Gootjes 136
    Catechism Preaching (Part 2) - N.H. Gootjes 153
    Christology and Mission - Alisdair I. Macleod 164
    Recent Criticisms of the Westminster Confession of Faith - R.S.Ward 184
    Redemptive Historical Preaching - H.M. Ohmann 203
    Remarks on Church and Tolerance - J. Kamphuis 213

Section IV—Miscellaneous   **ISBN 0-921100-49-3 Can.$9.95 U.S.$8.90**

Living in the Joy of Faith by **Clarence Stam**
The Christian Faith as Outlined in the Heidelberg Catechism

R.J. Rushdoony in *Chalcedon Report*: In a time of cheap grace, Stam makes clear what the results of redemption are: "Forgiveness is always combined with renewal" (p.178). He makes clear that the term *Holy Gospel* means the Bible, the whole of it, from cover to cover (p.45). It is God communicating with us. "A church that does not preach the Law of God diligently and squarely is an unfaithful church, giving its members false security and withholding from them essential facts, preventing them from leading a life of true happiness in the Lord!" (p.21). On one subject after another, Stam's is the authentic voice of the Reformed faith, speaking with power and with joy. This is a book to prize.   **ISBN 0-921100-27-2 Can.$39.95 U.S.$35.90**

Annotations to the Heidelberg Catechism by **J. Van Bruggen**

John A. Hawthorne in *Reformed Theological Journal*: . . . The individual Christian would find it a constructive way to employ part of the Sabbath day by working through the lesson that is set for each Lord's Day. No one can study this volume without increasing his knowledge of truth and being made to worship and adore the God of all grace. This book will help every minister in the instruction of his people, both young and not so young, every parent in the task of catechizing and is commended to every Christian for personal study.   **ISBN 0-921100-33-7 Can.$15.95 U.S.$13.90**

The Belgic Confession and its Biblical Basis by **Lepusculus Vallensis**

The Belgic Confession is a Reformed Confession, dating from the 16th Century, written by Guido de Brès, a preacher in the Reformed Churches of the Netherlands. The great Synod of Dort in 1618-19 adopted this Confession as one of the doctrinal standards of the Reformed Churches, to which all office-bearers of the Churches were (and still are) to subscribe. This book provides and explains the Scriptural proof texts for the Belgic Confession by using the marginal notes of the Dutch Staten Bijbel. The Staten Bijbel is a Dutch translation of the Bible, by order of the States General of the United Netherlands, in accordance with a decree of the Synod of Dort. It was first published in 1637 and included 'new explanations of difficult passages and annotations to comparative texts.'

ISBN 0-921100-41-8 Can.$17.95 U.S.$15.90

Augustine, The Farmer's Boy of Tagaste
by P. De Zeeuw, J.Gzn

C. MacDonald in *The Banner of Truth*: Augustine was one of the great teachers of the Christian Church, defending it against many heretics. This interesting publication should stimulate and motivate all readers to extend their knowledge of Augustine and his works.

J. Sawyer in *Trowel & Sword*: . . . It is informative, accurate historically and theologically, and very readable. My daughter loved it (and I enjoyed it myself). An excellent choice for home and church libraries.

for age 9 - 99   **ISBN 0-921100-05-1 Can.$7.95 U.S.$6.90**

This Was John Calvin by Thea B. Van Halsema

J.H. Kromminga: "Though it reads as smoothly as a well written novel, it is crammed with important facts. It is scholarly and popular at the same time. The book will hold the interest of the young but will also bring new information to the well informed . . . . This book recognizes the true greatness of the man without falling into distortions of the truth to protect that greatness."

It has been translated into Spanish, Portuguese, and Indonesian. This is its fourth printing.

for age 12 - 99   **IP1179 Can.$9.95 U.S.$7.95**

William of Orange - The Silent Prince
by W.G. Van de Hulst

F. Pronk in *The Messenger*: If you have ever wondered why Dutch Reformed people of former generations felt such strong spiritual ties with Dutch royalty, this is a "must" reading. In simple story form, understandable for children ages 10 and up, the Dutch author, wellknown for Christian children's literature, relates the true story of the origin of Dutch royalty. It all began with William of Nassau (1533-1584) . . . He dedicated his life and lost it for the cause of maintaining and promoting Protestantism in the Netherlands.

for age 9 - 99   **ISBN 0-921100-15-9 Can.$8.95 U.S.$7.90**

Love in Times of Reformation
by William P. Balkenende

G. Van Dalen in *The Trumpet*: This historical novel plays in the Netherlands during the rise of the protestant Churches, under the persecution of Spain, in the latter half of the sixteenth century. Breaking with the Roman Catholic Church in favor of the new faith is for many an intense struggle. Anthony Tharret, the baker's apprentice, faces his choice before the R.C. Church's influenced Baker's Guild. His love for Jeanne la Solitude, the French Huguenot refugee, gives a fresh dimension to the story. Recommended! Especially for young people.

for age 14 - 99   **ISBN 0-921100-32-9 Can.$8.95 U.S.$7.90**

Three Men Came To Heidelberg
and *Glorious Heretic* by Thea B. Van Halsema

From the sixteenth-century Protestant Reformation came two outstanding statements of Faith: The Heidelberg Catechism (1563) and the Belgic Confession (1561). The stories behind these two historic documents are in this small book.

Frederick, a German prince, asked a preacher and a professor to meet at Heidelberg to write a statement of faith . . . The writer of the Belgic Confession was a hunted man most of his life. Originally he wrote the confession as an appeal to the King of Spain . . .

for age 12 - 99   **IP1610 Can.$7.95 U.S.$5.95**

About Inheritance Publications

Inheritance Publications is a small company which has been established to provide Biblical Reformed literature. We want to maintain the antithesis between right and wrong, between true and false christianity. It is also our desire to give God the honour and glory due to His Name because of His covenant faithfulness. Remembering the great deeds of God in the history of His Church will always cause God's children to stand in awe for His Majesty. It is our aim to reach children with storybooks about the history of the Church, and adults with books on the doctrine of the Church. May God's Name be glorified and the readers edified by the reading of our books.

WHAT IS THE ADVANTAGE OF BECOMING A MEMBER OF THE *INHERITANCE BOOK CLUB*?

* As a member you will get the new books of Inheritance Publications at a special price (usually at about 15 % discount) sent to you within about thirty days after publication.
* You have the right to return new I.P. books within 10 days from the day of delivery.
* You don't have to send an order each time a new book is published.
* Members can obtain at any time any number of current I.P. or Premier books at the original special Publication Price, unless the book has been out of print.
* There is no postage charge!

You can join different categories.
Cat. A: Selected new books from Inheritance Publications (about 5 books per year)
Cat. B: Selected new children- and adult-fiction books from I.P. (about 3 books per year)
Cat. C: Selected new study books from I.P. (about 2 books per year)
Cat. D: Selected new books from I.P. and Premier Publishing (about 7 books per year)
Cat. E: Selected new study books from I.P. and Premier Publishing (about 5 books per year)
Inheritance Publications reserves the right to terminate a membership.
Our books are usually based on historical facts or contain sound biblical doctrines.

Titles that are currently available at special prices to I.P. Members:

Title	reg. price	I.P. member price	
Balkenende, William P. - Love in Times of Reformation	CN.$ 8.95	CN.$ 7.60	U.S.$ 6.60
Bootsma, P.M. Rustenburg - Mighty Fortress in the Storm	CN.$11.95	CN.$10.15	U.S.$ 9.25
Bouma, Hendrik - Secession, Doleantie, and Union: 1834 - 1892	CN.$15.95	CN.$13.50	U.S.$11.90
Bowen, Marjorie - W&M 1 - I Will Maintain	CN.$17.95	CN.$15.25	U.S.$13.50
Bowen, Marjorie - W&M 2 - Defender of the Faith	CN.$15.95	CN.$13.50	U.S.$11.90
Bowen, Marjorie - W&M 3 - For God and the King	CN.$17.95	CN.$15.25	U.S.$13.50
Coray, Henry W. - Against the World, Athanasius	CN.$ 8.95	CN.$ 7.60	U.S.$ 6.70
Deddens, K. - Where Everything Points to Him	CN.$12.95	CN.$10.95	U.S.$10.10
Erkelens, L. - The Crown of Honour	CN.$11.95	CN.$ 9.95	U.S.$ 9.25
Faber, J. - Essays in Reformed Doctrine	CN.$19.95	CN.$16.95	U.S.$14.95
I.C.R.C. - Proceedings I.C.R.C. 1993	CN.$ 9.95	CN.$ 8.50	U.S.$ 7.50
Keizer, P.K. - Church History	CN.$12.95	CN.$10.95	U.S.$ 9.95
Kloosterman, N.D. - Relation Between Chr. Liberty & Neighbor Love	CN.$11.95	CN.$ 9.95	U.S.$ 9.25
Knepper, J.A. - Wholesome Communication	CN.$ 9.95	CN.$ 8.50	U.S.$ 7.50
Los, D. - Thou Holdest My Right Hand	CN.$ 9.95	CN.$ 8.50	U.S.$ 7.50
Plantinga, T. - Christian Philosophy Within Biblical Bounds	CN.$ 7.95	CN.$ 6.95	U.S.$ 5.95
Prins, Piet - Anak, the Eskimo Boy	CN.$ 6.95	CN.$ 5.95	U.S.$ 4.95
Prins, Piet - Shadow 4 - the Partisans	CN.$ 7.95	CN.$ 6.75	U.S.$ 5.95
Prins, Piet - Shadow 5 - Sabotage	CN.$ 7.95	CN.$ 6.75	U.S.$ 5.95
Prins, Piet - Struggle 1 - When the Morning Came	CN.$ 9.95	CN.$ 8.50	U.S.$ 7.50
Prins, Piet - Struggle 2 - Dispelling the Tyranny	CN.$ 9.95	CN.$ 8.50	U.S.$ 7.50
Rang, William R. - It Began with A Parachute	CN.$ 8.95	CN.$ 7.60	U.S.$ 6.70
Rook, An - Judy's Own Pet Kitten	CN.$ 4.95	CN.$ 3.95	U.S.$ 3.60
Stam, Clarence - Living in the Joy of Faith	CN.$39.95	CN.$31.95	U.S.$29.90
Stretton, Hesba - Jessica's First Prayer & Jessica's Mother	CN.$ 8.95	CN.$ 7.60	U.S.$ 6.70
Vallensis, Lepusculus - Belgic Confession & Biblical Basis	CN.$17.95	CN.$15.25	U.S.$13.50
Van Bruggen, J. - Annotations to the Heidelberg Catechism	CN.$15.95	CN.$13.50	U.S.$11.90
Van De Hulst, W.G. - William of Orange, the Silent Prince	CN.$ 8.95	CN.$ 7.60	U.S.$ 6.70
Van Der Waal, C. - Hal Lindsey and Biblical Prophecy	CN.$ 9.95	CN.$ 8.50	U.S.$ 7.50
Van Der Waal, C. - The Covenantal Gospel	CN.$17.95	CN.$15.50	U.S.$13.50
Van Doornik, C.J. - Susanneke	CN.$ 4.95	CN.$ 3.95	U.S.$ 3.60
Van Genderen, J. - Covenant & Election	CN.$11.95	CN.$10.15	U.S.$ 9.25
Van Oene, W.W.J. - Inheritance Preserved	CN.$24.75	CN.$21.00	U.S.$18.90
Van Reest, Rudolf - Israel's Hope and Expectation	CN.$19.95	CN.$16.95	U.S.$14.95
Van Reest, Rudolf - Schilder's Struggle for the Unity of the Church	CN.$29.95	CN.$25.50	U.S.$22.50
Van Rongen - Our Reformed Church Service Book	CN.$15.95	CN.$13.50	U.S.$11.90
Vogelaar, Alie - Tekko 1 - Tekko and the White Man	CN.$ 7.95	CN.$ 6.75	U.S.$ 5.85
Vogelaar, Alie - Tekko 2 - Tekko the Fugitive	CN.$ 7.95	CN.$ 6.75	U.S.$ 5.85

INHERITANCE BOOK CLUB MEMBERSHIP FORM

Name _____ Date_____

Address_____

City & Province_____

Postal code _____ Tel._____

Membership Category _____ Signature _____

Please complete the membership form and return it to:
Inheritance Publications Box 154, Neerlandia, Alberta T0G 1R0 Canada